NEW WORKS IN ACCOUNTING HISTORY

Richard P. Brief, *Series Editor*

Leonard N. Stern School of Business
New York University

A Garland Series

THE STRUGGLE FOR
STATUS

A History of Accounting Education

Glenn Van Wyhe

Garland Publishing, Inc.
New York and London 1994

Copyright © 1994 by Glenn Van Wyhe

Library of Congress Cataloging-in-Publication Data

Van Wyhe, Glenn.
    The struggle for status : a history of accounting education /
Glenn Van Wyhe.
        p. cm. —(New works in accounting history)
        Includes bibliographical references.
        ISBN 0-8153-1654-2
        1. Accounting—Study and teaching—United States—
History.
I. Title. II. Series.
HF5630.V34   1994   93–39293
657'.071073—dc20

All volumes printed on acid-free, 250-year-life paper.
Manufactured in the United States of America.

Design by Marisel Tavarez

Dedicated to Dwight Zulauf, beloved professor of accounting and respected elder colleague, whose kindness and goodness have inspired a multitude of students and fellow professors

CONTENTS

ACKNOWLEDGMENTS

The author wishes to express sincere appreciation to Charles Burgess, Loyd Heath, Donald Williams, Dwight Zulauf, and Robert Van Wyhe for their assistance. They read over the manuscript and provided valuable suggestions. I especially thank Dr. Burgess for his guidance on the overall direction of the work, and Dr. Heath for his carefulness and encouragement to achieve discipline and brevity. These men have much to do with the good things present in this book, but I take full responsibility for any of the less successful elements.

Grateful acknowledgment is made to the American Institue of Certified Public Accountants, the American Accounting Association, the Ernst & Young Foundation, the School of Accountancy at the University of Missouri-Columbia, and the University of Pennsylvania Press for their permission to print various materials in this book.

INTRODUCTION

The winds of change appear to be blowing through the field of accounting higher education. Whether real change will in fact take place is not yet certain. A study of the history of accounting education reveals much about the roots of the present attempts at reform, and about the possibilities of success.

History acts as the laboratory for educational policy, and therefore the best way to begin to study the effects of educational policy is to study its history. There is a saying by George Santayana—not a cliche though often quoted—that those who are ignorant of history are doomed to repeat it.

History is a conversation where the opposing sides are often acting rather than merely talking, and thus the real implications of their positions can be more easily seen. A careful study of history has two very important virtues: (1) it helps the scholar avoid a too limited view of the issues, because it takes notice of a wide variety of opinions—wider than most individuals would perceive by their own lights alone, since such opinions come from a wide variety of people; and (2) it helps the scholar avoid an overly unrealistic idealism, because it often documents the practical results of previous idealisms and shows where such idealisms did not take adequate account of reality—in particular, of human nature.

Educational policy studies for accounting education have not adequately recognized the fact that historical study is a vital part of deriving educational policy. Some efforts may consider a bit of historical background, but typically this is brief and comes from the "official" perspective and provides little or no insight into trends or motivations or conflict development.

An important part of the way to understand the past, as well as the present, is to learn the opinions and philosophies of those who have in the past given direction to accounting educational policy. This can be done either by reading their writings, or by interviewing or surveying them. The present fashion of restricting quotations to brief snippets has been abandoned in this present study. Extensive quotes, if judiciously selected, give the reader a flavor for the manner and mood of expression, which moves the reader a step closer to the original writings and the spirit of the times. Furthermore, paraphrases which move far from the exact wording of a document often and inescapably misrepresent the intent of the document. True students of history prefer to read the exact words of those who made history, and are not content to rely completely upon the summations of the historian.

The Motivation for Historical Actions

The ingredients of an historical analysis do not lend themselves to experimental conditions. Historical data are deeply embedded in a unique historical context which cannot be reconstructed. The objective of historical analysis is to discern significant influences through the use of "historical insight," an ability to recognize developmental patterns through familiarity with similar patterns in other historical situations. There are two tests of historical insight: are all significant influences considered? and is there a strong consistency to the pattern such influences form? Such consistency and completeness is the test of evidence provided by historical analysis, and it is by that test that we can come closest to determining "historical causality"—i.e., why things happen. Of course, different levels of insight lead to different levels of quality in historical analysis.

A critical aspect of historical insight is the attempt to understand the motivations of the participants in the historical development. As much as possible, the words of the participants should guide the understanding of their motivations. But words are subject to interpretation, and it is also sometimes necessary to go behind the participants' words when it seems obvious that they appear to be attempting to present themselves in a favorable but not entirely honest light. If a person is assumed to be logical, and if that person's arguments are shown to be nonsense when subjected to logical analysis, then it must be assumed that there are hidden reasons for that person's position.

Much of the motivation for the developments in higher education in accounting arises from the efforts of accountants to establish their vocation as a profession. The rise of higher education in accounting and the rise of accountancy as a profession both take place in the half-century following 1880. That was the era of the Progressive Movement, when many Americans believed that the salvation of the country lay in the hands of those with "scientific" expertise.

In fact, the great allure of the professions in the period between 1880 and 1920 was that they could restore American democracy from the corruptions and excesses to which it was allowed to sink during the Gilded Age. Progressive reformers viewed the rise of bureaucratic organizations staffed by trained experts and employing scientific objectivity as the only way to sustain and renew the best of American democracy. For leaders such as Woodrow Wilson, representative government easily came to mean government by the ideal of nonpartisan expertise. "Nonprofessionalism is nonefficiency," he exclaimed.[1]

The exaltation of the scientific professional made the title of "professional" extremely attractive to anyone wishing to be exalted.

In more recent years, the infallibility and even motivations of professionals have come under attack, and opposing views of professionalism have arisen.

> There have been those who claim to have discerned in certain professions, chiefly medicine and law, such immutable and presumably edifying traits as altruism, a spirit of public service, and a code of ethics. More recently, some sociologists have focused on professionalization as an effective, though not particularly praiseworthy means of establishing and maintaining hegemony and occupational control.[2]

One group has seen professionalization as attempting to meet the goal of providing the best possible services to people. Another group, with a more jaundiced eye, has seen professionalization as attempting to meet the goal of unfairly increasing the incomes of professionals.

Donna Kerr sums up the latter revisionist position on how professions develop.

> There must be a base of "cultural capital," to borrow Alvin Gouldner's term. That is, there must exist an extraordinary stock of those human inventions we call

knowledge and know-how. In particular, it is crucial that this stock exceed what would be acquired by persons in the course of their general knowledge.... Essentially, there are two ways to develop cultural capital. One is to guard not-so-esoteric know-how as if it were beyond the reach of the nonspecialist. The second is to actually generate abstruse technical knowledge.[3]

Kerr goes on to speak of the "purposes" or "goals" of a profession, all of which are for the ultimate goal of acquiring cultural capital for the sake of buying power, or making "a power play."[4] The goals of a profession, then, are entirely political and consist of three strategies: (1) the use of "distancing" or the acquisition of cultural capital through the use of a special language, the use of propaganda making special claims for the occupation, the use of scientific research, and the effort to persuade governments to exclusively license practitioners; (2) "monopolizing," which increases cultural capital ("beyond what its cultural value would bring naturally in the marketplace") by controlling admission standards, acquiring the role of sole judge of knowledge claims, gaining control over the craft's technological tools, limiting practice to the legally qualified, and determining the range of actions over which their knowledge justifies exclusive control; and (3) "socializing," which is the guarding of the cultural capital by ingraining into new practitioners protective habits (which "hides the fact that not all professional knowledge is beyond common ken," for example).[5]

It can hardly be denied that some professionals act out of the motives ascribed to them by the revisionists, and therefore such motives must be guarded against. It is not clear, however, that all or even most professionals are so ethically inferior to their critics or so single-mindedly venal as their critics suggest. That all professionals conspire with each other to "unfairly" (on a competitive market-based standard) inflate their income and status is, I hope, unlikely. That some professionals who have risen to high levels of power within a profession are strongly inclined to seek additional power and glory for themselves, and therefore for their professions, is not such a far-fetched notion, however. It is a serious accusation which must be judged in the light of a careful historical study.

The Focus on Curriculum

The central issues for a study of educational policy surround the matter of curriculum, because curriculum is the content of education. Out of this subject matter of education, the other issues do or should derive.

The central issue of curriculum design is that of accommodating huge quantities of information (particularly in the professions) in the *limited time* available. The approach of expanding the time available for learning is not necessarily the best solution.

> Underlying many of the curricular issues of professional education is the simple matter of accommodating the expanding body of relevant knowledge into the curriculum. Knowledge accumulates so rapidly that, even if human tolerance of study would permit, lengthening the curriculum would be insufficient.... Young people do not relish the thought of waiting until their mid-thirties to complete their formal education.[6]

Nor is it merely student distaste for extended studies that is the central problem involved.

> Serious social problems are involved in the steady extension of preemployment education. There are curtailments of earning capacity, maladjustments in personal and family life, and an often unrecognized selection of individuals whose parents are in the social and economic groups which can afford the large capital investment required to complete a long professional course of study.[7]

Since not everything can be included in a professional education program which prepares people to enter the profession, the question of what to include becomes a question of *prioritizing subject matter*. In this respect,

A particularly vexing problem for professional education is the relative importance of theory and skill. The question as to which of these two aspects of professional concern should be emphasized has had an almost pendulum-like quality. Currently there is evidence that a number of professional schools have moved too far in the direction of theory, and some reform now represents attempts to moderate that swing. However, professional schools can and have erred in the direction of overemphasis on practice, resulting in a "how-to-do-it" procedure that limits members in adapting to changed conditions.[8]

One aspect of this problem is the question of the *role of* research in professional education.

Practitioners expect schools to provide replacements and to service a number of their applied needs. But a school dominated by research people will consider application and practice as inferior activities which interfere with the important work of the school—research and the prepar-ation of future research workers.[9]

Another aspect of this problem is the question of the *role of the liberal* arts in professional education. Lester Anderson refers to an "almost universal agreement that professional practice rests on a relative mastery of a body of fundamental knowledge. This knowledge is the substance of those subjects which we call the liberal arts." But then he reveals that, even if there is such agreement, important curricular questions remain to be answered.

Which of the liberal arts should be taught for which of the professions? when and where? to what ends and how?

With that inevitable factor, *time,* as a dimension of education, choices have to be made as to which subjects are more fundamental. Criteria for making these choices are not so easily derived. By what criteria, for example, might psychology be chosen or excluded as preparation for the practice of medicine, or biology in the education of the teacher? Traditions weigh heavy. Should the substance of the liberal arts be taught to prospective professionals without reference to any specific profession or to the professions in general? For example, should there be one type of course in economics as prelegal education and another for accounting? Should there be physics for engineers, physics for dentists, physics for physiotherapists, or just physics in preprofessional curriculums? ...To what extent should the liberal arts be taught independently of the professional schools, i.e., in the liberal-arts college, or to what extent should it [sic] be incorporated into the curriculum of the professional school?[10]

Anderson's questions ignore an even deeper question: what are the liberal arts and what is their purpose?

The Structure of the Present Study

McGrath, writing in 1959, identified five stages in the growth of professional education in the United States: (1) the apprentice stage, (2) the proprietary school stage, (3) the university school stage, (4) the preprofessional requirement stage (where subjects were required which were not specifically professional but were considered directly necessary for professional success), and (5) the general education stage (where subjects not directly related to practice were considered desirable—often to the point where professional education becomes a postgraduate education).[11] Whether or not this presentation is strictly accurate, it is apparent that there is a movement from less to more formal education, and then to ever higher formal education.

This book will give only a brief summary of the development of the proprietary school stage and the early university school stage. There are certainly interesting and instructive aspects of this development, so it cannot and should not be ignored, but it is the development since World War II which has had the most impact upon the present. As a result, the focus of the present study is on the most recent half-century. The effort to expand accounting education beyond the regular college degree and toward McGrath's stage five is a prominent aspect of that period.

Notes

[1] Nathan O. Hatch, "Introduction: The Professions in a Democratic Culture" in *The Professions in American* History, ed. by Nathan O. Hatch (University of Notre Dame Press, 1988), p. 6.

[2] Roger Soder, "Studying the Education of Educators: What We Can Learn from Other Professions." *Phi Delta Kappan* (December 1988): 301.

[3] Donna H. Kerr, *Barriers to Integrity: Modern Modes of Knowledge Utilization* (Boulder, Colorado: Westview Press, 1984), pp. 38, 39.

[4] Ibid., p. 46.

[5] Ibid., pp. 42-45.

[6] Lewis B. Mayhew and Patrick J. Ford, *Reform in Graduate and Professional Education* (San Francisco: Jossey-Bass Publishers, 1974), pp. 23-24.

[7] Earl J. McGrath, *Liberal Education in the Professions* (Teachers College, Columbia University, 1959), p. 3.

[8] Mayhew and Ford, *Reform*, p. 5.

[9] Ibid., p. 23.

[10] G. Lester Anderson, "Professional Education: Present Status and Continuing Problems" in Education for the Professions: The Sixty-first Yearbook of the National Society for the Study of Education, Part II, edited by Nelson B. Henry (Chicago: University of Chicago Press, 1962), pp. 20-21.

[11] McGrath, *Liberal Education*, pp. 28-34.

THE STRUGGLE FOR STATUS

A History of Accounting Education

Chapter 1

The Beginnings of
Collegiate Accounting Education

Education has long been a means of establishing status. In general, those who have higher status have often become more highly educated, and those who have become more highly educated have often had higher status. While no such generalization is infallible, of course, higher education and status have often gone hand in hand.

The ancient Greek citizens of Athens educated their children in the liberal arts. This education included oratory and such other skills as marked their elite status as political leaders. Greek philosophers such as Plato and Aristotle argued for a "liberal arts" education which was liberal in the sense of being free from physical necessity. It was not concerned with the matters of the flesh, the necessities of life, but rather with the free intellect and the deep issues of philosophy and justice. The citizens of Athens had such freedom because their needs were met by their slaves and by resident foreigners who were craftsmen and businessmen. The citizens of Athens were an elite ruling class.

This vision of education as a liberal arts education pervaded theories of education, particularly theories of higher education, for millennia. It has had a formative impact on higher education in the United States, and upon higher education for business and accounting. In the United States, education has especially been a way of achieving status, rather than a mark of the class-status into which one was born. With so much at stake, then, it was inevitable that education would become the focal point of battles between different philosophies of life. The United States has had in general a very practical bent, for example, and so it was inevitable that the ancient regime of the liberal arts would be challenged by more practical disciplines.

The Vision of Ben Franklin

The eminently practical Benjamin Franklin was the first to seriously challenge the traditional approach to formal higher education. In 1749 he fired the first shot in the revolution of formal education by advocating a new approach to high school, which was higher education for most Americans in those days. In his *Proposals Relating to the Education of Youth in Pennsylvania*, Franklin described the ideal education for the new breed of American. He called his new institution an academy, and it was to be made up of the traditional Latin grammar school, with its college-preparatory purposes, and also an "English grammar school," where English would be the language taught (rather than Latin) and the subjects would be "useful."

Skillful writing in English was crucial to Franklin, and students would write letters and abstracts of things they had read, and essays in prose and verse.[1] They would read and explain the best English writers and translations of the best classical writers. Franklin included rhetoric and public speaking in his academy, and logic was to be taught as well as morality.

Franklin believed that learning should be enjoyable to students, as it was to him. He envisioned the academy building surrounded by a garden, orchard, meadow, and fields, and filled within by books, maps, globes, and scientific apparatus. More importantly, "He painstakingly planned instruction so that one subject would lead naturally to the next. History was the central discipline."[2] Through history students would be introduced to geography, chronology, ancient customs, morality, the effects of oratory (both oral and written), and the necessity of "Publick Religion" and good government. Along with the readings in natural history would come practical experiences in agriculture. "The history of technology and actual experiences with machines would contribute to a knowledge of the applications of science to the arts of commerce, inventions, manufactures, machines of war, and to the improvement of civilization."[3]

Everything taught in the academy was to be useful. Mathematics was certainly to be in the curriculum in the form of arithmetic, bookkeeping, geometry, and astronomy. Natural science was

> a necessary accomplishment for merchants and mechanics in order that they might know more about their commodities and materials; for physicians to help them understand drugs and aid in preserving health; for ministers as an aid in strengthening their proofs of Divine Providence; and an improvement of the conversation and instruction of all.[4]

Even the classical languages were to be learned--by those who could use them, such as ministers and physicians. Others could learn them but would not be forced to. Those intending to be merchants would be taught French, German, and Spanish.

Franklin's ideas met with widespread approval among middle-class merchants, and the academy was established in 1751. But his dreams were short-lived. The trustees, all prominent men in the community, displaced him as president of the board in 1756, having, as Franklin said, "reap'd the full Advantage of my Head, Hands, Heart and Purse, in getting through the first Difficulties of the Design, and when they thought they could do without me, they laid me aside."[5] Franklin's utilitarian aims were not long honored by the trustees.

> He wrote a long complaint in 1789 describing the various ways that his beloved English school had been starved and neglected in favor of the Latin school at the

academy. He discussed at length how the masters and trustees had not lived up to the intentions of the founders and of the charter, and how they had cut the English master's salary and increased his duties while paying twice as much to the Latin master to do half as much work and teach half as many boys. Thus, good Latin teachers were secured, and poor English teachers could not hold their own against the skillful Latinists who pled for more tutors and higher salaries and even plotted to do away with the English school entirely. Disappointed parents withdrew their children from the school and sent them to private teachers.

For these reasons Franklin then demanded that the English school be separated entirely from the Latin school, the stock divided up, and the corporation dissolved. He was ready to call a failure the first experiment in developing an education that would combine the values of the classical humanism and modern science and utility.[6]

Franklin had lost the first battle of the revolution, but the war had only begun. Other academies, patterned after his, were established to provide practical education for those not intending to go to college. King's College, when it was founded in New York, was led by Samuel Johnson, who had greatly admired Franklin's plans for the academy and who intended to provide a similar education at the college level.[7] William Smith, president of the newly-founded College at Philadelphia was similarly inclined, but neither Johnson's nor Smith's efforts were able to long stand against tradition, and the battle reverted to the secondary level of education and to the elementary level. In the nineteenth century there was increasing pressure to expand the elementary school curriculum beyond reading, writing, and arithmetic and teach more subjects useful for life.

The period from 1810 to 1840 has been called the age of the academy because during this time they sprung up all over the nation, so that by 1850 there were more than 6000 of them serving more than a quarter of a million students.[8] The Latin grammar schools were finding less favor with the practical-minded American people, and academies took over the task of secondary education--and included girls as well as boys in that education. In their expansion, however, the academies lost their original aim. They devoted themselves more to preparing students for college, and lost interest in the commercial subjects.[9]

The first publicly supported free high school in the United States was established in Boston in 1821. Its original purpose was to "furnish the young men who are not intended for a collegiate course of studies, and who have enjoyed the usual advantages of the public schools, with the means of completing a good English education and of fitting themselves for all the departments of commercial life."[10] Likewise, the founding of the first high school at Hartford, Connecticut, was to "furnish an education preparatory to the pursuits of commerce, trade, manufacturers, and the mechanical arts."[11] Such purposes were very short-lived.

> The high school came in the first instance as a result of public demand for instruction suitable for youth not destined for the professions. There is little doubt but that the original vocational objectives of these schools was soon changed by teachers and administrators, presumably by impressing upon pupils the desirability of a college education and the superiority of professional training over vocational training. By virtue of this type of influence...the high school soon came to have preparation for college as the primary function. Thus guidance in the high school was toward the college, without regard to the interests or capacities of pupils.[12]

The only commercial course taught in the early high schools was bookkeeping, and that was for the sake of its mathematical discipline.[13]

The Success of the Commercial Schools

As can be seen from the early history of the academy and high school in the United States, there was among many educators immense resistance to practical and commercial education. Status was still perceived to be found in traditional educational approaches. But in such a nation as early America was, where practicality was honored and competition in education was allowed, such resistance could not long succeed. Since both the multitude of academies and the few high schools were offering primarily college preparatory courses, students who wanted business training went elsewhere. The first of the independent commercial schools was founded by Benjamin Franklin Foster in Boston in 1827.[14]

> By 1850 there were about twenty private business schools in various cities throughout the East and Middle West. The instruction often consisted only of arithmetic, bookkeeping, and penmanship. The faculty sometimes consisted only of the owner, who often prepared his own textbooks.
>
> The students came primarily from the ranks of those employed in business houses, and much of the instruction therefore was given in the evenings. The students usually spent about three months taking courses.[15]

The idea of a separate school for business training was becoming generally accepted, and vocational schools (which had been providing services for a century) either dropped business training or else switched over entirely to business training.[16] The nation became more industrialized, and the rural boys and girls poured into the cities to find jobs. Many had an elementary education but needed some business training to gain an advantage. A short, intensive course of study was all they needed and all they could afford, and these people found their way to the independent commercial school. Adults, too, caught in the transition to an industrial economy, went to the commercial schools for retraining. The schools allowed them to enter the courses at any time, receive individual instruction, and have considerable freedom in deciding what subjects to study (allowing flexibility with regard to their defined curricula).

In 1853 the first school in the Bryant-Stratton chain of commercial schools was founded in Cleveland, and by 1863 the chain had more than 50 schools. It was the policy of Bryant and Stratton to establish schools in every city of at least 10,000 people.[17] The schools were provided with uniform textbooks, and a lifetime "scholarship"--with which the student was allowed to study as long as he liked until he decided that he had learned enough, and which was honored in any of the chain's schools.

While the Bryant-Stratton chain, with its widely visible schools and its complete set of textbooks and its management conventions with prominent speakers, certainly had the greatest effect upon the growth of business education, it was not alone. There were other chains of commercial schools, and there were some notable individual schools arising during this period.

A particularly interesting school was that founded by Harvey G. Eastman in Poughkeepsie, New York, in 1859. It soon became the most widely known and most attended commercial school in the nation as a result of Eastman's unique promotion efforts.[18] He spent enormous amounts of money on advertising, and annual registrations between 1862 and 1866 averaged between 2,000 and 4,000 students. He maintained a brass band which toured the country, played to a packed house in Chicago (with Horace Greeley orating and General Sherman in the audience), and secured the highest place of honor in the parade in the capital at Lincoln's second inauguration. He distributed a million circulars to Civil War soldiers still in the field. He employed outstanding lecturers (at one time he had as many as 60 faculty) and communicated his own unbounded confidence to his students. He did more than any one man to popularize business education.

The Bryant-Stratton chain fell apart into its individual components in 1865, largely due to its transferrable life-scholarship plan (poorer schools were selling many scholarships which were being redeemed in the better schools)[19] and due to the fact that Bryant and Stratton treated different managers differently, which led to widespread dissatisfaction among them.[20] Individual commercial schools, however, prospered. In 1861 Congress had passed the Morrill Act, which set a very high tariff rate to protect U.S. businesses, and that tariff plus the productive needs of the Civil War resulted in an enormous expansion of industry, which found outlets for its goods after the war through the aid of the expanding railroads (mileage doubled in the eight years after the war). Civil War veterans returned home to booming business and often sought retraining in the commercial schools. As the population of the country grew, so did the number of school-age children, many of whom found the commercial schools useful. In 1876 there were 137 commercial schools in the nation; by 1886 there were 239; by 1900 there were 373.[21] By 1893 more than 115,000 students were being served.[22]

While bookkeeping, arithmetic, and penmanship continued to form the core of the commercial curriculum, some other subjects were being added, such as business correspondence, business law, business ethics, and political economy--though such subjects were not added universally.[23] With the invention of the typewriter, typewriting was added and shorthand became more popular.

As the nineteenth century was nearing its end, the independent commercial school was strong and healthy. It was a businesslike nation's original response to an educational need. Along with its rapid growth came problems, of course. Unscrupulous commercial school operators offered poor-quality instruction and admitted students who were too young. The commercial schools were criticized for their lack of standards, for their loose instructional approaches, and for their lower-quality (less-educated) students. On the other hand, they were not tied to tradition or ancient ways of doing things, and they could and did rapidly respond to new needs. They served a set of students whose needs were not recognized by the other available educational institutions, and they served them efficiently and with care for the individual. Yet their popularity was their undoing, for there were eyes upon them which coveted what they had.

The Colleges and Business Education

The colleges could not help but notice the success of the commercial schools. After the Civil War, American colleges desperately wanted more students. Since the time of Andrew Jackson, college enrollments had been static in a nation whose population was growing. "During the 1870s attendance at twenty of the 'oldest leading colleges' rose only 3.5 per cent, while the nation's population soared 23 per cent."[24] Business was booming and the colleges were not participating in the increase in wealth. Business was booming and success could be had without a college degree. Indeed, business leaders were often convinced of the uselessness of higher education, and the well-publicized words of Andrew Carnegie merely added fuel to an otherwise blazing fire. Carnegie said:

> While the college student has been learning a little about
> the barbarous and petty squabbles of a far-distant past,
> or trying to master languages which are dead, such
> knowledge as seems adapted for life upon another planet
> than this as far as business affairs are concerned, the
> future captain of industry is hotly engaged in the school
> of experience, obtaining the very knowledge required for
> his future triumphs.... College education as it exists is
> fatal to success in that domain.[25]

The mood of the country had progressed to the point where the concern for usefulness had led to a lessening of respect for the college graduate and for the college professor.[26] That was not a state of affairs which was enjoyable to the underpaid college professor. The decline in status was intolerable.

The implication of the Jacksonian democracy which had ruled the nation for decades began to make itself felt in higher education. "Real life" became exalted over the "cultivated life," and the individual's right to choose was expressed in the elective system pioneered in the later 1800s at Harvard by its president, Charles W. Eliot. Eliot went farther than others dared follow, but the use of the elective approach for at least the last two years of college study, and often even much of the two first years, became increasingly popular among colleges and universities in the last few decades of the nineteenth century. An elective system presumes that no particular subject is more worthwhile to study than another. The old justification for the liberal arts as being the best subjects to train the mind began to break down. Before long, only tradition kept any and all possible subjects from being included in the curriculum.

Colleges became universities, as new subjects were allowed. The government added fuel to this movement, beginning with the Land Grant College Act (Morrill Act) of 1862 which broke with the classical approach to education and economically supported applied sciences and technology--including agricultural instruction. If technical training for farmers was acceptable for higher education, could technical training for business leaders be far behind? After a couple of abortive attempts at other schools, a successful business school was finally established at the University of Pennsylvania in

1881, when Joseph Wharton made a gift of $100,000 for that purpose. A significant amount of money proved to be sufficient incentive to create support for business education.

Accounting Education and Theoretical vs. Practical

Just as collegiate business education effectively began at the Wharton School, so did collegiate accounting education. Indeed, Wharton himself specified that the faculty of the school should include "One Professor or Instructor of Accounting or Bookkeeping, to teach the simplest and most practical forms of bookkeeping for housekeepers, for private individuals, for commercial and banking firms, for manufacturing establishments and for banks...."[27] In 1883 the first accounting course was offered, taught by "a bookkeeper who was very familiar with the principles of debit and credit."[28]

After a two-year period in which the teaching of accounting courses was discontinued, the teaching of the subject was renewed in the fall of 1887 under a new instructor, and the course was described in the following terms:

> A course in the Theory of Accounting, to which are devoted four hours a week throughout the junior year. Practical work is insisted upon only so far as it is necessary to understand the theoretical aspects of the subject and the general principles which underlie all special systems.[29]

In this course description can be seen the desire to construct a "liberal arts" accounting course, where theory is stressed and practice minimized. This type of course would enhance the status of accounting among the liberal arts faculty.

For the next few years at Wharton, accounting was supervised by Roland Post Falkner. Falkner had received his Ph.D. from the University of Halle in Germany in 1888, and studied teaching methods in accounting in some of the higher French commercial schools before returning to the U.S. He considered the methods in the French commercial schools superior to the methods used in American commercial schools. While "American texts on elementary bookkeeping began with day-book entries" the "French school's approach to the subject was by means of account analysis."[30]

The great advantage of the account analysis method was not only that it was more conceptual, but also that it effectively set the teaching of collegiate accounting apart from the teaching of accounting as done in the popular commercial schools. Wharton's dean, in his report to the provost in February 1890, said, "The instruction in bookkeeping which was open to criticism in previous years has been put upon a new basis and is now one of the features of the department."[31]

During the next decade accounting education, along with business education in general, was shown by Wharton to be a legitimate collegiate activity. With the ground broken, others naturally joined in. In the fall of 1897, the University of Chicago offered a course in Railway Accounts, Exchanges, etc., to be taught by a newly-minted Ph.D. named Henry Rand Hatfield. Two years later a course simply titled "Accounting" was offered by the same instructor and listed in the catalog as:

> A study of the underlying principles. Some practice work under the guidance of an expert auditor of accounts will be given but only with a view to illustrating the principles discussed in the lectures. Emphasis will be placed on the interpretation of the balance sheets and the problems implied therein.[32]

Once again, the stress was clearly on concepts and not on practice. In the elementary course taught by Hatfield "accounts were studied and interpreted from the point of view of the business man rather than that of the professional bookkeeper."[33] Hatfield published one of the earliest American books on accounting entitled *Modern Accounting* in 1909.

Hatfield's approach, however, was early recognized as a "departure from the regular method of teaching the elementary course."[34] While the theoretical approach is useful in legitimizing a subject with the liberal arts faculty, once the subject has been accepted there is less pressure to continue to stress a liberal arts approach. The course in Theory of Accounts offered at Ohio University for some years after the fall of 1896 was described as follows:

> Ample practice is given in the systems of accounts used
> in various kinds of business from retailing to modern
> banking. It is the aim of this course to give the student a
> wide acquaintance with business methods and to secure
> proficiency in opening and closing books, journalizing,
> rendering statements, tracing errors, analyzing accounts
> and drawing business papers.[35]

The description is that of a practice-oriented bookkeeping course.
Likewise, beginning in 1900 the courses in accounting taught at the
Graduate School of Business Administration, known as the Amos
Tuck School of Administration and Finance, at Dartmouth, "stressed
the practical side of accounting."[36]

The issue of whether to teach accounting more in terms of theory
or in terms of practice continued to be raised, and the battle was
fought separately in each university. By 1900 there were thirteen
universities and colleges giving college-credit courses in accounting,
and the practical approach appeared to be favored over the theoretical.

> The courses were taught largely by the laboratory
> method supplemented by class discussion. Sets were
> worked out under the direction of an instructor and
> ample drills were given in the preparation of forms and
> the working of exercises.[37]

Though seemingly prevalent in the early years, what may
anachronistically be called the "laboratory method" was not
universally accepted. A course in the Science of Accounts was offered
by the Economics Department of the University of Michigan in the
fall of 1901, for example, and its instructor was requested by the
Chairman of the Economics Department to stress theory rather than
practice.[38]

The Growth of Accounting Education

An extremely important set of events in the history of accounting
education began with the formation in New York of the American

Association of Public Accountants in 1887, the first professional organization of accountants in the U.S. It took an immediate interest in education, and by early 1892 it had plans to start an educational institution for business students and accountants. The New York Board of Regents, however, objected to the idea of a business school, so the accountants scaled back their request and asked that they be allowed to offer simply a professional school for accountants--and they guaranteed financial support for the first two-year provisional period.[39] By December of 1892 the New York School of Accounts had been founded.

The school closed in mid-1894 due to a lack of students, but the idea of improved education for public accountants did not die. Something which greatly helped achieve that educational goal was the passage in 1896 in New York of the first state legislation to legally establish and protect the title of certified public accountant (CPA). The legislation required that any accountant certified by the state must pass a qualifying examination. Other states quickly followed New York's lead. The passage of the CPA laws made public accounting a governmentally-recognized profession--a profession which required comprehension of a specified body of knowledge. Members of the new profession quickly took advantage of their increased prestige.

> In November of 1899, the New York State Society of Certified Public Accountants adopted a resolution authorizing the president of the society to consult with the officials of Columbia University, the University of the City of New York, and other collegiate bodies with a view to establishing university training in accountancy because "it is the sense of this Society that it is expedient and necessary to the development of the profession of Public Accountancy that the same should be established primarily upon an educational basis, as in the case of other professions." Two sentences from letters of the then president of the society, Charles Waldo Haskins, are indicative of what lay in the minds of professional accountants at the turn of the century: "The grave and urgent necessity for a carefully educated body of public accountants has been demonstrated" and "The establishment of the profession of accountancy upon an

> educational foundation is manifestly its only safe-
> guard."[40]

To ultimately be recognized as a true profession, public accounting
would have to require higher education of its practitioners. Motion
toward that goal began. In the fall of 1900 the School of Commerce,
Accounts and Finance was founded at New York University (NYU),
with Haskins as its first dean. The business school was founded at the
insistence of prominent public accountants, with the expressed
purpose of preparing men for the profession of accounting.
"Accounting practitioners served as guarantors against any and all
financial loss and agreed to furnish a large part of the necessary
faculty."[41] The same approach would be imitated by other public
accountants in other states.

The establishment of the New York school fully legitimized
accountancy in higher education, and even allowed it to dominate the
rest of business education. It was the newly professionalized field of
public accounting which forced an accounting curriculum upon higher
education. Furthermore, the fact that the passage of the first CPA law
and the establishment of the first Department of Accounting in higher
education were so closely related in time and place and in the
personalities involved had strong implications for the accounting
curriculum. The subject matter of the New York CPA exam was the
subject matter of the curriculum at NYU.[42]

Theoretical vs. Practical Revisited

The public accounting practitioners who were instrumental in
establishing the business school at NYU were strong supporters of a
conceptual approach. Charles Ezra Sprague, the banker and public
accountant most responsible for the passage of the New York CPA
law and the establishment of the NYU business school,[43] became a
professor of accounting at NYU and offered a course called
Philosophy of Accounts in 1902. In this course,

> accountancy was considered from the standpoint of
> science. Illustrations were freely used but the emphasis
> was upon the philosophy of the subject as a phase of

economic theory. During the course the various arts
which depended upon this science were defined and
differentiated. The account was defined and analyzed,
and accountancy was reviewed. Critical opinions were
gathered from different writers as to the purposes of the
account, the information furnished, forms of accounts,
and the results of accounts. Various theories of debit and
credit were studied and used as a basis for argument and
explanation.[44]

Sprague published a book called *The Philosophy of Accounts* in 1907,
and the book revolutionized accounting by making it systematic
(based upon the "accounting equation" of Assets equal Liabilities and
Owner Equity) rather than an assortment of actions learned by rote.

NYU did not use the "laboratory method" but was "founded upon
the use of textbooks and courses of lectures, supplemented by the
careful employment of a system of quizzes designed to aid the
student's memory."[45]

Nevertheless, the majority of accounting educators rejected the
emphasis on theory and philosophy which the thoughtful practitioners
and pioneers of accounting education desired. As early as 1907 many
schools were requesting practitioner-teachers because "professional
subjects must be practically applied" and "theoretically oriented
professors could not handle accountancy in a professional manner."[46]
By 1912, when Sprague died, the character of the average accounting
instructor had become clear:

> very few of the most skilled practicing accountants are
> qualified to conduct class work, and even if they were,
> the average school could not afford to pay the price
> demanded for such services; therefore the school
> considers itself lucky when it can secure the services of a
> qualified accountant who can teach well and impart what
> he knows to others, even if he has not had the practical
> experience of the ablest accountants.[47]

Apparently the average accounting instructor was a former
practitioner who was not very skilled and not theoretically oriented.
The old saying that those who cannot do something teach it instead

seems to have been justified in accounting education after the pioneers were gone. A person who is not skillful in practice will, however, tend to take on the mantle of a theoretician who is "above" the "unimportant" details. The results of this theoretical approach by instructors who were deliberately chosen because they did not have a theoretical approach, can be easily surmised. Apparently there were by 1912 a number of professors who were teaching "theory" (something having little relation to practice), and there were a number of practitioners who were wanting more practical approaches.[48]

On the other hand, there were a number of practitioners who did not believe that the colleges could prepare a practical accountant. In 1914 John C. Duncan opened an address to the national association of public accountants with a lament that, although practitioners he had talked with confessed the desirability of a college course,

> [I have] yet to find a practitioner who believes that it is possible for any university to give one in accountancy anything more than a most general preparation for actual practice. More than one practitioner and members of examining boards have told the speaker that the best that any university course can do is to give the student a theoretical training which he must unlearn in the office before he is any good.[49]

This attitude among practitioners--considering theoretical training useless--inspired an eloquent defense of theoretical training by Seymour Walton, who argued "that theoretical accounting is not a form of thought disjoined from the actual facts of business, but is a summation and systematization of such facts."[50] What Walton did not mention is that everything, of course, depends upon how well the theory is formed and taught.

Duncan suggested his own solution to the problem. He sympathized with the practitioner, admitting that "experience may be the best teacher, but we shall all have to admit that experience is a very wasteful pedagogue."[51] He advocated "substituting for the unsightly cribbage of individual experience the harmonious shaft of the science of administrative criticism" and suggested a series of research articles on topics he named. He also proposed to add another course (which he himself had already done when teaching at the

University of Illinois) which trained the accounting student in "professional technique" by giving him "a man-size task" which needed to be done "in a workmanlike manner." "Since these courses must be designed to teach a man how to work, the author called them laboratory courses."[52] Such courses would be eminently practical, but in a theoretical and scientific kind of way--not looking at every different type of business and its way of keeping books, but rather at a single set of generalized books.

Duncan was not the only one to whom this solution suggested itself. Robert H. Montgomery, a prominent public accountant and accounting teacher at Columbia University and author of the first American book on auditing, also proposed an "accountancy laboratory" in 1914, claiming that the accounting student needed the equivalent of a medical student's clinic in order to overcome a deficiency in practical experience.[53]

Montgomery appealed more to the practical vision which was being popularized in progressive education. Though Montgomery did not explicitly say so, the laboratory method, where extensive practice sets were used, would seem to be justified by John Dewey's "pragmatic" educational philosophy, which was popularly interpreted as excusing a more vocational approach to education. Perhaps accounting instructors found additional support by looking at the law schools, where the "case method" was reforming the curriculum in a deliberate departure from the traditional stress on theory.[54]

The reason Montgomery explicitly used to justify the introduction of an accounting laboratory was the high failure rate of prospective accountants who took the CPA qualifying examination. Entry to the public accounting profession was through the CPA examination and so, not suprisingly, most academicians taught students how to pass that exam--much to the continuing dismay of many thoughtful practitioners and academicians. In the new accounting programs springing up around the country, "The introduction of [a course in] the study of C.P.A. problems in almost every case closely followed the passage of the state C.P.A. laws."[55] Though many practitioners criticized the CPA examinations as narrowly technical, academicians took the passage rates of their students as a measure of their teaching success.

Montgomery argued for the laboratory method as a way for students to gain practical experience in the schools, short-cutting the real experience requirements and allowing students to pass the practical accounting sections of the CPA exam. He faced the argument that practical experience could not be gained in a generalized course in college with this rebuttal:

> Now if practical experience means a given number of years' clerkship in an office (other than that of a public accountant) we, to a certain extent, contradict our claim that accountancy is a science. If its principles can be acquired and assimilated only by contact, as is the case with bricklaying, it would be very discouraging to attempt to short-cut the process of training students.[56]

Montgomery, of course, was convinced that accounting was a "science" that could be entirely taught in the schools, so long as students had contact with "actual transactions" just as medical interns have contact with living patients. Montgomery installed an accountancy laboratory at Columbia.

> The laboratory consisted of accounting records and some complete sets of books of business enterprises which had been discontinued by dissolution or bankruptcy. In addition there were a few "model" sets of books and collateral records, such as minute books, stock certificate books, and transfer books.
> The laboratory also included a file of annual reports and statistical data from leading companies, together with organization charts, descriptions of systems in use, and similar material. Also the laboratory was expected to maintain an exhibit of office appliances, bookkeeping machines, and so on. All this was designed to give the student contact with the real world of accounting, as well as with the theory of the subject.[57]

Many academicians believed that the laboratory method would make the schools self-sufficient for preparing professionals. Many leading practitioners were not convinced. To their way of thinking, theory was what was to be learned in higher education and practice was what was to be learned in accounting practice. Education was not complete until both were learned, and education was therefore not complete at college graduation. F.C. Belser in 1927 complained about the fact that graduates were impatient with working their way up from the bottom ranks through an "apprenticeship" process, and he appealed to teachers to give their students a better picture of reality in public accounting,

> to make clear to the graduate that his schooling has not made of him a finished accountant, but has only taught him how to learn to the end that he may approach his period of practical training in the attitude of one who is merely completing his education.[58]

Belser recognized that some practical training was necessary in college--indeed, he expressed the fear that "instructors in accountancy schools have a tendency to become rather too academic"--but he also stated that "what is needed is more theory, and a sounder education, not only in accounting, but in related science.... What is still more important, the student needs a sounder fundamental education, particularly in English and rhetoric."[59] Schooling had its function, which was primarily in providing theoretical education, and experience had its function, which was primarily in providing practical education.

> [I]t should be emphasized that there is required a long period of experience in practical work if any success whatever is to be achieved. This fact is sufficiently recognized by teachers in that they seek to have their accountancy course duplicate, as nearly as possible, the practical work of the accountant. Of course, the schools cannot actually duplicate the conditions which confront the accountant in his practical work, and it is therefore essential that the schooling in theory be supplemented by experience in practice.[60]

This request to academic accountants to stick more to theory, however, fell on deaf ears.

Academicians felt no need to change their direction. They were awash with success. By 1921 all the states had CPA laws. Those laws required at most a high school education with some experience in order to qualify to take the CPA exam and become licensed to practice. But colleges and universities were the likely agents to prepare the "serious" students who wanted to enter the new profession. While there were only thirteen colleges teaching accounting in 1900, there were 52 in 1910, and 335 by 1926. Only two schools (NYU and Wharton) had offered a baccalaureate in accounting in 1910, but by 1926 at least 60 schools were providing it. Only NYU had offered a master's degree in accounting in 1910, but 30 schools did by 1926.[61] "By the mid-1920s, 36 percent all native-born practitioners had college degrees."[62]

Bossard and Dewhurst Re-evaluate Developments

The status of accounting in business education was high. When James Bossard and Frederic Dewhurst (both of Wharton) completed their landmark study of business education in 1931, they had this to say about accounting:

> Accounting was the first, and is now one of the most specific and well defined fields of business for which collegiate schools of business attempt to prepare their students. In some respects it may be described as the original *raison d'etre* for university instruction in business. ...
> Accounting is, undoubtedly, the most fully developed subject or field of study in our collegiate schools of business. The objectives of accounting departments are usually well-defined and clear; the courses in accounting and their content are relatively standardized. Accounting is usually the first "business" subject to be introduced in college curricula. In fact, to many persons accounting stands in a peculiar sense as the Alpha of business education. ...All of the schools offer courses in accounting. It is generally recognized as an essential and integral element in business education.[63]

Bossard reported that accounting was commonly one of the two most popular majors of undergraduates at the schools he studied.

Yet underneath this bright surface there remained the tension between the theoretical and practical. Indeed, the tension was present not only in accounting education but in the whole of business education. Bossard and Dewhurst gave an insightful analysis of the origins of that tension.

> Business curricula have been developed in a certain measure to meet the demands or to avoid the antagonism of the arts faculty; sometimes such demands having been given more consideration than the obvious needs of the students. In other words, these curricula are a compromise between liberal arts insistence and the business school judgment. The result is an academic structure lacking, in some cases completely and in other cases in certain respects, in coherence from either point of view.
>
> ...If the liberal arts college is the grandmother, then the department of economics has served "in the dual capacity of father, and midwife" to the collegiate school of business. The attitude of the economists has constituted a second factor of primary importance in the evolution of the business curriculum.... The attitudes of the economists toward the business schools are not so clear cut as those of the liberal arts faculties. ...To the extent that there is anything like a common or typical attitude, it may be likened to that of a petulant father who is partly proud of, partly envious of, partly skeptical of, or even antagonistic toward his offspring, who has outgrown him or is threatening to do so.
>
> There are various results of this tension. One could name four or five schools where the development of the business subjects seems to lag because of a petty domination by the economics group. There are institutions where the relationship is described as one of "more or less constant tension between two groups working in fields not sharply distinguished." At other institutions, the economists appear almost peevish,

preferring the non-business atmosphere of the college of liberal arts, or, if within the fold of the business school, longing to resume their liberal arts connections. And finally, at some schools there is a clear-eyed vision of the importance of a constructive integration of the work of both business and economics departments, in which each profits by service through critical co-operation with the other. ...

...Another factor in the development thus far of some collegiate schools of business and of their curricula has been the attitude of the general university administration, particularly with reference to financial support. Certain schools of business have been considered too much in the light of a good thing, financially. They have been utilized in a number of cases to make a net financial contribution to the general university budget. At places they have been exploited specifically for the benefit of the liberal arts college. At other places, they have been starved, consciously and purposively, to prevent their development as competitors to other schools and programs of the university.[64]

In spite of such adversity, business education was phenomenally successful and rapidly growing from the end of the first world war to the great depression. This popularity seems to have allowed the practical side to gain the upper hand over the theoretical side. The most important criticism Bossard and Dewhurst made of the business schools had to do with the proliferation of specialties and courses:

The number of separate undergraduate courses in some of the older schools varies from 60 to 100, and in one case exceeds 200. ...Specialization in the business curricula runs riot--at least so far as differentiated curricula and faculty preferences are concerned. Of a total of 353 curricula announced by 38 undergraduate schools, 132 different titles appear. Twenty-three of these 38 schools offer eight or more fields of specialization. ...Much of the specialization is window dressing.[65]

What could be said of business education could also be said of accounting education. In accounting education, too, there was sometimes an excessive proliferation of extremely specialized courses. If business education was popular, then so was accounting education. Even during the depths of the depression in 1933 it could be reported that there was

> striking evidence of the importance which is attached to accounting training and the stability with which it has been so far maintained in face of business difficulties of the most extraordinary severity. Our "volume of business," if we may call it that, has fallen off very little--probably not over 10 per cent at the outside. Our "working forces" have suffered virtually no impairment, and our "wage scale" is practically untouched.[66]

Academic education in accounting had been wildly successful, and there seemed little reason to believe that it could not conquer any problem. Accounting academicians formed themselves into a group in 1916, meeting concurrently with the American Economic Association. In 1923 they first met separately from the economists and declared their independence in Hatfield's address to the meeting entitled "An Historical Defense of Bookkeeping." This address "was to influence others that the subject matter of accounting was worthy of recognition as an academic discipline."[67] In 1926 the first issue of the group's scholarly publication, *The Accounting Review*, appeared--complete with a detailed and ambitious "research agenda."

The College Requirement for a CPA

An event in 1929 enhanced the position of accounting academicians, and thereby attracted to them the attentions of other academicians (especially economics professors, who felt paternalistic stirrings toward academic accountants). In that year the New York state legislature passed a law which required that after January 1, 1938, everyone taking the CPA exam for that state would have to have "satisfactorily completed the course of study in a college or school of accountancy registered by the department."[68] Before this, the educational requirement for sitting for the CPA exam had been high school graduation and three years of experience in bookkeeping (with a school of accountancy degree accepted as the equivalent of two of those years).

The New York requirement was a bolt out of the blue. Even insiders were surprised that its sponsor had proposed it, except to note that he must have been convinced "that certified public accountancy was growing up as a profession and that it was due to its status as a profession that it should, like medicine and dentistry and other professions, be based upon college and university training."[69] A desired increase in status seems to have figured prominently in the reasons for forcing prospective accountants to graduate from college before they could become certified. Whatever the reason, New York's position as the financial center of the nation would once again inspire other states to follow its lead, but much more slowly this time.

There were some who were not happy with what the New York legislators had done. The "Abraham Lincoln approach" was much honored in the nation at that time; it was believed that a person's opportunities should not be restricted by requiring a formal education, but rather that people should be left free to educate themselves in whatever ways worked best for them. A college degree, however, carried more status than self-education, and, where education confers more status than experience, such notions were doomed.

The realization that collegiate instruction soon would be required of anyone desiring to be a public accountant seems to have inspired accounting academicians and economics professors to rethink the relationship between accounting and the liberal arts. For the next six or seven years articles on that subject regularly appeared in the *Accounting Review*. The discussion was directed more toward the liberal arts college or university than toward the business and professional programs in a university, but the distinction between the "liberal arts" style of accounting and the "professional" style of accounting was being drawn nonetheless.

The first question, of course, was whether accounting belonged in a liberal arts curriculum at all. This was not an issue of whether to put it there, since it was already deeply entrenched as a collegiate subject, but rather an exercise in justification. The "classical" idea of liberal education as emphasizing languages and literature and history and some mathematics was attacked as subject-oriented. In the place of this outmoded idea, liberal education was defined to include all studies that were not vocationally or professionally concerned. According to an economics academician, any subject could be taught (or at least any "professional" subject), including accounting, so long as it was not taught with vocational or professional objectives, "but with cultural, citizenship and disciplinary objectives."[70]

Vagueness about the goal of liberal education was very useful in excusing the presence of accounting. One writer, claiming with considerable justification that his "conception of the purpose of liberal education...is as comprehensive as any that can be found," opposed the idea of liberal education as emphasizing the development of the mind, since "all educators and schools, professional as well as liberal arts, lay claim" to doing that. Instead, he defined the purpose of liberal arts as

> seeking the discovery of truth in every field of human life without attempting to prepare the student for any special activity. Liberal education therefore may be said to be a training for the practice of living, developed by a study of man and his environment in their relation to contemporary life and of all the problems growing out of that life, with the objective of aiding youth to deal masterfully with existing conditions. ...If liberal education is training to deal masterfully with the problems of contemporary life, in which economic and business experience plays a large and vital part, accounting is a legitimate and necessary study in the program.[71]

In the same words, yet quoting another source, another writer defined the purpose of education as being "to train youth to deal masterfully with existing conditions" and then continued:

> It is significant that accounting as a profession grew with the development of corporations and large-scale production. Its introduction into the curricula of colleges came as a result of the necessity for accounting in the operation and management of business enterprise of the

new type. It grew as a skill, a technique, a method, and
as such became indispensable to modern society. This,
then, is our justification for including the study of
accounting in the liberal arts college.[72]

Once the presence of the indispensable accounting in the liberal arts
curriculum was adequately justified, the next question to be asked
was, what was the "liberal arts" way of teaching accounting? To the
writers it was clear that accounting should be

taught from a point of view and in a manner to
contribute most toward the purpose of liberal education
and least toward a professional purpose. Concerning the
teacher it is clear, for example, that he should have a
rich background in economics and probably should not
be a certified public accountant.[73]

The approach advocated by some of the writers harkened back to the
theoretical approach to accounting used by the pioneers, but with a
greater antipathy toward the mechanics of bookkeeping and the public
accountant.

It is doubtful if the student need spend much time
puzzling over the details of recording and the books of
original entry. ...In a general course in accounting,
much attention should be given to a study of the
financial statements--their preparation, analysis, interpretation, and general relationships. The student will
accomplish more if he becomes familiar with the type of
business for which the statements were prepared and the
multiplicity of ways such statements may be used than if
he has a knowledge of the forms from which they were
prepared. The case method, here, might be particularly
useful. ...This amounts, perhaps, to teaching business
organization through accounts rather than accounting
itself, but where limited time is available, I believe it
yields to the student much fundamental knowledge.[74]

Speaking to the same issue, another writer said,

> When we have tried to do anything for the general
> business student, it has usually been to put him through
> the initial stages of our program of specialist training.
> ...From the standpoint of accounting teaching, this
> seems to me our most important problem--the develop-
> ment of a brief but effective program of instruction in
> the fundamentals of accounting for all those who are
> training themselves for work in the business field.[75]

This more conceptual approach to teaching accounting was suggested
for general and business students, but not for preparing accounting
students, since "we are already doing this job well." Apparently the
elementary course in accounting was of poor educational value to
everyone except those who intended to ᵇe accountants.

In teaching the liberal arts accounting course the value of
exposing the students to controversy and to the variety of possible
methods was also defended.[76]

Finally, once the right sort of accounting was considered
allowable in the liberal arts curriculum, the last question was how
much accounting was justifiable. The writers tended to agree that "not
much" was the best answer to that question. The chairman of the
Department of Economics and Social Institutions at Princeton,
thought that "accounting should be taught in the liberal arts course as
a part of the program in economics, not as a part of the program of a
school of commerce or of business administration, and not as an
independent department or field of study."[77] If accounting were just
one area of economics it should not command much time by itself, he
thought. An assistant professor of economics agreed.[78]

The problem was that there already were several courses in
accounting in the college curriculum, and it would not be easy to
dislodge them. Bossard reported that "accounting curricula are more
narrowly specialized than those in any other [major] offered in the
business schools."[79] All of the business schools which he studied
offered an elementary and advanced accounting course and a cost
accounting course; all but a few offered auditing and income tax
courses; about half offered an accounting systems course; and other
courses offered by 9 to 15 of the 38 schools were: problems of

the CPA, case problems, governmental accounting, management accounting, and financial statement analysis.[80]

A Fifth Year of College for CPAs

The tension between the need to claim that an accountant must be liberally educated (or why require college at all?) and the need to offer a large number of specialized courses in accounting beyond the major in business, seemed to have an obvious resolution. In 1936 Roswell McCrea and Roy Kester announced that Columbia University was establishing, within the framework of the business school, a college of accountancy which would cover a three-year course in technical training based upon a two-year course in a college of liberal arts. So before the first state requirement for a four-year college degree became effective (and before any other state indicated that it would follow in that direction), the five-year approach was born. The approach was modeled very self-consciously upon the "schools of law, where usually the course covers a minimum of five years of work of collegiate grade, which three...are devoted to technical courses in law."[81] They made the following claim:

> because of the breadth of the field of business, which is limited only by the extent of human endeavor in the satisfaction of human wants, the accountant is required to be familiar with a broader field than, probably, is the lawyer. A course of training, therefore, equal in intensiveness and extent to that of the law would seem to be a minimum requirement for the professional accountant.[82]

If the claim that the accountant, concerned with one aspect of business, needs more knowledge than the lawyer, concerned with the regulation of all aspects of society, seems just a trifle overblown, perhaps the real reason for the move to a five-year course of study might be more apparent in this later statement by Kester:

> From the standpoint of the development of professions out of their earlier stages, in which they may be called

trades or vocations, one might, I believe, with a high degree of accuracy, point out that the transition from the stage of the incipient or inchoate profession to the true profession, is usually marked by the taking over by the schools of the training necessary to prepare for the profession. Stated otherwise, it may be said that up until such time as a group of men working in a semiprofessional field become conscious of the shortcomings of training by the apprenticeship method and address themselves to the task of the organization of the basic subject matter of their field of practice in such a manner that definite and specific outlines of the field can be established and the subject matter made available for instructional use, such vocation cannot take seriously to itself the right to be called a profession.[83]

Here was the argument, to be voiced again and again in the coming years. If accountants want to be called "professionals" then they must understand that the key to being a professional is being schooled scientifically, and not merely trained through experience. The status accorded a professional is achieved through more education. Kester went on to say,

When high educational standards are required before admission to the practice of public accountancy, it seems reasonable to expect that state boards of accountancy will give suitable recognition to such training by lessening the amount of practical experience required before or after admission to the examination, but always before the issuance of the certificate for certified public accountant.[84]

In a profession, more schooling replaced experience, according to Kester.

The addition to the argument, implied by Kester, is: if schooling is the key to being a professional, then being more professional means being more schooled. Unless we are willing to call all college graduates professionals, we must require more than four years of college education in order for us to be called professional. Here then was the key to the plan which would allow accounting to move from being the "semi-profession" it was considered previously to being a "real profession." Like Pinnocchio, accountants wanted to become real, but like him they had some trouble keeping their noses from growing. Fortunately for them, there were so many wooden boys with long noses besides those in the field of accounting that it did not seem very unusual.

An influential accounting professor, historian, and theoretician, A.C. Littleton, while agreeing with the idea of reducing practice requirements for more education ("perhaps even to the extent of dropping them entirely for those with a master's degree in accountancy"), disagreed with Kester on the need for a five-year program. He attacked the "reasoning by analogy" which suggested that since accounting was a profession it should have similar educational requirements to those of law and medicine and other such professions. His analysis of the history of medical and legal education led him to the following conclusion:

> The pressure of a vast growth in the quantity and complexity of materials has forced medicine and law into schools of specialization under teachers who are also specialists. But there is no comparable pressure in accountancy of accumulated special subject matter or of the subdivision of specialties.[85]

Littleton did say that someday there might be so much material in accounting and the techniques so complicated that separate accounting schools might become desirable. The argument that such a complex time had finally come would be used periodically by accountants over the following years.

Most accountants of the time, however, focused their attention upon the requirements for a four-year college degree in accounting. A study of CPA examination results for New York State (where about a third of all CPA candidates were examined) from 1929 to 1934 showed "a striking uniformity" between the examination scores of those who were college-educated and those who were not. The writer who reported these results commented:

My experience in examining applications for examination and in rating answer papers has convinced me
that in far too large a proportion of the cases of failure
the primary cause is the inadequacy of the candidate's
secondary or high school education and that quite often
the superstructure of a college course upon that weak
foundation has made a bad situation worse. Bad English,
not alone in rhetoric but in grammar and spelling and in
the unwise selection of big words; failure to recognize
that a question in costs was merely a problem in practical
arithmetic; muddled thinking; those were the causes of a
very large proportion of the failures.[86]

In the writer's experience, college did not help. Nevertheless, in the
very next paragraph the writer said:

May we expect that the educational requirement effective
after next New Year's will overcome this situation? In
my opinion not for a considerable period, several years,
perhaps a decade, though I do hope for improvement
within that time.[87]

The writer went even further to hope for a time when collegiate study
of accountancy would be post-graduate work, as at Columbia. He
neglected to address the problem of how an ever higher superstructure
on the same faulty foundation would help.

Accrediting the Right Program

The committee on education of the American Institute of
Accountants (the public accounting practitioners' national
association), with Kester of Columbia as chairman, issued a report in
1936 which considered New York's requirement and agreed that "four
years of collegiate training beyond the high school" should be the
minimum. The committee, however, thought that courses in
accounting should take up 38 semester hours rather than the 24 which
New York required.[88] More than that, the committee suggested that

the public accountants should begin accrediting programs; it proposed:

> That the committee on education attempt to develop, formulate, and present in their 1937 report a set of standards--covering at least: (a) courses and their content; (b) faculty personnel; (c) library and laboratory equipment; and (d) financial resources--to be used as a basis for measuring or rating the various schools offering professional training in accounting.[89]

The governing council of the American Institute in 1937 went even farther than its committee on education, favoring the "highest practicable standards of preliminary education, similar to those effective in other professions, such as law or medicine," and stating forthrightly that the desirable standard was completion of a full course in a college of liberal arts plus graduate work in courses designed to train students for public accountancy.

The council favored forcing prospective accountants into college through the gradual requirement of additional experience in cases of prospective CPAs who were not college graduates. But the vision of the U.S. as a land of opportunity still prevailed enough at that time to cause the council to oppose rigid requirements which would prevent someone with quality apprenticeship training from becoming a CPA.

The council also favored courses specifically designed to train students for public accounting practice, and told the committee on education to develop standards which would allow the council to judge whether courses in any given educational institution met with its approval. The notion of accreditation was born.[90]

Following the council's recommendations, the Institute's committee on education went into a flurry of activity--analyzing catalogs of business schools, surveying deans of business schools, surveying practitioners. But by 1940 resistance to this activity developed. Many academicians were unhappy with having practitioners develop detailed curricula and standards for the accreditation of accounting courses in the business schools.

One academician voiced his rebellion against the notion of accreditation in general, with special emphasis on the practice of setting a quantifiable measure to determine how many accounting, business, and cultural credit hours were best.

> This recommendation [of the American Institute requiring 60 hours for cultural subjects and 60 for accounting and business] seems to be dangerous from several aspects.
>
> From the standpoint of the teacher and school administrator it may encourage a belief that students sufficiently exposed to accounting and business courses automatically become qualified for public accounting. The yardstick for evaluating the accounting curriculum might become a specified number of semester hours rather than the type of courses offered and the quality of training given during those hours. There might develop a false sense of satisfaction with a curriculum which would probably be hard to change.
>
> ...Of course, the effectiveness of such a rating of schools which offer professional accounting training would not be lasting; for as soon as it became known that a certain school which did not meet the formal standards was nevertheless doing an excellent job of preparing men for the profession, public accounting firms would turn to that school for personnel in spite of the fact that it did not meet the standards of the Committee on Education.[91]

Whether the Institute shared this faith in the market is not known, but Kester stepped down as chairman of the committee in 1941, and the new chairman backed off from establishing standards; instead the committee would tell educators what practitioners wanted in general and would let the educators determine how to meet the profession's requirements. In fact, in 1944 the committee was deliberately composed only of practitioners, rather than including educators as it previously had. This was part of a move to require the committee to work with the AAA and to approach educators only through the committee on education of the AAA.[92] This concession of a kind of veto power over educational matters to the academicians was very important in setting the stage for the following years.

Notes

[1]   Gerald L. Gutek, *Education in the United States: An Historical Perspective*, (Englewood Cliffs, N. J.: Prentice-Hall,1986) p. 36.

[2]   Edited and with introductions by David B. Tyack, *Turning Points in American Educational History* (Waltham, Mass.: Blaisdell Publishing Company, 1967), p. 53.

[3]   R. Freeman Butts and Lawrence A. Cremin, *A History of Education in American Culture* (New York: Holt, Rinehart and Winston, 1953), p. 79.

[4]   Ibid.

[5]   Tyack, *Turning Points*, p. 55.

[6]   Butts and Cremin, *History*, pp. 80-81.

[7]   Ibid., pp. 82-83.

[8]   Ibid., p. 239.

[9]   Benjamin R. Haynes and Harry P. Jackson, *A History of Business Education in the United States* (Cincinnati: South-Western Publishing Co., 1935), p. 11.

[10]   Ibid., p. 42, quoting Emit Duncan Grizzell, *Origin and Development of the High School in New England Before 1865* (New York: The Macmillan Company, 1923), p. 42, quoting J. W. Edmunds, *English High School Semi-Centennial Anniversary* (Boston, 1871), p. 76.

[11]   Ibid., p. 43, quoting Isaac L. Kandel, *History of Education in the United States* (Boston: Houghton Mifflin Company, 1930), p. 434, quoting O. B. Griffin, *The Evolution of the Connecticut State School System*.

[12]   Edwin G. Knepper, *History of Business Education in United States* (Bowling Green, Ohio: Printed by Edwards Brothers, Inc., 1941), pp. 33-34.

[13]   Ibid., p. 31.

[14]   Jay W. Miller, *A Critical Analysis of the Organization, Administration and Function of the Private Business Schools of the United States* (Cincinnati: South-Western Publishing Co., 1939), p. 17.

[15]   Haynes and Jackson, *History*, p. 26.

16 Knepper, *History*, p. 35.

17 Haynes and Jackson, *History*, p. 27.

18 Knepper, *History*, p. 48, and Haynes and Jackson, *History*, p. 29.

19 Haynes and Jackson, *History*, pp. 27-28.

20 Knepper, *History*, pp. 52-53.

21 Miller, *Analysis*, p. 18.

22 Haynes and Jackson, *History*, p. 36.

23 Knepper, *History*, p. 62.

24 Lawrence R. Veysey, *The Emergence of the American University* (Chicago: University of Chicago Press, 1965), p. 4.

25 U.S. Com. Ed., *Report*, 1889-90, II, 1143. Cited in Ibid. pp. 13-14.

26 Veysey, *University*, pp. 4-7, 13-16.

27 Cited in Robert G. Cox, "Accounting," in Frank C. Pierson and Others, *The Education of American Businessmen: A Study of University-College Programs in Business Administration* (New York: McGraw-Hill Book Company, Inc., 1959), p. 355.

28 Jeremiah Lockwood, "Early University Education in Accountancy," *The Accounting Review*, June 1938, p. 135.

29 Annual Report of the Provost of the University of Pennsylvania, including reports of Departments for year ended October 1, 1887, cited in Lockwood, p. 136.

30 Lockwood, p. 136.

31 Report of the Provost of the University, 1890, p. 73, cited by Lockwood, p. 137.

32 Registers of the University of Chicago, 1897-1900, cited by Lockwood, p. 138.

33 C.E. Allen, "The Growth of Accounting Instruction Since 1900," *The Accounting Review*, June 1927, p. 154.

34 Ibid.

35 Bulletin--Ohio University, Athens, Ohio, 1896-1897, cited by Lockwood, p. 139.

36 Lockwood, p. 140.

37 Allen, p. 152.

38 Lockwood, p. 140.

39 Harold Q. Langenderfer, "Accounting Education's History-- A 100-Year Search for Identity," *The Journal of Accountancy*, May 1987, p. 305.

[40] Sidney G. Winter, "What is Proper Training for Accountants?" *The Accounting Review*, June 1941, pp. 183-184.

[41] Gary John Previts and Barbara Dubis Merino, *A History of Accounting in America* (New York: John Wiley & Sons, 1979), p. 140.

[42] Lockwood, p. 140.

[43] Previts and Merino, pp. 100, 139-140.

[44] Allen, p. 154.

[45] Ibid., p. 152.

[46] American Association of Public Accountants, "Report of the Committee on Education," Yearbook 1912, pp 137ff, cited by Previts and Merino, p. 154.

[47] R.J. Bennett, "Educational Training of an Accountant," *The Journal of Accountancy*, January 1912, p. 188.

[48] Ibid.

[49] John C. Duncan, "Some Scientific and Educational Problems of the Accountancy Profession," *The Journal of Accountancy*, October 1914, p. 260.

[50] Seymour Walton, "Practical Application of Theoretical Knowledge," *The Journal of Accountancy*, October 1917, p. 279.

[51] Duncan, p. 268.

[52] Ibid., p. 272.

[53] Robert H. Montgomery, "An Accountancy Laboratory," *The Journal of Accountancy*, June 1914, p. 407.

[54] Previts and Merino, p. 154.

[55] Allen, p. 155.

[56] Montgomery, pp. 107-108.

[57] John L. Carey, *The Rise of the Accounting Profession: From Technician to Professional, 1896-1936* (New York: American Institute of Certified Public Accountants, 1969), p. 99.

[58] F.C. Belser, "How the Universities Can Aid the Accounting Profession," *The Journal of Accountancy*, October 1927, p. 42.

[59] Ibid., p. 40.

[60] Ibid., p. 38.

[61] Allen, pp. 156, 163.

[62] Previts and Merino, p. 215.

[63] James Bossard and Frederic Dewhurst, *University Education for Business: A Study of Existing Needs and Practices* (Philadelphia: University of Pennsylvania Press, 1931), pp. 43, 390.

64 Ibid., pp. 318, 319, 321.

65 Ibid., pp. 322, 323.

66 Howard C. Greer, "The Present Status of Accounting Teaching," *The Accounting Review*, May 1933, p. 64.

67 Gary John Previts and Thomas R. Robinson, "In Search of an Identity," *Accounting Education News*, January 1991, p. 2.

68 Norman E. Webster, "Higher Education for Public Accountants," *The Accounting Review*, June 1938, pp. 117, 118.

69 Ibid., p. 119.

70 Stanley E. Howard, "Accounting Instruction in the Liberal Curriculum," *The Accounting Review*, June 1930, p. 147.

71 L.L. Shaulis, "Instruction in Accounting for Liberal Education," *The Accounting Review*, September 1930, pp. 223, 224.

72 L.O. Foster, "Accounting in the Liberal Arts Curriculum," *The Accounting Review*, March 1933, p. 22.

73 Shaulis, p. 224.

74 Foster, p. 24.

75 Greer, p. 66.

76 Stanley E. Howard, "Accounting in a Liberal Arts Curriculum," *The Accounting Review*, June 1936, p. 154. See also Foster, p. 24.

77 Ibid., p. 147.

78 Foster, p. 24.

79 Bossard and Dewhurst, p. 392.

80 Ibid., pp. 394-395.

81 Roswell C. McCrea and Roy B. Kester, "A School of Professional Accountancy," *The Journal of Accountancy*, February 1936, p. 108.

82 Ibid., p. 109.

83 Roy B. Kester, "Education for Professional Accountancy," *The Accounting Review*, June 1936, p. 99.

84 Ibid., p. 104.

85 A.C. Littleton, "The Professional College," *The Accounting Review*, June 1936, p. 114.

86 Webster, pp. 121-122.

87 Ibid., p. 122.

88 Schools registered by the New York State Department of Education devoted approximately 50% of their efforts to liberal arts and sciences, and the department specified that candidates for the

CPA exam would have to have completed 24 semester hours of study in accounting, 8 hours in business law, 8 hours in finance, and 6 hours in economics. The committee on education of the accounting professors' association, the American Accounting Association (AAA), quickly followed the American Institute's lead in 1937, deliberately conforming to the practitioners' proposal but adding a minimum of 24 hours of accounting and a maximum of 48 hours. The AAA committee specified which courses in "social economics" (which were placed in the liberal arts category), business, and accounting should be taken, and even provided course descriptions. It also recommended that liberal arts courses, business courses, and accounting courses be intermingled throughout the four years of college rather than segregated (e.g., the first two years in liberal arts and the last two in business). Herman C. Miller, "A Suggested Program of Education for the Accountant" and "Syllabus of College Preparation for Accountancy," *The Accounting Review*, June 1938, pp. 191-198.

[89]   Stephen Gilman, "Is College the Only Way?" *The Accounting Review*, June 1937, p. 106.

[90]   John L. Carey, *The Rise of the Accounting Profession: To Responsibility and Authority, 1937-1969* (New York: 1970, American Institute of Certified Public Accountants), p. 260. See also Thomas W. Leland, "Educational Prerequisites for the Certificate," *The Accounting Review*, April 1945, p. 198. See also John L. Carey, "Toward Higher Educational Standards," *The Journal of Accountancy*, December 1937, pp. 403-405.

[91]   Richard S. Claire, "Training for the Public Accounting Profession," *The Accounting Review*, April 1944, pp. 152, 153.

[92]   Carey, pp. 260-262.

Chapter 2

Accounting Education
in the Early Post-War Years

The American view of the world changed radically as a result of the second world war, and the decade and a half which followed was a period of transition. There was a deep shift away from the communal or even socialist thinking which had been popular at the beginning of the century and a return to the older American heritage of individualism. The great depression, the war against evil dictators, and the continued threat of communist dictators had badly shaken the faith in inevitable progress so popular at the beginning of the century.

Rebelliousness became the mood of the land--particularly against the large organizations which had previously symbolized socialized progress. Big government was opposed by increasing numbers of people. Big business was questioned as well. Though its "scientific management" was credited with helping to win the war and was highly respected as a result, big business came under attack as dehumanizing in a series of articles and books, such as *The Organization Man* by William H. Whyte, Jr. The establishment was the enemy, and the hero was the rebel--from the beatnik hipster to James Dean to Marlon Brando to Elvis Presley.

The popular rebellion focused on individual pleasure as opposed to social stability. The soldiers came home from the war with an aquired taste for pictures of pin-up girls. *Playboy* magazine was introduced in the early 1950s and was followed by a host of girlie magazines; movies were filled with sex goddesses such as Marilyn Monroe and Bridgit Bardot; an epidemic of out-of-wedlock pregnancy swept the land. Popular Freudian psychology saw anxiety as caused by efforts of the "superego" to repress the subconscious sexual desires of the "id"; the popular solution for such anxiety was to stop repressing those sexual desires and oppose the superego (which represented the demands of social forces such as parents, church, etc.). Popular philosophy rejected the passionless rationalism of socialized progress for the passionate embrace of the existential moment; in the adsurdity of this life, neither the past nor the future means anything, but only the act of individual personal decision in the present.

This change in world-view had its effect on education. Efforts to "socialize" students through schooling (called "life-adjustment" education) were attacked by educational thinkers such as Arthur Bestor, who opposed social conditioning by the state and argued that schools should strive solely to develop personal intellectual competency. The call to a concern for personal excellence was compelling for the time, and the stress on individual creativity eclipsed the stress on the group-centered approach. There was also growing opposition to narrow "vocational" education and growing support for expansive "liberal" education.

"Professional" Accounting Redefined

The rebelliousness of the time made itself felt even in accounting education. An article in the January 1945 issue of the *Accounting Review* began:

> By professional accountant is meant any one who
> practices accounting on a professional level as contrasted
> to a strictly clerical or routine bookkeeping and

procedural level. As such it would include the work
of internal accounting and auditing as well as the professional practice of the independent public accountant.[1]

To most people, the term "professional accountant" meant something
much less inclusive than that.

Professional accounting had always been considered synonymous
with public accounting. Public accounting was the area of accounting
which was considered of such importance to the public good that it
was regulated by government through CPA laws. Public accountants
had been the ones who had felt the need for collegiate training and
had pressed for and established accounting programs in higher
education. Many, and probably most, of the university teachers of
accounting had come out of the practice of public accounting rather
than out of private company jobs. In fact, it would not be unfair to
say that higher education in accounting had been directed almost
exclusively to the needs of public accounting. The redefinition of
"professional" accounting was nothing short of the opening shot in a
rebellion against this domination. The rebellion against public
accounting would define the post-war period.

This rebellion among academicians quickly built up steam. By
1951 the American Accounting Association (AAA), the organization
for academic accountants, argued:

> In adopting the term "professional accounting" the
> [Standards Rating] Committee intends to use the
> expression in the broadest sense rather than the narrowly
> conceived and limited sense having applicability only to
> professional public practice.[2]

Not only were private company accountants to be considered
"professionals" but the previous monolithic accounting education had
to be divided up into a track for public accounting and a track for
"industrial" accounting--indeed, some suggested numerous tracks for
different types of industrial accounting.

So began the effort to build the field which would come to be
known as "managerial accounting"--a field in opposition to the
"financial accounting" which was dominated by public accounting.

The motivation to overthrow domination was not the only motive in the rebellion, however; there were also more down-to-earth ones.

The reward for those willing to devote themselves to the job of becoming accounting executives is indicated by a quotation from a report that presented the results of a survey of business executives conducted by *Fortune* magazine: "As for the fact that 94 per cent of the executives like their present positions, *Fortune* concludes that 100 per cent of those polled were well paid 'successes' and that the successful are proverbially happy."[3]

Executives are rich and happy; that was the word on the street. If it was true, then it was obviously desirable that accountants become executives. So private company accountants should redefine themselves as "accounting executives" and business leaders should accept such redefinition:

> Business leaders are beginning to realize that it is just as important to have highly trained accounting technicians on their accounting staffs as it is to have lawyers on their legal staffs and engineers on their engineering staffs. These business leaders have learned through costly audits, system installations, federal tax assessments, and the like, that the old type "bookkeeper" (who knew little more than a debit from a credit) was, despite his low salary, a costly investment. They have found that their business will fail to prosper as it should unless their accountants can grow with it, assume new responsibilities, revise systems to meet operations, and help guide the business through the intricacies of modern government taxation and regulation.[4]

If business leaders should acknowledge such a change in status for private accountants, so then should education. In 1950 the comptroller of Humble Oil & Refining Company called for a change in educational approach and sketched an outline for such change in his suggestion

> that perhaps a little less emphasis be given in the curriculum to financial accounting and preparation for the CPA examination and that a little more emphasis be

given to managerial accounting, budgeting, cost analysis, methods and procedures, principles of organization, human relations, and report writing. I wish there were some way for our industrial accountants to come to us with a little more of the viewpoint of the low-cost operator and a little less of the viewpoint of the financial accounting theorist. ...The really ideal solution...would be to have some way of helping the student choose either public or industrial accounting early in his schooling. Then he could be given a curriculum tailored especially to prepare him for the career of his choice.[5]

In summary, the reasons for the creation of the new area of managerial accounting were simple. Business management had high status, and was well-paid and happy. For private company accountants to join the ranks of business management they would have to orient themselves more toward the concerns of management, and their education would have to include more about how to meet the concerns of management. Their education should thus focus on something called "management" accounting.

These reasons were entirely practical and, as such, of little use in an academic environment. Academic accountants had to provide a theoretical and non-practical reason for increasing the focus on management accounting.

The Arguments for Management Accounting

First the ground had to be cleared. This was done with an attack upon the concept of accounting as a "science." The practitioners of a science discover eternal truths. The truths of science do not change; water does not begin to run uphill. If accounting were a science, its truths could not change. How could accounting take on the flexibility needed to serve managment in changing circumstances if it were a science?

Edward G. Nelson used a wry wit to debunk the idea that accounting is a science. He suggested that the idea began because science had very high status during the first quarter of the century, and accountants wanted that status.[6] To counter that idea, he quoted Thorstein Veblen, Bertrand Russell, Alfred North Whitehead, and John Dewey, then made reference to the ancient Greeks, quoted the accounting historian A.C. Littleton as saying that, "Accounting is relative and progressive," and finally noted that Montgomery emphasized the adaptive nature of accounting. To complete his picture of truth as changing when its surroundings change, he chronicled the end of what he called accounting's "romantic period":

> But the idea that there was little truth in accounting gained such currency as the sun set on the 1920's that, when subsequent events proved disastrous to investors, a Congress, perhaps already convinced, was easily induced to grant authority over much financial accounting to a governmental agency.
>
> The fall from grace during the 1930's was not accompanied by an immediate about-face. The culture defined the goals of accountants in terms of a mechanistic science, and many found it impossible to abandon their appeal to "nature."[7]

Nelson saw this inability to face reality as due to a longing for prestige and "honor." He then analyzed the effect of this longing.

> A science of accounting has a function in a society where science has status; it helps to satisfy the needs of many individuals; it is an incentive to important, useful work; and it helps to develop individual responsibility to society.
>
> But status systems are also disruptive. They tend to distort the evaluation of individuals; they inhibit leadership and morale; and they limit adaptability in an adaptive society. A science of accounting is in grave danger of becoming a middle-class ritual--a ritual in which the participants fail to analyze the facts, to reason from them, and to develop insight and inventiveness.[8]

The strength of Nelson's ridicule of accounting as science would make it impossible for academic accountants (deathly afraid of having

their status reduced by being ridiculed) to ever again seriously argue
for "truth in accounting" or for scientific principles in accounting.[9]
Within a year another article in the *Accounting Review* argued again
that the fact that accounting was systematic did not mean that it was a
science, nor that it was able to establish a "fundamental truth."[10] It
was now clear that status did not come from discovering truth but
rather from some other activity.

Fredrick Horn of Columbia made the new source of status clearer
in his 1951 discussion of how the public accountants came up with
their definition of accounting:

> There was much discussion as to whether accounting was
> a science or an art. The technical mechanism was
> stressed while the creative skill and ability which the
> accountant brings to the application of his knowledge to
> a given problem was given little emphasis. In fact, it was
> not until 1941 that these authorities recognized this
> attribute....[11]

Horn lamented the fact that "Very few texts stress the fact that the
accountant's first duty is to management," and advocated reducing
emphasis upon the first part of the definition of accounting (i.e.,
"Accounting is the art of recording, classifying and summarizing in a
significant manner and in terms of money, transactions and events
which are, in part at least, of a financial character...") and instead
increasing emphasis on the last phrase added in 1941 (i.e., "..and
interpreting the results thereof."). He even put the two phrases in
opposition to each other.

> [L]et us eliminate the *narrow view* toward accounting--
> the necessity for an exact, balancing and chronological
> historical record of financial events and stress the *broad
> view*--that accounting is a presentation of useful
> information.[12]

Horn announced that Columbia was developing an introductory course
in accounting (for all business students, whether accounting or non-
accounting majors) which had a managerial emphasis. Accounting was

not a science but an art, a broad art of communication--could one even say a liberal art?

Such a broad view of accounting required that academicians avoid a narrow focus on accounting and consider the correlation of accounting instruction with that of other business fields and attempt to focus on the interrelationships among business courses.

> The purpose of integration is to reverse the usual emphasis and come out with "management skills" rather than only "technical skills." ...This kind of training produces not specialists but "generalists." ...The purpose of correlating accounting instruction with other courses is to make accounting graduates more generally useful to employers. This purpose differs from that of training professional accountants.[13]

Accounting must change with the times. It must become responsible, purposeful, and flexible (with the implication that it had previously been none of these).

> [T]he world of the intense individualist, the domineering boss, and the ruthless seeker of profit is rapidly giving way to the responsible administrator with a strong sense of duty toward society. Today's business leader, by necessity, must possess the broad view. His problem solving and decision making take place in a disorderly world defiant of logic and upsetting of principle. And this world is vastly bigger than it once was. The compulsion to "get along" and to cooperate with people is more urgent than ever....
>
> Students in accounting classes should be encouraged to think in terms of management's need for business facts. Such facts become useful in relation to an immediate problem or as they underlie a decision. Purpose must underlie the keeping of accounting records. It is in this area of purposeful action that the correlation of accounting with other business courses is so badly needed. Figures for the sake of figures is a sterile concept.

The attention of the embryonic accountant should be turned away from the emphasis upon what is "right" and into the area of diagnosis and choice of alternatives. The world of the administrator is one of choices and decisions. These involve value judgments in which the distinctions between right and wrong are not always clear. ...Accounting students should realize that business facts arise from situations involving human beings. ...The well-trained accounting student will realize that figures are a means, not an end.[14]

Accountants had once stressed an independence from management--a determination to present the honest truth no matter what management wanted. Now it was time to "get along" with management, and make the effort to please them. All this was supported (as every argument for change is) with the argument that the world was dramatically changing and what once worked no longer could.

By January of 1953 the arguments for managerial accounting in the curriculum had reached an amazing level of rhetorical flourish. The argument that accounting was not an unchanging science became the argument that accounting changes so rapidly that there are no settled principles and no point in teaching any. One author advocated, in a very "liberal arts" approach, an unstructured process of "learning how to learn" using an orderly problem-solving method.

[This] approach would place less emphasis on conventional course content as pertains to both subject matter and method of teaching. In the beginning there would be little apparent presumption of a fixed body of subject matter to be covered or learned, but the instructor, of course, would have an abundance of subject matter at hand. This is based partly on the belief that the candidate to a major profession cannot know long in advance much about what the later requirements of his profession will be. The student must discover these objectives as his educational development unfolds, and his opinions will not be held for long. Most of this curriculum would be prescribed with but few elective courses. Instead of subject matter to be taught, the

> learning process would be the focus of attention. ...The instructor's function would not be to dispense information any more than it would be the function of the student to perform prescribed educational chores. The instructor's function would be to create situations designed to force the student to apply his present mental powers to the acquisition of new powers. Success in a course would be judged not by the student's interest, but by his acquired power to perform. This is measured by the difference between his power at the end of the course and that which he possessed at the beginning and minus that which he would have acquired anyway as a result of having spent his time elsewhere and becoming just a little older.[15]

Such would appear a daunting measurement task even for an academic accountant, but too much could not be asked of a field upon which, another author asserted, civilization itself depended.

> Communication as a problem of administration of economic units, political institutions and other societal organizations has long been dealt with in its occurrence in actual situations. It has been demonstrated in the past that the downfall of empires and civilizations may be traced to the dissolution of the communications systems of these orders. ...Accounting, then, as a communications problem is one of the highest order.[16]

Another author spelled out an agenda for accounting academicians which exalted the civilized aims of "integration" and "living communally" and similar "policies of progressive education."

> Among the practical objectives which may be suggested for the consideration of accounting educators are the establishment of amicable relations among nations, expansion of national income without sharp disturbances, attainment of substantial equity in the distribution of real income, the safeguarding and expansion of personal freedoms.[17]

By taking responsibility for world peace, national economic policy, national redistribution of income, and civil rights, accounting education would have become pretty nearly maximally broad. Accounting for the providential activities of God seems not to have been suggested, but the teaching of "national income accounting" (which was better titled "national income statistics" and considered as an economics course[18]) continued to be advocated.[19]

Nelson attempted to shame those who were not convinced about the value of the new broader and non-dogmatic accounting.

> The individual accountant, as others, has not always adapted himself readily to changes in the accounting society, and many find themselves greatly disturbed when they fail to understand their own relation to the profession and to the society in which accounting lives. There is comfort in the ritual of a mechanistic science, and there are individuals who seek personal satisfactions resulting from the manifest resemblance of accounting and mathematical physics. Individuals struggle to retain their personal comforts. Leaders in a movement for change may expect to be the focal point of an attack which, adorned in the dazzling dress of an apparent logic, is, in reality, an individual release of tension and a fight to maintain personal equilibrium during the process of methodical selection.[20]

The academic accountants seeking a broader role for accounting did not restrain themselves from calling upon fashionable psychological concepts for support. One author predicted dire personal consequences if his suggestions favoring "broad" rather than "narrowly technical" education were not heeded:

> An important consideration remains to be mentioned. The psychological needs of the professional accountant require a comprehensive and expressive understanding of business problems. Only through integration of the individual in relation to social integration principles can this need be adequately met. A blocking of this personal

> development will be reflected in nervous irritation and
> psychoses, or alternatively in the development of
> protective inertia. In either case the individual will fall
> short of his maximum contribution to his own personal
> life.[21]

So not only would world peace hang in the balance, but the
accountant's personal fulfillment would be frustrated if broadness
were not the guiding light in accounting.

It was not enough for the proponents of the new accounting to put
down ideas; it was also necessary to put down the public accounting
profession. Since collegiate accounting education had always been
oriented towards public accounting, in order for there to be more
emphasis on managerial accounting there must be less emphasis on
public accounting.

> [W]hat is wrong with the typical accounting curriculum?
> When these curricula were originally set up, public
> accountants had a principal part in the effort. ...We
> believe that these close contacts [between teachers and
> public accountants] and the concomitant emphasis on the
> CPA examination have contributed to such deficiencies
> as...lack of training of students in the solution of
> business problems and the proper analysis of more
> complex business situations (overemphasis of the how of
> doing things over the why).[22]

It was argued that the managerial accountant was superior to the
public accountant because his responsibilities were greater:

> The public accountant often can confine himself to the
> recording, analyzing, and interpreting of historical
> transactions. He can be the watchdog for fraud,
> embezzlement, and the execution of existing contractual
> and other legal relationships. In the past the general
> accounting curriculum seems to have been dominated
> excessively by this point of view. ...As an aid to
> management the industrial accountant has responsibilities
> which exceed those of the public accountant. If historical

> records have value as guides to the future, it is based on
> the assumption that the future will be a continuation of
> the past. But the crucial problem always is to decide how
> or why the future will or will not be a continuation of
> the past. ...This problem might not be one for the public
> accountant, but I would make it the province of the
> industrial accountant....[23]

While the public accountant was a mere historian, the managerial
accountant was a prophet--not merely recording and accumulating the
forecasts of others but actually making them himself. A prophet must
have deep knowledge of historical cause and effect (not to mention
divine revelation), and obviously needed a broader education.

> As presented in some classrooms [accounting] is perhaps
> merely a highly specialized technique of little
> fundamental educational value. However, it is becoming
> increasingly clear as we investigate the basic concepts of
> accounting in its administrative phases that it is an
> intellectual discipline of great depth and scope. ...By
> associating the accounting problem with the qualitative
> aspects of the business (or administrative) problem, the
> currently developing accounting curriculum is becoming
> a far more important discipline than has been envisaged
> heretofore.[24]

By implication, accounting education associated with preparation for
public accounting was unimportant, non-intellectual, and of little
educational value. It was presented as mechanistic, procedural, and
mere technique.

Where were the public accountants while these academic
accountants were belittling them, pretending to have discovered for
the first time that accounting was supposed to be useful, and filling
the air with grandiose schemes and psychobabble?

The main reason that public accountants had no real problem with
the direction the academic accountants were charting was that the
more radical revolutionaries could easily be ignored and the less wild
change agents were doing just what the public accountants wanted
anyway. Back in 1944 had come the announcement of a new interest

for public accountants which made them very sympathetic with the efforts of academic accountants to teach administrative accounting:

> Today there are two words that are buzzing with all the spark and elusiveness of an electric charge in some public accounting firms--business consultant. They are also buzzing with even greater elusiveness at some schools. It is a reflection of a rapidly increasing realization on the part of public accounting firms that many of their clients have been in need of and, in some instances, have been paying for diagnosis whereas they were getting little more than an annual reading of temperature. In order to grow, and perhaps just to survive, public accountants will have to provide added services in the future. They are in an ideal position to provide business consulting services and if they do not fill the need some other group will.[25]

If the very survival of the profession depended on management consulting, then a prospective public accountant should certainly learn the principles and practices of business "to the end...that he may give advice concerning the desirability of effecting any proposed transaction or series of transactions when they are in the formative stage [as well as] that he may obtain the best possible evidence" for audit purposes.[26] By 1955 things seemed clear:

> The accountant who is capable only of making an audit will pass out of the picture and make way for the professional business and financial advisor.[27]

If, through the new "management accounting," private accountants were trying to enter the world of management and advise management on major business decisions, so too were the public accountants in their search for lucrative new opportunities.

Therefore, it would seem that both types of accountant would need to know the same things about managing a company. As early as 1948, at a conference attended by business school deans and public accountants and controllers, there was "apparent agreement that there need be no substantial difference between the training for those going into private accounting and those going into public accounting."[28] Even among people championing the cause of managerial accounting in the academic realm, some did not see a need for different education depending upon the type of accountant a student might become.

> This distinction between internal accounting and public accounting for basic educational purposes may be a transient development. The "pure" approach to controllership problems may disappear as the element of administrative emphasis sifts its way down to the elementary and intermediate levels of accounting instruction. Then, there will be less need for separate offerings for administrative accountants and for public accountants. In theory, there is no fundamental distinction worthy of a schism between the two in our educational curricula.[29]

The Push for the College Degree Requirement

While it was true that the public accountants were not opposed to the direction of the managerial accountants, it was also true that the public accountants would not easily give up their pride-of-place in accounting education.

The major weapon the public accountants had to keep accounting education focused on public accounting was the fixation that academicians had on the CPA examination. The exam was largely a test of academic preparation, and the ability of a school's program to enable a student to pass the test ("enter the profession") was easily and unavoidably measured.

The CPA exam had been around since it was established by the first CPA law, and it had always been successful in dominating the curriculum of accounting education. Indeed, it had been so successful that, when the Institute sought to strengthen its hold over education, it turned again to the same concept.

In 1941, after the Institute had backed away from the accreditation issue and its attempt to specify a desirable collegiate curriculum, it began instead an effort to achieve uniform standards through a uniform testing process it designed. In 1947 it first gave an "orientation" (aptitude) test and an achievement test; the achievement test was for college graduates or for candidates for junior or semi-senior staff positions in a public accounting firm. By using a test to select qualified students, public accountants could indirectly influence what was taught and how it was taught.

But when the tests were given, the results varied widely among colleges, which suggested (whether correctly or not) that not all college programs were of equal quality. When colleges and universities discovered that the tests could be used to spotlight apparently inferior programs, many of them refused to administer the tests.

If a voluntary testing program was not going to be successful in bending colleges to the Institute's will, there was still the uniform nationwide CPA exam designed by the Institute. That was not voluntary, and colleges had long used it as a measuring stick for comparing educational programs.

Public accountants were proud of the CPA exam. They took pride in the fact that "the difficulty of attainment of the CPA certificate is the principal reason for the prestige enjoyed by certified public accountants." But they also had to admit, "Qualifying standards cannot be so difficult or so rigid as to suggest monopolistic intentions on the part of the profession."[30] Low passage rates on the exam were cause for concern.

Only about 20 percent of those who took the exam successfully passed it. The standard explanation for this was that a college degree was not required to take the exam. Twenty years after New York State decided to require a college degree (and a decade after it actually began requiring it) it was still the only state that required it. In 1944 California began requiring two years of college and New Jersey began requiring "the completion of a program of study of accountancy." In 1945 Kansas required the completion of two years of college work or its equivalent and Illinois passed a law which would require one year of college. The rest required only a high school degree with experience requirements (e.g., three years in public practice). A considerable number of states, however, were willing to reduce the experience requirements in exchange for college work.[31]

The effort to prove that college preparation was necessary to enter the profession (i.e., pass the CPA exam) had early hit a snag: the disappointing results of college graduates on the CPA exam during the period 1929-1934 (where they performed no better than non-college graduates, as discussed in the last chapter). If college education did not improve exam scores, then there would seem to be no point in a college education. A follow-up study of the period 1938-1942 fortunately showed that college graduates did better on the exam than people who had not graduated from college.[32] The public accountants analyzed the results of the CPA exam rather closely for the years 1948-1950, and discovered that those with college education seemed to do better on the exam than those without.[33]

So the ultimate cure for the poor passage rate on the CPA exam seemed obvious to many: require college education. That this position involves the odd idea of requiring people to do better on exams never seems to have been discussed. If the exam honestly tested what a CPA should know, and if a person passed it, then logically that person should be allowed to be a CPA--regardless of whether he had a college degree or not. Why should a person who could pass the exam without a college education be required to get a college education? This was the once-widespread view that everyone should have an opportunity to try to enter the profession without being blocked by artificial barriers.

Though a few voices defended this "Abe Lincoln" approach to entering a profession, it was generally either ridiculed or ignored. There were two overpowering reasons for restricting a potential public accountant's freedom. The first was the old argument that public accounting could never have the status of a true profession unless it at least required a college degree. Second, if public accounting required a college degree while private accounting did not, the interest of those in higher education would be pulled toward public accounting.

Nevertheless, the Institute had not been remarkably successful in getting states to require a college degree to become a CPA. Failing that, the Institute tried other approaches to encouraging college education. In 1937, when the Council of the Institute had advocated graduate education for public accountants and accreditation standards designed by public accountants, it had also come out in favor of requiring additional experience of applicants for the CPA certificate who had not completed satisfactory courses in accountancy of collegiate grade. By 1945 the Institute's committee on state legislation had suggested that states legislate that "a candidate may qualify for examination by roughly six years' preparation, which may be in part college training and part experience, or may be wholly experience in practice."[34] This would have doubled the required experience for high school graduates. It would require two years experience from a college graduate and one from a graduate of a five-year program. The proposal, however, received little support from state legislators.

Another approach to motivating candidates to get a college education, even though state laws did not require it, was a suggestion that a preliminary examination be required for CPA exam candidates. Once again the required exam approach was attempted--this time an exam required to take an exam. It was proposed that the preliminary exam test commercial arithmetic, business English, advanced bookkeeping, commercial law, (preliminary) economics, commercial geography, banking and finance, office organization and systems, accountancy, and business history--the desired background which was believed to be available in collegiate courses in business.[35]

These suggestions, however, were merely tactics designed to achieve the objective of requiring a collegiate degree for all CPA candidates. It was the college degree that mattered. The main argument advanced was that it would increase the status of the profession--it would impress people, such as management. It would "provide this basic background of general, cultural, and disciplinary training so essential to provide poise, confidence, and capacity to meet on any level with future business and professional contacts."[36]

The Importance of Liberal Education

A more generally acceptable argument was that accountants needed to have the liberal education which only a collegiate program provided. Without it, some claimed, new accountants were virtually unable to write, speak, or think.

The complaint about accountants' communication and analytic skills was actually of long standing. Around 1920 the deficiencies of the junior public accountant were said to include:

1. Lacking in many of the rudiments of business arithmetic constantly recurring in commercial transactions,

2. Unable to use correctly everyday business terms,
3. Unable to write a clear and concise business letter,
4. Unable to grasp simple business problems quickly,
5. Not thinking clearly. ...[37]

The situation was even worse a quarter of a century later, according to at least one author, because the rigor of a high school education had declined over that period. Less English, less mathematics, less history, and less science were required, and the situation had been made even worse when high school authorities created two routes: one for college and professional preparation, and the other for "terminal education and a trade--the latter program being less difficult and permitting for local political reasons practically any one to graduate who attends classes better than 70% of the time and whose intelligence is slightly above that of a high-grade moron."[38] The obvious solution to the problems created by high schools seemed to be to require college.

Not that all was well in collegiate education. The report of a 1948 conference of business school deans, public accountants, and controllers, voiced the concerns of many:

> On one thing the accountants all seem to agree: that is, that nowhere along the educational line do our graduates pick up a really adequate command of written and spoken English. Maybe this is just an easy flaw to pick, maybe it's just another signal for buck-passing, down to the high schools. Maybe, on the other hand, some college faculty, somewhere, will one of these days really figure out what to do about it, and earn the very real gratitude of the profession."[39]

The chairman of the Virginia state board of accountancy echoed:

> One of the most disturbing defects of the average candidate is their [sic] seeming inability or unwillingness to think. ...Closely following disorderly thought is its consequential result--inadequate speech and writing.[40]

The Committee on Auditing Education of the academic accountants reported from a survey in 1954 "that public accountants are more distressed by the deficiency of college graduates in the area of oral and written communication than any other single weakness."[41]

Various reasons were given for these poor communication skills. Some blamed the CPA exam.

> A concomitant effect of the emphasis on the CPA examination has been the lack of ability among students to analyze actual business situations with a view of using their findings by means of oral or written reports. This deficiency has been pointed out by business executives time and again. As long as accounting instruction continues to "drill" students on the procedural aspects of accounting, there is little chance for analysis and the proper presentation of its results.[42]

Another suggestion was that students with poor communication skills are attracted to accounting due to a misunderstanding of what accountants really do.

> I sometimes wonder whether the public at large, and particularly the young people in college who may select public accounting as a career, do not look upon it perhaps as the one vocation where they will never have to be troubled with the written word and can bury themselves for life in a mass of figures--a safe refuge where such dragons as the split infinitive, the dangling participle and the awkward phrase will never catch up with them. In other words, how many people may enter public accounting in part because of the difficulty--as opposed to facility--in self expression, feeling that here of all places is a field where self expression is not required? I merely ask this as a question; I don't know the answer.[43]

The answer to the question was not hard to find. A study of students at the University of Texas showed that those who chose accounting (about 3% of those expressing a career choice) made a fairly high numerical score and a fairly low verbal score with the result that their median was 75 (compared with an over-all median of 82).[44]

By 1957 the solution to the problem seemed obvious to many. Speaking of college graduates, a partner in one of the largest public accounting firms argued:

Not enough are displaying qualities of leadership--executive ability, if you like.

Why don't enough of these people "make the grade"? I can cite a number of reasons, all of them based on actual cases in our firm. Some never learn to express themselves clearly--to communicate their good ideas--orally or in writing. Some make good progress up to a point, then suddenly shy away from taking on new and important responsibility. Some seem unable to discipline their thinking so as to cast aside irrelevant detail and concentrate on important points. Some can't seem to get along with clients; others cannot direct the work of subordinates without causing friction; others can never make themselves look the boss in the eye and say, "I don't agree with you." And unfortunately, some of them seem more concerned with the money they are making today than with the satisfactions (as well as the financial rewards) that can be obtained by devoting oneself to the professional concept of service.

When a staff member progresses to the point where he is being considered for admission to partnership in our firm, technical qualifications are taken for granted. Other factors now become important--those qualities which I just mentioned as being missing in too many of the young men who come to us, plus integrity, judgment, ability to train others, personality, and so forth. No one person can have all of these qualities to the highest degree, but many of them are present in what is often termed "a broad, well-rounded person."

So you see, we would like today's graduates to have more of those many intangibles which cause us to think of someone as a "broad, well-rounded person." How can they be provided? The answer is obvious--we've heard it many times before and we'll hear it many times again: more liberal education, more emphasis on the humanities, on studies that tend to produce a cultivated person.[45]

The broad education was the apparent solution. It was believed that public accounting could be saved from all its sins and weaknesses by liberal education. The messianic fervor of this faith in the humanities was, of course, perfectly in keeping with the times, but it is striking nonetheless. It was heard over and over again that liberal education, almost magically, produced a person with powerful analytic skills, deep maturity of judgment, unshakably high ethical standards, and a pleasing personality. Could there be any question that an accountant should be college-educated with a course of study filled to the brim with liberal arts?

Requirements for Entering the Profession

There was a wide-spread agreement that collegiate education was necessary. As noted before, the low passage rates on the CPA exam were early causes of concern, and the fact that college graduates were more successful in passing the exam was being noted. In January of 1947 the Board of Examiners of the Institute requested that the AAA study the CPA exam, and in February 1948 the Committee on the Uniform CPA Examination was appointed.

A preliminary report of the Committee published in early 1949 supported the idea that collegiate education should be required, but it added another notion which would haunt the public accounting profession for decades. It suggested that a college student be permitted to take the CPA exam before the experience requirement was met and, if successful, a CPA certificate should be awarded even though that person had no practical experience.[46] The fact that the academic accountants were apparently looking upon the passage of the CPA exam and the awarding of the CPA certificate as a "professional degree" may have served the public accountants' immediate goal of controlling the academic process through control of the exam, but the ramifications of this belief would later prove to be quite unacceptable.

In 1949 the Institute's Committee on State Legislation set about preparing a revised accountancy statute[47] including education and experience requirements, and the Association of CPA Examiners appointed a committee to study education and experience as prerequisites for the CPA examination. Such a variety of opinions was found regarding these issues that Donald P. Perry, who had become chairman of the Institute's Board of Examiners in 1949, proposed at its annual meeting in 1951 that the Institute appoint a commission whose "responsibility should not be confined to the initial task of formulating standards for the present, but should be a continuing endeavor to see that the standards are changed with changing conditions and raised as rapidly as will meet with general acceptance."[48] Also, in January of 1952, a committee formed by the New York State Department of Education to study the CPA law of that state proposed that an independent study be made of the entire process of preparing people to become competent CPAs.

The Institute followed Perry's recommendation, and Perry became chairman of the Institute-sponsored Commission on Standards of Education and Experience for Certified Public Accountants. While the Commission had been formed at the instigation of the Institute and many of its members were from the Institute, it also included many outsiders and was considered an independent organization with a broad constituency--just the thing to solve the problems the profession was facing, and to attract the attention of academicians to public accounting.

An article Perry published in the *Journal of Accountancy* was perhaps the best brief summary of the forces at work in accounting education at the time, and it held forth the promise that the work of the Commission would be similarly eloquent.

Perry reviewed the forces of change (including the expanded scope of services of the CPA) and noted that "There is a great underlying social need for comprehension and competence in those who provide, select, and interpret the information required in administering business." He elegantly and tightly tied together professional status and higher education.

Certified public accountants have gone far in meeting the criteria used in recognizing professional status. They are expected to provide leadership in the community and more and more are dedicating their skills to the welfare of society. Personal integrity and character, together with honest adherence to a code of professional conduct, are as important as a high degree of competence. The public accountant should be able to view his work in broad perspective and to think clearly in a world of ideas that is far wider than the particular disciplines of his craft. All such characteristics of professional status should be given weight in setting the aims of educational training.

As a consequence, we already find increasing emphasis on general cultural education in preparation for the accounting profession.[49]

There was "general agreement," he said, that broad general cultural education helps develop imagination, clarity of thought, flexibility of mind and awareness of situations, powers of oral and written expression, character and personality--not to mention "equal social and intellectual footing" with other professionals which increases the accountant's "influence and usefulness." His message was as clear as he could make it: broad college education equals higher status.

Perry spoke of the "consolidation and better integration" of business and accounting studies with humanistic studies (suggesting a course in industrial history). He persuasively displayed the ideals of public accounting and how those ideals require business administration studies:

In auditing services alone the certified public accountant needs a broad understanding of industrial practices, methods of business administration, and economic processes. He cannot intelligently examine statements of a public utility, for example, without an appreciation of the powers and practices of the regulatory commissions. Nor can he pass upon statements to be used for financing purposes without knowing the requirements of commercial banks, investment houses, and the Securities and Exchange Commission.

The auditor must, as well, have general familiarity with the laws governing business and be able to recognize situations where legal questions may be involved. He should also be aware of the interests of the various readers and users of financial statements. If accounting is to be useful as a measurement of economic relationships and is to facilitate low-cost production and a fair distribution of economic income, the accountant-- whether in public or in private industry--should have some understanding of general business relationships. In short, he must have an understanding of our whole involved capitalistic system, in which business and industrial leaders exert their skill and resourcefulness to expand production and distribution, to lower costs, and to increase profits and intangible values.

Aside from strictly accounting fields, the certified public accountant is often regarded as a qualified business advisor on many other problems for which his experience has given him valuable background and familiarity. The American Institute's CPA Handbook, based on replies to a questionnaire, lists the following subjects upon which accountants often give advice: financing, accounting personnel, insurance, forms of business organization, governmental regulations, reorganizations, values of business enterprises, budgeting, office organization and administration, renegotiation and termination of contracts, and internal auditing procedures. It further indicates that a minority of those replying to the questionnaire also have advised on nonaccounting personnel, factory management, marketing and merchandising, contractual relations, pension plans, incentive plans, and rate regulation.

While primarily a business tool, accounting does not exist in and for itself.

The person applying it needs considerable understanding of the purposes it can serve. ...[50]

Perry concluded that accounting education should not be divorced from business education generally, and that the needed education for public accounting would require more time than that available in the typical four year collegiate course. "The conclusion reached by many is that we need a postgraduate professional program organized in the university schools of business specifically for preparation of the certified public accountant."

Perry was confident that his efforts were regaining academic ground for public accountants.

> Since the collegiate schools of business provide majors in subjects other than accounting and since 80 per cent of collegiate accounting majors do not go into public accounting, it is only natural that many schools should place the special needs of public accounting in a low category.
>
> Now is the time to see that the public accounting profession is effectively recognized in educational programs. Programs aimed towards preparation of CPAs will tend to be developed more rationally and uniformly as a result of the substantial current interest in this educational field--particularly from the studies of the Commission on Standards of Education and Experience for CPAs.[51]

There is no doubt that Perry's efforts helped public accountanting regain its momentum. The attention of academic accountants was riveted on the Commission's efforts, which were very straight-forwardly concerned with the preparation of public accountants. Indeed, as Perry described them, the responsibilities of the public accountant included not merely the preparation of financial statements but all of the area claimed by the managerial accountants as well, and even a good part of that claimed by non-accountant business managers. If public accountants required the broadest education of all, then everyone desiring broad accounting education should focus upon the needs of the public accountants.

Professional Schools of Accounting

Just what the educational needs of public accountants were had already been addressed fairly often by this time. Of most concern was the desired mix among the three categories of required education: cultural, general business, and accounting. In 1937 the Institute and the AAA had agreed that half of a four-year college education should consist of professional subjects, formalizing the intuitive belief that cultural and professional studies were equally important. Although the New York state law which started that whole discussion required only that 20 percent of the collegiate studies be in accounting, the Institute advocated that about 32 percent be given to accounting studies, and the AAA agreed and added that the minimum would be 20 percent and the maximum 40 percent. In 1949 the AAA's Standards Rating Committee, reflecting the increasing recognition of the importance of general business studies, reduced the recommended amount of accounting to 25 percent, formalizing the intuitive belief that general business and accounting studies were equally important.[52] This balanced 50/25/25 pattern, with its strong intuitive appeal, held firm against challenges and was in fact followed by many universities (with accounting actually having slightly less than 25 percent).[53]

One early challenge to the balanced pattern came from a public accountant editorial writer already in 1951. He believed that the AAA's program was too heavily weighted with business and technical subjects and advocated 75 percent for liberal arts and sciences and 25 percent for business subjects and general accounting. This approach suggested that the advanced accounting courses would "be recognized as subjects for graduate study, or, alternatively, on-the-job training. This approach is similar to the educational programs of law and medicine."[54]

The push for making professional accounting a subject for graduate study had been going on since the Institute's Council in 1937 had surprisingly advocated, based on the stated desire to be like law and medicine, four years of liberal arts in college and graduate work in accounting. The Council had also favored courses specifically designed to train students for public accounting practice rather than for accounting in general. This gave rise to discussion about the merits of schools of public accounting and five-year programs. Some considered the emergence of the schools inevitable even as early as the mid 1940s,[55] while at the same time others opposed them, arguing that public accounting was not that different from private accounting and should not be separated from schools of business.[56] In 1947 the New York State Society of CPAs advocated separate schools for training public accountants. In 1949 Columbia completely dropped its undergraduate program in business and became a graduate school of business, thereby raising accounting to the graduate level as well.[57] Also in 1949 the University of Texas announced that it was offering the degree of Master in Professional Accounting, a five-and-one-half-year course for public accountants.[58]

An editorial in the national journal of the Institute in 1950 expressed the desire for a school of accounting which was separate from the business school (and from managerial accountants).[59]

By 1956 a survey revealed that public accountants overwhelmingly (94%) approved of the idea of a professional school of accountancy, and so did accounting professors and controllers (76%). Business school deans, however, were overwhelmingly (88%) opposed to the idea, because they did not want to see accounting separated from the business school. On one thing everyone, however, even the deans, were in agreement, "namely, a professional accounting training cannot be crowded, along with liberal arts and the core business curriculum, into four years!"[60]

The Commission's Report

In August of 1956 the Institute-sponsored Commission on Standards of Education and Experience for Certified Public Accountants issued its report, and there were plenty of surprises for everyone. Many of the important issues debated in the 1950s were addressed.

The Commission's long-range goals for preparation for entry into the profession were, in chronological order:

1. College graduation. There was no specification of content or proportions (except that there should be "a substantial amount of general and cultural courses"). The recommendations of the Standards Rating Committee of the AAA were considered satisfactory.

2. A qualifying examination. This nation-wide exam would test the college graduate's intellectual capacity, academic achievements,

and aptitude for public accountancy. Its purpose was to eliminate the problem of dealing with collegiate programs of varying quality.

3. A postgraduate professional academic program. Without specifying the curriculum, certain areas of study were recommended: oral and written communication, auditing and other phases of the practice of public accountancy (such as taxes, systems and controls, ethical standards, and practice administration), accounting principles and their application, and business policy. A new accrediting organization would be required, but the programs would be offered "within the framework of collegiate schools of business administration."

4. An internship program. Saying that it "recognizes the value of practical experience" the Commission recommended that an internship be a required part of the professional education.

5. Passage of the CPA exam.[61]

Two of the Commission's recommendations caused considerable uproar. The first was that the postgraduate professional accounting programs be "within the framework" of business schools. While it was not entirely clear what that meant, it was decidedly contrary to the idea of separate schools of accounting. The business school deans on the Commission had apparently won that point. Many continued to support separate schools, but the rapid acquiescence of academic accountants to the Commission forced such supporters to finally admit that they were apparently in the minority.[62] A survey of accounting department chairmen in 1957 showed that 87 percent believed that a professional program could be implemented within the framework of schools of business administration.[63] Slowing down the movement toward separate professional schools of accounting was, apart from generating conversation, perhaps the only lasting effect of the Commission.

The second Commission recommendation that caused great concern was its recommendation that the CPA certificate be received after successfully passing the CPA exam, and that the CPA exam be taken immediately after graduation. In other words, experience in public accounting (other than the internship) would no longer be necessary for gaining the CPA certificate and for entering into the profession. This recommendation generated considerable uproar among practicing public accountants.

Trouble on this recommendation was immediately apparent in the vigorous dissents of four of the 24 Commission members. Traditionally, the CPA certificate signified that its holder was qualified to practice as a principle.[64] The recommendation to convert it into something like an academic degree was strongly opposed by most public accountants. The Commission must have known that it was asking for trouble because even a cursory review of history would have revealed that public accountants had always jealously maintained that formal education alone was insufficient to prepare a person for public accounting.

The Commission's recommendation came as a surprise to many. In 1955 Perry himself had said,

> One of the best arguments for an experience prerequisite for the CPA certificate is that only on the job can an accountant learn to recognize, handle, and evaluate the raw data which take so many forms in bookkeeping records.[65]

Why, a year later, the "Perry Report" was opposing an experience requirement was unclear. Moreover, the Association of CPA Examiners, one of the forerunners of the Commission, recommended in its 1952 report (as the Commission was forming) that:

1.   A successful candidate...be issued a certificate as a public accountant, but not as a certified public accountant.
2.   The certified public accountant certificate...be issued after the successful candidate has had a minimum of three years' public accounting experience.[66]

Since it was so obvious that most public accountants opposed dropping the experience requirement, where did the recommendation come from? This was clearly a victory of the accounting academicians. Recall that an AAA committee had recommended this in 1949. After the Perry Report was issued, it was found that 97 percent of the accounting department chairmen surveyed "endorsed the proposal to allow graduates of professional programs to take all parts of the C.P.A. examination...before obtaining practical experience...."[67] Taking the position that a college education alone (rather than college plus experience) was enough to prepare a person for public accounting would certainly enhance the prestige of collegiate accounting education. But this victory by the academicians discredited the Commission and drained its authority.

It did not help that the arguments advanced by the Commission to support the dropping of the experience requirement were so flimsy. Its argument that admission to the bar in the legal profession required no experience simply made public accountants belatedly aware that their profession was different from the profession of law. Its argument that the quality of various experiences was too hard to objectively evaluate was even more of a disaster. As two of the dissenters pointed out, the Commission did not similarly argue that because the quality of various educational programs was too hard to objectively evaluate, the value of education should be ignored. Again, the Commission, to soften the blow, said that "there are not likely to be many individuals who would undertake to establish their own practice without first obtaining experience with an established firm." As the same dissenters pointed out, the Commission was essentially saying that public accountants would have enough sense to not take seriously the Commission's view that experience was not necessary to practice as public accountants. The contradiction between the fact that the Commission disavowed the need for experience but then recommended that an internship be required was not lost on its critics either. What no critic at the time seems to have noted was that the Commission appealed to the invisible hand of the market to weed out the inexperienced and incompetent young CPA who dared "hang out his shingle" too soon, but did not similarly appeal to the market to weed out those without any formal education or who had not taken the CPA exam. Their faith in the market was quite selective.

Although the Commission's arguments were poor and its position unpopular among public accountants, the report did raise some interesting questions. What was the value of experience; is there really any value to having some years of undefined experience; and how could the value of experience be assured? One person, at least, asked some penetrating questions.

> [T]he issue that practitioners must face is this: Will they honestly undertake to provide experience as professional training, or do they still regard this as a cheap pool of labor? ...Many educators, while recognizing the value of experience, agree with students who have long viewed this requirement as a form of cheap labor apprenticeship and a barrier placed in the way of becoming a CPA, the purpose of which is to exploit them for a couple of years. ...I favor continuing an experience requirement, but one redefined, with provisions for standards and accreditation.[68]

The Institute did later form a committee to study ways of setting standards for qualifying experience, but its report was ignored.[69]

As if the Commission's position on experience were not bad enough, it was quickly pointed out that its idea of requiring an internship of all accounting students was simply impractical. The Institute had been proclaiming the value of internships since the 1940s, and most people seemed to approve of them, but a study reported in 1954 that only about 5 to 16 percent of accounting students availed themselves of voluntary internship programs.[70] Sixty percent of the accounting department chairmen surveyed after the Commission's report "did not regard an internship as necessary but a significant number (almost 50%) of those who answered in the negative commented that an internship would be desirable."[71] The logistical difficulty of gaining an internship in public accounting for every student interested in entering that profession was surely a factor in the opposition to the requirement.

The impracticality of the Commission's recommendation for a nation-wide qualifying examination was reflected in the fact that only 12 percent of the accounting department chairmen considered it necessary, and 24% were quite sure their schools would not accept such a qualifying exam as a criterion for admittance to post-graduate studies.[72]

The Real Issue of Reform

Even the recommendation of the Commission with which most people agreed--the recommendation that a post-graduate professional program be required--came up against criticism. Earl McGrath, who had recently been the U.S. Commissioner of Education, cautioned the profession about "the practice of constantly extending the period of formal education to accommodate more and more liberal and professional subject matter." McGrath pointed out that the medical profession, which had gone from two years to eight years beyond high school in a relatively short time, was rethinking its approach. Johns Hopkins had announced a program to reduce the period by two years, through eliminating some instruction and renewing emphasis on broad principles rather than on details.[73]

The issue of broadness versus detail was an aspect of reform which the Commission did not really address. There had, of course, been calls to get rid of the details and mechanics and focus on theory, and those calls came not only from those attempting to establish the position of managerial accounting. They had come from the very pioneers of accounting education, and had gathered force in the 1930s from those concerned about liberal education. In the 1940s even the public accountants became aware of the problem, approaching it from a different angle and trying to bridge the "gap between the accountant, who prepares or certifies financial statements, and the policymakers, untrained in accounting, who must interpret the statements." They suggested that a course in the "understanding and interpretation of accounting" be created for non-accounting majors.[74] That thought was carried further by a speaker in 1948:

> Less debiting and crediting would seem to be the answer at least for the non-accounting major. This may lead to the necessary inference that the introductory course work required of all should be divided into two sections: one preparing the prospective accounting major for subsequent concentration; the other emphasizing the measuring and control aspects for the non-accounting student. ...I am not sure, at this point, that the broader approach would not be more beneficial to even the accounting majors.[75]

In its report in January 1956, the AAA's Committee on Standards of Accounting Instruction said that it believed that

> the first course in principles is the keystone to the whole accounting structure. It is to be observed that offering the first course at the freshman level may tend to encourage emphasis on accounting techniques rather than meaningful principles. ...To avoid these negative consequences, the quality of teaching in these areas is especially important.[76]

Another writer in 1956 agreed with this assessment of the importance of the first course.

> Perhaps the most vital part of the accounting program is the first one-year course commonly required of all business students. It is here that the student gets his initial impression of what accounting is all about, is attracted or repelled by his experience, and decides at the end of the course whether to continue his preparation for entrance to the profession. A highly technical routines-and-procedures course will attract the [plodder with a fair mind, little imagination, no curiosity], but in order to persuade [the highly intelligent, mentally agile student with a high degree of intellectual curiosity and creative imagination] that the profession is a challenge to his high ability, accounting must be clearly presented as a complex, flexible, and highly useful tool in the solution of business problems and in the measurement and appraisal of operating results. ...[H]ow do we meet simultaneously the educational requirements of the general business student and the student who will enter the accounting profession? ...[With] a first year course of the kind just described, this problem will disappear. Regardless of the student's ultimate choice of a business or profession he will, in my opinion, be learning what he needs most to know about accounting--its objectives, uses, and processes--and he will be best prepared to

choose intelligently between the accounting profession
and other fields of endeavor.[77]

McGrath, though obscurely, also pointed out that

it is not necessary to introduce the student to all the
details of a subject to have him gain a knowledge of its
key ideas and principles. On the assumption that students
had to learn everything about a subject or nothing, basic
courses have included vast bodies of detail which could
have been omitted not with a loss, but with a positive
gain in effective learning. ...First courses in physics,
chemistry, and biology are designed as if all students
were dedicating their lives to the subject. ...Broad
courses are needed emphasizing the unity of knowledge
and its meaning in the life of the average citizen.[78]

At the end of the era, another writer tried to settle the issue.

Within the five-year accounting program there is no
place for different introductory courses in accounting for
accounting "majors" and non-accounting "majors." The
introductory course in accounting should explain the
logic which underlies accounting conventions. It should
clearly define the role of accounting as an interpreter of
the business process. It should deal with concepts and
theory. The entire theme of the introductory course
should be, "Why?"[79]

But all of these voices went blowing in the wind, too small and lonely
to be heard above the roar of the Commission. All that could be heard
was "post-graduate professional education." There were cautionary
warnings thrown in the path of the juggernaut:

the shift to a five or six year program should be made
when convincing evidence exists that the four year
program cannot accomplish the objectives satisfactorily.
At the present time little such evidence exists. Many
people think that four years is not enough. However,

demands for graduates from four year programs which are accomplishing a high level of professional education remain extremely strong. Furthermore, recent graduates appear to be able to progress without undue delay in most areas of accounting.[80]

A survey of business leaders showed that many were satisfied with the status quo, and did not see a great need for change. They strongly desired more English composition and public speaking, a bit more mathematics and business statistics, and strongly desired more cost accounting. Otherwise, more than 80 percent of the time, they were satisfied, and "over 90% of the businesses responding to the survey felt that a four-year college course, assuming quality in instruction, is adequate in giving the accountant his educational background for employment."[81]

A survey of accounting department chairmen, on the other hand, disclosed that 73 percent of them agreed with the Commission on the need for a fifth year of formal education for certified public accountants. "Seventy-five per cent regarded the five years of formal education to be composed essentially of 3 years of business and accounting and 2 years of liberal arts, and only 14 per cent believed the overall program would consist of 3 years of liberal arts and 2 years of business and accounting." This prompted the reporter to consider an important problem:

> It seems reasonable to expect that the additional year of business and accounting will eliminate many of the deficiencies of baccalaureate degree graduates in these areas, but it may be asked: How will the existing deficiency in liberal arts training be overcome? In the opinion of the writer this can be accomplished by improving the quality of undergraduate liberal arts training and by placing a higher premium on oral and written communication in business and accounting courses.[82]

Apparently liberal arts teachers would be able somehow to increase the quality without increasing the quantity, but business and accounting teachers could not be relied upon to do so.

Another author took a good look at the times and pointed out:

> The [Perry] Report, in the long run, proposes to shift the
> primary burden of preparation to formal education. In so
> doing it comes at a peculiarly inappropriate time, since
> institutions of higher learning are faced with heavy
> burdens of increasing enrollment and are in addition
> dominated, and perhaps properly so, by a trend back to
> fundamentals and away from the emphasis on specialized
> and particularly so-called "vocational" studies.[83]

The Climax

Both the Institute and the AAA formed committees to study the
report of the independent Commission, and both committees reported
their findings in 1959. The AAA's Committee on Professional
Education in Accounting made it clear that the term "professional"
should not be restricted to public accounting and "that basically the
same educational preparation is necessary for a professional career in
any of these four areas of accounting [public, industrial,
governmental, academic]." The Committee's position on the need for
post-graduate instruction was also clear.

> The over-all collegiate program of professional education
> envisioned by the committee may be accomplished
> within a four to six year time period. Four-year
> programs presently offered by some departments of
> accountancy may be accomplishing substantially a high
> level of professional education. Other four-year
> programs may require only minor modifications and
> revisions to attain the objectives desired. ...While a five-
> year program does not presently appear necessary to
> accomplish a desirable level of professional education,
> an evolution of four-year programs into five-year
> programs appears likely.[84]

The AAA Committee also recommended "some kind of advisory
accreditation committee" which would be "persuasive in nature and

would have to recognize the several possible sound approaches to achievement of the goals anticipated."

The Institute's committee to study the Commission report sought out the opinions of various groups and individuals and recommended that the Commission's view of the CPA certificate be rejected; the traditional meaning of the CPA certificate as evidence of competence to practice public accounting without supervision should be continued, and the experience requirement should be retained as the "overwhelming majority" of practitioners felt. The Institute's committee (called the Bailey Committee, after its chairman, George D. Bailey) agreed that students could take the CPA exam immediately after meeting educational requirements, but not actually become certified until the experience requirement was also met, and the level of the exam should remain at the level of testing "competence required for conducting the medium-sized engagement or for general practice in a medium-sized community."

The Bailey Committee agreed that college graduation should be a requirement for becoming a CPA, and added, "For those studying accountancy at this level, education for public accounting should differ little, if any, from education for careers in industrial and governmental accounting." The Committee said that post-graduate education was "highly desirable" but recognized that "there is always the problem of time and expense of attending school." The Committee recommended that "as soon as it is feasible postgraduate study devoted principally to accountancy and business administration [should] become a requirement for the CPA certificate." Unlike the Institute's 1937 resolution, four years of liberal education were not contemplated as the norm, but rather the Commission's suggestion of an undergraduate accounting major with one year of post-graduate study was expected to be more common. The Bailey Committee gutted the rest of the Commission's major recommendations. It did not support a qualifying examination as a screening device; it did not support requiring internships; it did not support the formation of a new organization for accreditation purposes.[85]

The Institute's Council approved the recommendations of the Bailey Committee with few dissents. It was now the official policy of the Institute that not only a college degree be required but that post-graduate studies also be required.

Why was the Institute determined to require a four-year college education to become a CPA? At the time only four states (New York, New Jersey, Florida, and Connecticut) had such a requirement. In spite of that, "Of those who had received their CPA certificates in the years 1941-1945, 66.8 per cent held college degrees, and more than 25 per cent had been awarded both a Bachelor's degree and an advanced degree."[86] Moreover, "Of all candidates for the May 1953 examination, 74% were college graduates."[87] In 1957, 80% of new CPAs were college graduates.[88] It appeared that the market was handling its needs without formal requirements. Why then should a college degree be required of everyone? The answer was obvious. How could accounting be considered a true profession when it did not even require a college education? The profession was seeking prestige, not education. Education was only a means to an end.

If there was no substantive reason to require even college graduation, then what explains the Institute's commitment to postgraduate education? Again the answer is prestige. A college degree or less may be sufficient for other types of accountants (e.g., managerial), but to be a public accountant post-graduate work was necessary. The five-year program would enhance their status. Academic accountants, also concerned about status, would unavoidably have their attention drawn to the high-status public accounting program. Public accountants had regained control of accounting education--or at least so it seemed.

The Disaster

Unfortunately for the public accountants, 1959 also saw another set of events occur. Two significant reports on business education were published almost simultaneously. The first, entitled *The Education of American Businessmen*, was financed by the Carnegie Corporation and authored by Frank C. Pierson (with some others contributing). The other, entitled *Higher Education for Business* and financed by the Ford Foundation, was authored by Robert A. Gordon and James E. Howell. These reports (which became widely referred to as "the Foundation Reports") set the public accountants back on their heels.

The authors of both studies were economists and were strongly in favor of post-graduate instruction in accounting[89]--not because they thought accounting education needed more time on top of an extensive undergraduate major, but because they wanted to remove accounting as far from the undergraduate curriculum as possible. This is how the public accountants summed up the message of the reports:

> Many accounting courses were said to contain too much descriptive material of a vocational-training type, and too little of the type of instruction that would encourage an individual's maximum intellectual growth. Financial accounting and auditing were regarded as inferior to managerial accounting as subjects for academic study.[90]

Pierson did not even consider accounting a "functional core subject" but rather a "quantitative core subject" akin to statistics. He criticized the core accounting course for stressing the mechanics rather than the managerial uses of this tool.

> Presumably, introductory courses in accounting and statistics developed along these lines are thought to provide the best preparation for students who want to do more intensive work in these two areas, though even from the viewpoint of future majors such courses are being increasingly questioned. From the point of view of nonmajors, however, there seems little doubt that the emphasis on mechanics and techniques is a serious mistake. Indeed, attention ought to be centered on accounting and statistics as aids to management in reaching decisions, with special reference to their uses as tools for coordinating different aspects of management decision making. Viewed in this light, accounting becomes an extremely important instrument for analyzing sales policy questions, pricing problems, capital expenditures programs, debt-financing methods, etc.[91]

In Pierson's suggested undergraduate curriculum, only six semester hours were to be given to "quantitative methods (accounting-statistics)" with an optional three-hour elective.

Robert Cox, who wrote the Carnegie Report's chapter on accounting, was a bit more lenient, suggesting three hours in "Accounting Fundamentals" and two more in "Applications of Accounting Data to the Administrative Process" Accounting majors would be allowed ten additional hours in accounting, four of them in "Administrative Controls and Analysis" but none of them in auditing. Furthermore, the focus of the desired accounting was clear, and it was in line with the book's stated idea of "managerial decision making as an organizing concept."

> A growing number of leaders in the field of accounting education are concerned over the tendency of the curriculum to become more and more technical, with excessive emphasis upon a narrow concept of public accounting. ...The profession of public accountancy can ill afford to accept an educational program for students intending to go into public practice which is lower in quality and more narrowly oriented than that designed for students who will seek employment as accountants with industrial organizations.[92]

Similarly, the Ford Report focused on the beginning accounting course, noting both "universal acceptance" of its necessity and "considerable dissatisfaction" with its content.

> The principal conflict concerns the extent to which students should be able to omit the procedural detail in the introductory course and move on to what is called managerial or interpretive accounting. ...We have the impression that, for both the accounting major and the general business student, there is a good deal of waste motion in the elementary course. Even more important, the general business student does not get the training he so badly needs in how to use accounting as a managerial tool.[93]

In their suggested undergraduate curriculum Gordon and Howell allowed 9-12 hours for "managerial accounting" and "statistical analysis and related topics." For accounting majors, "under no circumstances should the work in accounting constitute more than twelve hours beyond the elementary course."

Obviously, such undergraduate programs would not meet the requirements of those states requiring a college degree as well as specified numbers of hours in accounting to take the CPA exam. Unflinchingly, the reports said that students would simply have to take some graduate study or night courses to make up the shortcoming.

Public accountants watched in shock as years of status-building evaporated overnight. The 1960s promised to be a tumultuous time.

Notes

1 C. Aubrey Smith, "Education for the Professional Accountant," *The Accounting Review*, January 1945, p. 17.

2 Hermann C. Miller, "Interim Report of the Standards Rating Committee," *The Accounting Review*, January 1951, p. 19.

3 Fladger F. Tannery, "The Requirements and Opportunities in Industry for Students of Accounting," *The Accounting Review*, October 1948, p. 384.

4 Ibid., p. 377.

5 Gay Carroll, "Some Challenges to Accounting," *The Accounting Review*, January 1951, pp. 17-18.

6 Edward G. Nelson, "Science and Accounting," *The Accounting Review*, October 1949, pp. 354, 355.

7 Ibid., p. 357.

8 Ibid.

9 That is not to say that the terminology of the scientific ideal did not occasionally resurface, but it was not really defended. Harry Kerrigan ("Some Current Problems in the Teaching of Accounting," *The Accounting Review*, January 1952, p. 79) hoped "to see formulated, along scientific lines, a body of definitive principles, the hallmark of all disciplines which have come of age." But he left his hope at that comment, not defining or discussing it further.

[10] Curt Gruneberg, "Is Accountancy a Field of Science?" *The Accounting Review*, April 1950, p. 161.

[11] Frederick E. Horn, "Managerial Emphasis in Elementary Accounting," *The Accounting Review*, July 1951, p. 308.

[12] Ibid., p. 309.

[13] Karl A. Boedecker, "The Correlation of Accounting Instruction With Instruction in Other Business Fields," *The Accounting Review*, January 1951, pp. 70, 71.

[14] Ibid., pp. 71, 72.

[15] Russell Bowers, "Curriculum Building for Prospective Industrial Accountants," *The Accounting Review*, January 1953, pp. 58, 59.

[16] G. Winston Summerhill, "Administrative Accounting in the Accounting Curriculum," *The Accounting Review*, January 1953, p. 74.

[17] Harvey T. Deinzer, "Specialization or Integration as the Objective of Graduate Accounting Instruction," *The Accounting Review*, April 1953, p. 250.

[18] A good critique of such "social accounting" can be found in A.C. Littleton, "Accounting Rediscovered," *The Accounting Review*, April 1958, pp. 246-253.

[19] J.E. Smyth, "A Case for National Income Accounting in the Accounting Curriculum," *The Accounting Review*, July 1959, pp. 376-380.

[20] Nelson, p. 359. Nelson wanted the accounting associations to champion his cause, and take the heat.

[21] Deinzer, p. 257.

[22] Harold Q. Langenderfer and Ernest H. Weinwurm, "Bringing Accounting Curricula Up-To-Date," *The Accounting Review*, July 1956, pp. 423, 424.

[23] Bowers, p. 61.

[24] Summerhill, pp. 64-65, 71.

[25] Richard S. Claire, "Training for the Public Accounting Profession," *The Accounting Review*, April 1944, p. 155.

[26] H.T. Scovill, "Education for Public Accounting on the Collegiate Level," *The Accounting Review*, July 1946, p. 263.

[27] Malcolm L. Pye, "The Undergraduate Accounting Curriculum," *The Accounting Review*, April 1955, p. 287.

28 Leo A. Schmidt, "Employers' Conference Evaluates Accounting Curriculums, Recruitment, Placement," *The Journal of Accountancy*, October 1948, p. 293.

29 Summerhill, p. 75.

30 "Are CPA Examinations Too Hard?" *The Journal of Accountancy*, June 1947, p. 457.

31 Thomas W. Leland, "Educational Prerequisites for the Certificate," *The Accounting Review*, April 1945, pp. 192, 193.

32 Norman E. Webster, "College Education as a Requirement for Certified Public Accountants--The New York Experience," *The Accounting Review*, October 1946, p. 447.

33 See in *The Journal of Accountancy*, "How Education and Experience Affect Examination Results" (November 1949, p. 370), "Students' Department" (February 1950, p. 177), "New Study Reveals Reasons for Failure to Pass Uniform CPA Examination" (June 1950, pp. 540-542), "Education Plus Experience Only Way to Pass CPA Examination" (September 1950, pp. 269-270), "Better Educated Candidates in 1949 Were More Successful in CPA Exams" (March 1951, p. 467), "Education for Professional Accounting Practice" (May 1951, pp. 673-674).

34 "Accounting Education," *The Journal of Accountancy*, September 1945, p. 163.

35 "Students' Department," edited by Thomas W. Leland, *The Journal of Accountancy*, May 1947, p. 440.

36 Smith, p. 19.

37 Sidney G. Winter, "What is Proper Training for Accountants?" *The Accounting Review*, June 1941, p. 185.

38 Smith, p. 18.

39 Schmidt, p. 292.

40 A. Frank Stewart, "Accounting Education--From the Viewpoint of a Member of a State Board of Accountancy," *The Accounting Review*, July 1953, p. 352.

41 "A Report of the Committee on Auditing Education," *The Accounting Review*, July 1954, pp. 467-468.

42 Langenderfer and Weinwurm, p. 426.

43 Rosecrans Baldwin, "A Practitioner's Plea for More Training in Written English," *The Accounting Review*, July 1956, p. 359.

44 Charles T. Zlatkovich, "Training For an Accounting Career: An Educator's View," *The Accounting Review*, April 1958, p. 197.

[45] Paul E. Nye, "Training For an Accounting Career: A Public Accountant's View," *The Accounting Review*, April 1958, pp. 188-189.

[46] "Accounting Teachers Evaluate the Uniform CPA Examination," *The Journal of Accountancy*, March 1949, pp. 254-255. See also, Hale L. Newcomer, "The CPA Examination," *The Accounting Review*, April 1949, pp. 128-135.

[47] The Institute has recommended its version of an ideal accountancy law to the states from time to time.

[48] Donald P. Perry, "Public Relations and Legislative Control of the Accounting Profession," paper presented at the 64th Annual Meeting of the American Institute of Accountants, p. 40.

[49] Donald P. Perry, "Training for the Profession," *The Journal of Accountancy*, November 1955, p. 67.

[50] Ibid., p. 68.

[51] Ibid., p. 71.

[52] Paul L. Noble, "A Quantitative Evaluation of Accounting Curricula," *The Accounting Review*, April 1950, p. 164.

[53] "Undergraduate Curriculum Study: Report of the Task Committee on Standards of Accounting Instruction," *The Accounting Review*, January 1956, pp. 37-39.

[54] "Advanced Education in Accounting," *The Journal of Accountancy*, January 1951, p. 68.

[55] Claire, p. 158; and Ralph L. Boyd, "A Suggested Program for College Training in Accountancy," *The Accounting Review*, January 1946, p. 53.

[56] Smith, p. 20.

[57] "Developments in Accounting Education," *The Journal of Accountancy*, October 1950, p. 356.

[58] C. Aubrey Smith, "University Offers Degree of Master in Professional Accounting (MPA)," *The Journal of Accountancy*, February 1949, pp. 140-141.

[59] Editorial in *The Journal of Accountancy*, October 1950, p. 280.

[60] C. Aubrey Smith, "The Next Step--A Professional School of Accounting," *The Accounting Review*, October 1956, pp. 567, 569.

[61] *Report of the Commission on Standards of Education and Experience for Certified Public Accountants* (University of Michigan, 1956), pp. 121, 127-136.

[62] Jim G. Ashburne, "The Five-Year Professional Accounting Program," *The Accounting Review*, January 1958, p. 106; and Peter A. Firmin, "The Five-Year Accounting Program--With Due and Deliberate Speed," *The Accounting Review*, October 1959, p. 591; and Arthur M. Cannon, "Education and the CPA Standards Report," *The Journal of Accountancy*, January 1957, p. 37.

[63] Walter G. Kell, "The Commission's Long Run Goals," *The Accounting Review*, April 1958, p. 200.

[64] A principle in a CPA firm is someone who can sign the audit report. Someone without a CPA certificate can practice only under the supervision of a principle.

[65] Perry, "Training," p. 69.

[66] Quoted by J. Earl Pedelahore, "The Case For the Dissent," *The Journal of Accountancy*, December 1956, p. 39.

[67] Kell, p. 204.

[68] Arthur M. Cannon, "Education and the CPA Standards Report," *The Journal of Accountancy*, January 1957, p. 39.

[69] John L. Carey, *The Rise of the Accounting Profession: To Responsibility and Authority. 1937-1969* (New York: AICPA, 1970), pp. 272-273.

[70] Quoted by Pedelahore, p. 41.

[71] Kell, pp. 203-204.

[72] Kell, p. 199.

[73] Earl J. McGrath, "Education, Profession and Public Affairs," *The Journal of Accountancy*, April 1958, p. 48.

[74] "Accounting Education for Nontechnical Students," *The Journal of Accountancy*, May 1946, p. 359. See also correspondence on this subject in *The Journal of Accountancy*, September 1946, p. 257.

[75] David A. Revzan, "What is a Balanced Curriculum in Accounting?" *The Accounting Review*, October 1949, pp. 410, 411.

[76] Report, p. 40.

[77] Willard J. Graham, "How Can the Colleges Serve the Profession?" *The Journal of Accountancy*, February 1956, pp. 47-48.

[78] McGrath, pp. 46-47.

[79] Peter A. Firmin, "The Five-Year Accounting Program--With Due and Deliberate Speed," *The Accounting Review*, October 1959, p. 598.

80   Arthur R. Wyatt, "Professional Education in Accounting," *The Accounting Review*, April 1959, p. 205.

81   Emory O. Sondereggen, "Qualifications for Accounting Students to Meet the Needs of Business Firms," *The Accounting Review*, January 1959, pp. 115-121.

82   Kell, p. 200.

83   Cannon, p. 40.

84   "Report of Committee on Professional Education in Accounting," *The Accounting Review*, April 1959, p. 198.

85   "Education and Experience for CPAs: The Report to Council of the American Institute of CPAs by the Special Committee on the Report of the Commission on Standards of Education and Experience for CPAs," *The Journal of Accountancy*, June 1959, pp. 67-71.

86   "Educational Background of Certified Public Accountants," *The Journal of Accountancy*, July 1949, pp. 4-5.

87   Lawrence L. Vance, "Education for Public Accounting: With Special Reference to the Report of the Commission on Standards of Education and Experience for Certified Public Accountants," *The Accounting Review*, October 1956, p. 577.

88   Cannon, p. 35.

89   They preferred post-graduate education in general business also, ideally following a liberal arts degree or broad engineering program and a couple of years of work experience. The popularity of the MBA owes much to the Foundation Reports.

90   Carey, p. 273.

91   Frank C. Pierson and Others, *The Education of American Businessmen: A Study of University-College Programs in Business Administration* (New York: McGraw-Hill, 1959), p. 210.

92   Ibid., pp. 378-379.

93   Robert Aaron Gordon and James Edwin Howell, *Higher Education for Business* (New York: Columbia University Press, 1959), pp. 194-195.

Chapter 3

In the Wake of the Foundation Reports

The Foundation Reports single-mindedly advocated "management." Because of this, the phrase "management accounting" had magic in it. But it was not yet clear exactly what management accounting was.

The AAA had set up its first committee on management accounting in January of 1957 "to clarify just what is meant by the term management accounting." Two years later it published its final report, which hinted at the difficulty of the task:

> Management accounting is not new in any sense of the word. It emphasizes a composite of numerous well-known concepts, techniques, and procedures which had their inception in the development of so-called scientific management and the over-all financial accounting structure as it exists today. The evolution of management accounting cannot be determined precisely. Nevertheless, lines of evolution with respect to certain concepts and procedures which are basic to management accounting have been traced with some precision. Among these concepts and procedures are: standard

costing, budgeting, break-even analysis, differential
analysis, and responsibility accounting.[1]

It was no easy task to carve out a whole new academic area using bits
and pieces from the formerly unified accounting area. Trying to find
something unique in the entirety of those fragments--other than the
term management--was difficult. Indeed, that difficulty is evident in
the committee's attempt to define management accounting:

> Management accounting is the application of appropriate
> techniques and concepts in processing the historical and
> projected economic data of an entity to assist manage-
> ment in establishing a plan for reasonable economic
> objectives and in the making of rational decisions with a
> view toward achieving these objectives.[2]

If the word "management" is omitted, that definition could arguably
be applied to financial accounting as well.

The problem was that the difference between management
accounting and financial accounting was seen as an opposition
between being user-oriented (management accounting) and being
procedurally-oriented (financial accounting). Only occasionally did
anyone come close to seeing that such opposition was not the
difference between management and financial accounting at all.[3]
Historically, accounting had been the act of reporting financial
information to users (i.e., decision-makers). As such it had always
had a user orientation, even if that was sometimes (by some teachers
and authors) buried under techniques. The real problem of identifying
the managerial approach with a user approach was that a whole set of
important users (i.e., owners and investors and lenders) and their
decisions would be ignored for the sake of the needs of other users
(i.e., management).

Management accounting as a separate academic course became
visible around 1956. At that time it was typically required only for
non-accounting majors, apparently because it was assumed that
accounting majors would pick up the material in following courses--
particularly "cost accounting."[4] It was largely a service course for the
business school and not yet a legitimate separate accounting area.

The Foundation Reports however seemed to consider it the *only* legitimate accounting area. For the accounting educators who still largely identified with financial accounting and for the public accountants as well, this was clearly a threat--certainly to their prestige and perhaps even to their livelihood.

Furthermore, the full logistical ramifications of the Foundation Reports began to also sink in:

> This means that the "ideal" educational program for professional accountants, established within the framework recommended by the Gordon and Pierson reports, would consist of an undergraduate program in the liberal arts, a two-year program in business (MBA), followed by whatever professional accounting work might be considered appropriate for the university to offer.[5]

Requiring seven or eight years of higher education would undoubtedly have an impact on the supply of accountants. Five years of higher education was one thing, but this was quite something else.

Reaction to the Foundation Reports

Articles in the April 1961 *Accounting Review* revealed the defensiveness of both academic and public accountants. The AAA's committee to study the Foundation Reports was not impressed by them. It said,

> Together they constitute over 1200 printed pages and in this volume they say almost everything that could have been said and also succeed in hedging just about every statement to which anyone could take exception.[6]

The committee continued:

> We reject the idea that uses and decision making can be taught without an understanding of techniques, but we agree that many elementary accounting courses could be

improved by a reduction of the procedural aspects and by a considerable increase in attention to interpretation and to managerial uses of accounting data. ...Many readers-- and this is certainly true of the members of this committee--reject the implication that all liberal arts courses are of greater value to basic education, to the development of the personality, and to training in analytical thinking than are courses in business administration. ...We do not feel that this defense of accounting is merely an emotional reaction, but that it touches a real factor to be carefully appraised lest the swing away from too much specialization go too far toward meaningless generalization. ...It is entirely possible that the deliberations of [AAA] committees have been more intensive and their recommendations on a better informed basis than those of the Ford and Carnegie reports. Intensive study of the problem since 1950 has resulted in the virtually uniform recommendation of 25% to accounting, 25% to other business, and 50% to liberal arts. ...Considering these factors this committee believes that the Ford and Carnegie recommendations regarding excessive specialization point in the right direction. We do not, however, approve their specific recommendations: we believe that they have gone too far.[7]

The committee was not happy with the cavalier disregard by the Foundation Reports for the responsibility of business schools to prepare their students to meet the requirements of state CPA laws. It also pointed out that "The larger C.P.A. firms are already well embarked on their own training programs which are admirably suited to give the specialized training that is really needed"[8]--thereby allowing the universities to be more general and conceptual, and more acceptable to the demands of the Foundation Reports.

A very prominent public accountant, in an article in the same issue of the *Accounting Review*, took a practical approach. Rather than trying to attack the Reports conceptually, as the AAA committee did, he expressed some agreement with the ideals of the Foundation Reports, but then added, "Realism suggests, however, that attainment of this ideal is still far off." And he complained, "Unfortunately, neither the Ford nor the Carnegie Report dwelt heavily on the means and mechanics of transition from our present levels to those recommended."[9] The Reports were simply not realistic. He brought up the cost/benefit consideration:

> Our problem then becomes one that is familiar to all accountants and particularly cost accountants. How great a cost in terms of time and effort can a young man afford to spend in formal education and how much should be left to be obtained through self-education and experience?[10]

Shifting the Burden

For all the protestations, however, the writing was on the wall. Specialization (other than specialization in the management of people) had lost favor in the business school, and the specialized field of accounting would have to find a way to deal with that. If the schools were now unwilling to provide as much technical training as before, then practitioners themselves would have to make up for the lack. The head of a university accounting department put it bluntly: "Practitioners have an inescapable responsibility to provide training in the areas which colleges cannot supply." He spelled out what he meant:

> Much of the responsibility for too much emphasis in the classroom on application of accounting procedures can be attributed to the accounting teaching faculties at the universities because of their lack of knowledge of the basic educational needs of professional accountants. A part of the responsibility lies in the lap of the employers of graduates of universities who have exerted strong pressures on accounting faculty members to give them a product that can perform a specific job immediately upon graduation. Without question, CPA examinations have had considerable influence on the type and content of courses offered. ...Knowledge must be applied to be

useful. Part of the application to specific problems can be accomplished within the university framework by clinical teaching, i.e., use of case method, etc. Part of the application must come through actual experience in applying the basic fundamentals learned to actual business problems. ...By reducing the number and variety of courses now offered during the traditional four-year program in the applied and mechanical areas in accounting as well as in other business fields and substituting fewer, soundly conceived courses, enough time in the four-year program would be released to provide space to meet most of the criticisms which attack the failures of present programs. These changes would permit the inclusion of enough of the cultural and humanistic areas of knowledge to satisfy professional needs.[11]

His argument was clear: more of the practical training should be done by employers of college graduates. The stated justification was that colleges could not do the whole job. This position was in direct opposition to the position taken by the Perry Report a few years earlier--the position that colleges could do all that was needed if they only had five years in which to do it, and that no further experience requirement was necessary. But this post-Foundation-Reports writer suggested reducing the accounting courses to only 12.5 percent of the four-year program--half of what had been accepted for many years before the Foundation Reports. He also advocated a fifth year of specialized accounting studies, to make up for the lack.

Another accounting professor went even farther. He recommended that accounting courses take up only 10 percent of the four-year program and that there be no fifth year at all. Instead,

The way to professional competence must be through real world experience, dealing with actual problems under the guidance of those who know those problems intimately, in a way no professor can. The university cannot produce trained and competent accountants....[12]

A partner in a large public accounting firm also defended the efficiency which could be achieved by teaching technique through practice:

> Considering the student's maturity and experience, the faculties and facilities available in the universities, the pressures of time, and parallel matters, a proper division of the responsibility for preparing students for accounting careers--as between the universities and the employers--should be based upon what each separate group can do most effectively. I believe the universities can deal more effectively with broad and basic concepts and principles, emphasizing the relation of the accounting function to all other aspects of business, economic, political, and civic environment, and thus preparing the student to be a thinking and learning man.... At the same time, methodology and specific techniques can, I believe, be imparted more effectively by the employer. Since this is done as an integral part of the employee's daily job activities, a substantial savings in time and effort is effected.[13]

It is no surprise that a public accountant was defending the necessity of experience for a complete education. What the Foundation Reports had done was cause academicians to agree--indeed, to advocate eliminating anything very practical from the curriculum. It was up to the public accountants to supply all things practical.

And, in the actual event, the public accountants were in fact going beyond simply relying upon experience to supply the lacking education. The American Institute of Certified Public Accountants (AICPA) had begun efforts to develop continuing education courses in 1956, and in 1959 established a full-time staff to develop a comprehensive adult education program.

The AICPA's committee on long-range planning also focused on the training of accountants *after* they left college. In a seminal article in 1961 a member of the committee, Norton Bedford, distinguished four areas of responsibility for the comprehensive education of an accountant:

1. The university should concentrate on general education, the preprofessional program and a professional program centered on the general principles and concepts of the technology. It should be directed to the development of critical and analytical thinking, with only those procedures included which are essential for understanding the concepts.

2. The staff training program should concentrate on procedures. While the student will be introduced to the basic procedures in the university professional program, the highly technical aspects and detailed procedures should be a part of the staff training program.

3. On-the-job training necessarily centers on the application of the procedures and principles to specific problems. This should be developed so the individual will get the maximum education out of experience.

4. The American Institute should provide the educational programs to keep the profession professionally competent in all phases of contemporary accounting practice. It would include courses at all levels. It might include further staff training classes for new employees of small firms. It might include experimental programs which would advance the profession into new areas. In general, the American Institute program should assume responsibility for leadership in developing the nonuniversity training program.[14]

In 1961 the long-range planning committee made an innovative suggestion for encouraging continuing education. Its proposal was introduced by an appeal which seems invariably to have influenced public accountants:

Why aren't CPAs yet recognized as a learned profession? Partly, no doubt, because of the youth of the accounting profession. ...But the recognition of certified public accountants as members of a learned profession is also delayed by the fact that the profession as a whole is not required to meet a high standard of learning. ...While only about a dozen states require a college education for the CPA certificate, it is estimated that about 85 per cent of the successful candidates in the CPA examination have college degrees. This in itself, however, does not necessarily meet the standard necessary for recognition as a learned profession. ...[I]t seems clear that a four-year undergraduate course is no longer a sufficient educational basis to command recognition of CPAs as a learned profession....[15]

Continuing education was proposed as the solution to the problem (at least until the hoped-for five-year requirement became reality). But "the question of incentive for continuing education arises. How many certified public accountants will study for the intangible, indirect benefits of self-improvement? Would some formal credit or recognition that might enhance their prestige and increase their earning capacity be an added incentive?"[16] The committee proposed a system of "higher accreditation" which would be "Some form of recognition within the profession of individuals who had demonstrated superior knowledge, ability and professional competence." A parallel to the specialty boards in medicine was drawn, and an elaborate system was suggested. Once again, increased status demanded that there be some form of higher credential required. But the idea went nowhere.

Is the Fifth Year Justifiable?

It seemed that the real hope for increased prestige for public accounting lay in the five-year requirement. Yet only a handful of states required even four years. The AICPA could make the point that graduate study in accounting better prepares people for their careers, and a study showed that people with graduate degrees were more successful than those with only bachelor's degrees.[17] But it was another matter to argue that everyone should therefore be required to have a fifth year of education.

Not all public accountants were sympathetic with the AICPA's efforts to force a fifth-year requirement on accounting students. A partner in a large accounting firm voiced this opposing position:

> I believe that none of us wishes to impose additional years of academic preparation on aspiring accountants unless, after the potentialities of the four-year program have been fully realized, it proves insufficient. Mounting costs of education, the increasing problems in attracting qualified faculties and in maintaining adequate facilities, and the probability that the four-year program is likely to be with us for some time to come indicate, at least to me, the need for further thought on what can be done within the framework of a four-year program to keep up with the changing needs of accounting education.[18]

The fact that there were practitioners who did not believe that there was an educational need for a fifth year did not stop the AICPA leadership from pushing for it, however.

The AICPA had been trying to justify the need for a fifth year using the same excuse that had been so successful in persuading many people to support the four-year college requirement: that an excessively high failure rate on the CPA exam could only be cured by more education. By the end of 1960, however, the Middle Atlantic Association of Colleges of Business Administration reported that, based on its studies in New York State, there was not in fact an excessively high failure rate.

> [T]he Association is not impressed that the fifth year will solve the problem of failures on CPA examinations. Results on the examination are influenced by the ability of the candidate, and the merits of the college training to which he has been subjected. An integrated four year course can and should provide the theoretical background needed for a well balanced program.
>
> Some very practical considerations work against the validity of the proposal for a required fifth year.

Students who seek careers in public accounting already constitute only a small minority of business administration enrollees. To require this group to complete an additional year will tend to divert potential CPA Candidates into alternate four year programs. The non-urban schools which offer a public accounting major will not be able to attract sufficient students to a fifth year course to support this operation.[19]

A powerful intellectual defense of the four-year program was made by Robert K. Mautz, a prominent professor. He argued that (1) it is popular as a major (and an extra year might endanger that), (2) it is successful as shown by the well-respected accountants it had produced and the high passage rate of college students on the CPA exam, and (3) it is economical for both the student and society. He then demolished the arguments for the five-year program.

He first attacked the argument "most commonly expressed [which] may be bluntly described as the 'prestige reason.'" He questioned the validity of "the contention that increased educational requirements will bring the desired prestige." He went on to say,

It seems to me there is something almost unethical about this kind of approach, particularly for the most ethical of professions. Unless there is a real need for the educational time, can we conscientiously advocate additional years of school on the part of candidates for the profession merely because it may add to their and our professional prestige?[20]

He reiterated how successful the four-year program had been, and suggested how it could be further improved.

Four years is a mighty long time. Four years devoted to education, if carefully planned and intelligently applied, can accomplish a great deal. ...If one has the courage to sweep out all the accumulated chaff, to eliminate outmoded materials, to condense, consolidate, and revise, there is a good deal of time in any four-year program.[21]

He explained how he and others at the University of Illinois had crafted a four-year program which "may be described as a very rigorous four years, with generous quantities of liberal education, sufficient accounting to give the student some real depth in that subject, and little opportunity for the student to dissipate his efforts in irrelevant electives."

> It is not enough to tell a man to take more courses in arts and sciences. Many of these courses are as highly specialized, as career oriented, as anything taught in a school of business. We have tried to avoid sending our students to this kind of course. Through discussions with representatives of other departments, we have either found courses especially suited to our students' needs or have had courses so designed. Please don't think this results in watered-down versions of standard offerings. In every case the course was designed, taught, and administered by the department charged with responsibility for developing that discipline; the business faculty serves only in an advisory capacity.[22]

Mautz then countered the argument that if four years of college is good, five years must be better. He was opposed to graduate study immediately after an undergraduate degree:

> I think much of the argument in favor of continued schooling is really an argument for holding the man from practice until he is a little older, until he has acquired something more in the way of maturity. If so, let me take a firm stand against it. Keeping a man on campus does not necessarily add to his maturity; education and maturity are quite different aspects of personal development. ...We keep grown men on campus in sneakers, T-shirts, and tight-fitting jeans until they are well into physical and intellectual maturity. Then we wonder why they have difficulty assuming responsibility. They need experience in accepting responsibility long before we give it to them; they need real-life

situations in which to face problems, make mistakes, and learn to do better. They are mature physically and mentally; they need activity, not more schooling. ...

...It occurs to me that a great weakness of a five year program, insofar as presenting professional education is concerned, is that it may take an inexperienced person into subjects which he is not competent to discuss and the implications of which may be entirely foreign to his previous activities.[23]

Mautz's view of education for professional accountancy called for three parts:

(1) a solid four-year undergraduate program thoughtfully developed to meet the needs of our society for quantities of accounting graduates, graduates who are prepared to accept their responsibilities as educated men in a technically oriented society, graduates who are equipped to enter public accounting or any other field of accounting activity

(2) a period of experience in public accounting sufficient to familiarize one with the profession and its problems, and to select those who have both a career interest and partnership potential

(3) a professional course offered by a limited number of selected and qualified schools and open only to CPAs meeting given standards of age, experience, and education[24]

Mautz's fifth year would be a one-year residency for people with significant accounting experience and a proven interest in public accounting--a kind of research sabbatical for public accountants.

Boom Times

It was not Mautz's ideas, however, which slowed the push for the five-year requirement. Rather, it was the fact that the 1960s were boom times for the accounting profession. Demand far exceeded supply, and college graduates were being hired as quickly as they were produced. There was absolutely no incentive for a student to take a fifth year.[25] Indeed, it was not long before public accounting firms reported such "great difficulty in hiring enough qualified university [accounting] graduates" that they were forced to hire people with majors other than accounting and to train them on-the-job.[26]

One very large problem with hiring non-accounting graduates was that they were not qualified (i.e., did not have adequate accounting credits) to sit for the CPA exam under some state laws. If they could not become CPAs, they could never legally become partners in a CPA firm. It was not easy, apparently, to persuade college graduates or MBAs to work for CPA firms in which they could never become partners unless they took additional accounting courses. The alarm was raised that CPA education standards should be lowered, or at least that state CPA laws should be made less specific about accounting requirements.

> Business school faculties have responded [to the Foundation Reports] with a critical revaluation of their objectives, curriculums, and course content--and with change. As a general rule, the better the school, the more likely it is to have changed.
>
> Two patterns of change in accounting education are of particular importance in their effect on the supply of high quality candidates for the CPA certificate. First, the undergraduate schools have been moving away from allocating to the major subject one-fourth or more of the hours required for a degree. The number of hours in the accounting major has been reduced, and reduced substantially, in many schools. Second, there are a number of good schools that have dropped the undergraduate major entirely and are concentrating their accounting education at the graduate level, where the quality of students is so good that they learn much more in the same number of course hours than does the typical undergraduate.
>
> Thus there are many highly intelligent and well-educated young people, whose university work included a sound core of accounting, who cannot, without taking

additional course work, qualify as CPA candidates in some states because laws or regulations are based on educational standards--often expressed in terms of hours or course titles--no longer accepted by the candidates' alma maters. Some of these universities are among the nation's finest institutions. It is not enough for the profession to say, "Then let them take additional work." We do not have so many well-qualified candidates that we can afford to treat them casually, nor, more importantly, is it at all clear that the educational standards of five or ten years ago are now appropriate.

...

Perhaps we should question the educational specifications in state laws.[27]

It was hoped that the problem of excess demand would go away as the baby-boomers began to graduate from college, but the Vietnam war heated up and many college graduates were drafted into the armed services or hid out in master's programs. Moreover, business education was not held in high esteem by the baby-boomers. By the last half of the 1960s, the fuse of rebelliousness lit in the 1950s had reached the powder keg of a multitude of people in their late teens, and the explosion rocked the nation. Anti-establishmentarianism ruled the media, the colleges, and much of American life. Business was part of the establishment, and as such it was not attractive to many young people. The straight-laced accounting establishment was perhaps least attractive of all. Accounting firms had to take whatever they could get.

So accounting practitioners made a virtue out of necessity. They hired more MBAs and made it look like they were living up to the high ideals of the Foundation Reports. They went a bit too far in their piety, at least for the taste of one accounting professor:

Quite frankly, I am disturbed (as are many other accounting professors) that some leaders in the profession (broadly) continue to downgrade the so-called "ivory tower approach" and continue publicly and privately to state that they would rather employ nonaccounting majors. The direct implication is that there is no solid academic base in accountancy essential in the academic community as represented by the university. Alternatively, it may be that these accountants take the view that an academic discipline can effectively exist *outside* the broader context of the university community. Contrary to this notion is the fact that a *discipline* only has real merit when it is operative, and justifiably so, within the context of an overall academic community. Nor will a discipline receive the type of recognition desired if that discipline is only "taught in our own firm."[28]

The Quest for Academic Respectability

The dissatisfaction which the practitioners were expressing towards accounting graduates was not entirely the result of a false piety, however. Actually a serious rift between practitioners and academicians had begun to appear. Academicians had begun to wander away from the issues which most concerned practitioners.

Some academicians have always resented the pressures which practitioners bring to bear upon the academic enterprise; they cherish their independence, perhaps excessively. In the 1950s the movement of academicians to gain independence from the public accounting profession marched under the banner of "management accounting" and the needs of non-public accountants. That banner became less useful when the public accountants moved dramatically into management consulting, making managerial accounting simply another area of public accounting. A fresh banner was needed, and at the same time a banner was needed under which academic accountants could enhance their tarnished status among other academicians. Such a banner, of course, was found.

In 1960 G. Leland Bach, dean of the graduate school of business and head of the department of economics at Carnegie Institute of Technology, had used the Foundation Reports as his starting point and charted out, with considerable prescience, the course of business education in the 1960s. His dream for business would strongly influence the dream for accounting as well.

He saw that management (or administration *per se*) would become a separate professional job, and that it would become "more analytical and scientific and the role of 'hunch' and even 'informed judgement' will become steadily smaller."

> At the extreme, this will mean increasing use of sophisticated analytical approaches to management decision processes such as mathematical programming and the extensive use of computers. In less extreme form, the critical change will involve increased clarification of the variables that need to be considered in making decisions, increased use of carefully considered quantitative information as to these variables, and increased use of rigorous analysis in weighting and combining the variables involved.[29]

Bach specified a set of major analytical tools which were beginning to emerge for management:

> First, the traditional, analytical tools of economics are still being used. …But there is a change in the flavor of the economics that is being taught in business education. There is a new emphasis upon the use of economics as a managerial tool--on managerial economics.
>
> Second is the area of quantitative methods. …[T]he tools of quantitative analysis are getting increased attention in business education, but the stress is increasingly on statistical techniques as well as on accounting, and often on cutting across the traditional fields covered by both.
>
> The third major tool is the behavioral sciences. In many respects this is the newest area of business education. It is the attempt to draw especially from psychology and sociology--the social sciences other than economics--fundamental knowledge that will help us understand individual behavior and how human beings work together in organizations.
>
> …A fourth new area is mathematics. In one sense, we can include mathematics with quantitative methods.

In another, this is quite incorrect. Mathematics does not
necessarily deal with quantitative data. It is a tool of
thinking in itself--a language.[30]

This was the direction in which business education was going; this
was the direction in which status within the business school could be
found. This was the direction in which accounting academicians, too,
could find status. Mathematical programming, the computer, decision
theory, management economics, statistics, behavioral sciences,
mathematical language--these were the areas that beckoned to a certain
breed of accounting professors--not the area of accounting theory. It
was even more apparent to them that the writing of textbooks--and
nearly everything to do with the field of accounting education--would
be of no value to them for their career advancement.

In 1961, Bedford, of the AICPA's long-range planning
committee, similarly encouraged this new direction. He especially
stressed that "the basic postulates underlying accounting procedures
must rest in [the] behavioral sciences."[31] He saw (in a vision which
he would bring back to haunt the profession twenty years later) a
New Accounting with a widened function of "measurement and
communication of economic data":

> Recent developments in applied mathematics and
> probability theory, which have been rather well received
> by the business world, point to the advancements in the
> measurement and communication function. The amazing
> growth of electronic data processing must also be
> included with any compilation of evidence to show that
> the accounting function is growing both in scope of
> activity and in the quantity of work performed.
> Suggestions from mathematicians that we may expect
> further advances in the use of mathematical methods in
> developing economic data for decision-making indicate
> that the tools to be available to the accounting profession
> may well encourage further expansion in the measure-
> ment and communication of economic data.[32]

The AICPA's dreamy vision of a greatly increased scope of practice,
however, was not what moved academicians. Their concern was with

their second- or even third-class status in the academic community--
induced by the Foundation Reports.

It was the eloquence of Mautz which charted the way to
salvation, when he spoke to the AAA meeting in 1962. The opening
paragraph of his call to arms is both revealing and fraught with
implications. It is clear that increased status for academic accountants
was the real motivation, but Mautz's strong ethical character would
not allow him or his listeners to leave it at that. Resoundingly, he
asked,

> Is accounting a social science? Such a question may be
> asked for any one of a number of reasons. To the
> suspicious, it may appear to be an effort to elevate
> accounting to a status it does not now have, to dignify it
> with the term "science," to class accounting with other
> accepted social sciences so we may share in whatever
> status they have attained. Like the rhetorical question:
> "Is accounting a profession?" often asked in the
> professional literature and always answered in the
> affirmative back in the days when there were still
> substantial doubts that public accounting could so
> qualify, a question of this kind is automatically subject
> to suspicion. My purpose here is not to claim unmerited
> prestige for accounting. Neither public practice nor
> academic accountancy can gain genuine prestige by
> debate or argument, however vigorous or scholarly it
> may be. We gain stature through service at a high level
> of skill, through rigorous research requiring continuing
> intellectual effort, through support of ethical and moral
> standards befitting the status we seek, and through a
> genuine humility that marks the person more interested
> in achievement than glory. Unless the purpose in asking
> this question is to seek ways to provide better service,
> expend greater intellectual effort, perform more
> fundamental research, hold ourselves to higher
> standards, and be ever more humble in our achieve-
> ments, any answers we discover will be little more than
> hollow rhetoric.[33]

While President John F. Kennedy was stirring the hearts of America's youth with his idealistic and self-sacrificial rhetoric, Mautz was doing the same to the hearts of young accounting academicians. He was making clear their place and purpose in the world:

> We do not expect practicing accountants to be social scientists any more than we expect practicing physicians to be physical or natural scientists. Their opportunity for service is of another kind, it lies in helping their clients or patients to the utmost of their professional abilities within the scope of ethical practice. Practitioners are not expected to do research, although some of them find time to do so. They are expected to make use of the research performed by the scientists in support of professional practice, and, where possible, to feed back to those scientists case studies and empirical data that will help the scientist to extend the bounds of human knowledge.
>
> ...There is a compatibility of education and research just as there is an incompatibility of professional practice and research. Not only are the essentials of a research environment found most commonly in the university community, but traditionally the academic burden of class meetings, office hours for student consultation, and committee service are intentionally lightened to provide opportunity for scholarly pursuits, of which research should be an important part. And there is additional incentive. The conscientious teacher, if he is meditative and contemplative in his approach, challenged as he must be by his students, has problems brought to his attention that literally cry for inquiry and investigation. At the same time the inquiring mind of the research man should be stimulating to students, thus making the researcher a good teacher.
>
> Thus the opportunity, the freedom, the stimulus, the time are all available to the teacher. The practitioner, on the other hand, has none of these advantages.[34]

Academicians saw now that they had a special purpose in the world, and that purpose required a friendly separation between academicians and practitioners--a separation of responsibilities enabling both to do better at their tasks and both to improve the wide world of accounting. As the new world opened up before the eyes of his listeners, Mautz assured them that it was an untouched continent (occupied only by savages) waiting only to be cleared by the hard-working hands of dedicated pioneers. It was truly a New Frontier.

Now what is the situation in accounting? First, let us look at the relationship between academic and professional accounting, for if we are to find social scientists anywhere in accounting it will be in the ranks of the teachers. An outsider looking at accounting today would find a situation quite contrary to that suggested above. He would find the organization of educators, the expected social scientists, engaged in no great research projects, either as an organization or its members as individuals. On the contrary, he would find the professional organization [i.e., the AICPA] heavily committed to an extensive research program encompassing not only the solution of the every day problems of practice but the development of a theoretical structure for all of accountancy and a proposed study of the scope of a common body of accounting knowledge. It already has a substantial record of practical research eagerly accepted by the teachers as educational material for their students. Instead of two arms, research and practice, cooperating but independent, and making relatively equal contributions, we find one far outweighing the other, dominating it to an unfortunate degree. To anyone seeking to establish accounting as a social science, this comes as an unpleasant fact and one warranting attention.

...Except for such outstanding early efforts as the Paton and Littleton monograph, relatively little sustained research has been done by educators in many years; here again the practitioners have dominated. And this is not due to particularly aggressive action on their part; they have won the field by default. As a matter of fact, their entry into the field of pure theory is a rather severe indictment of our own lack of progress. If we had been more productive as social scientists, there would have been less need for such an entry on their part. If any group must sustain the burden of criticism for failure to develop accounting theory, it must be the academicians....

It is not enough, of course, to cry that we have insufficient research and piously hope that this will bring more. We must find why there has been so little and seek remedies for whatever the fault may be. Here one man's conjectures are probably as good as another's. Mine follow along this line. To the question: "What are the best minds in accounting education doing instead of research?" I would be forced to answer: Young or old, most of them are either writing textbooks or engaged in part-time practice.[35]

The key to the promised land for accounting academicians was embodied in one word: research. This was research which did not involve such things as writing textbooks or engaging in practical efforts. Research--that was the banner under which academic accountants would march to independence and glory.

Mautz would come to rue the implications of his own words, but once the beast was awakened it could not be controlled by its maker. Some researchers tried, as Mautz wanted, to change accounting from "an art, a way of doing, with rules, procedures, and conventions" to "an organized body of knowledge with basic assumptions, concepts, definitions, and techniques, each one closely related to the others." Most researchers, however, saw that the call of status and increased independence came from another direction. Research which involved statistics and computers, and not research involving philosophy and logic, was the doorway into the kingdom of academic heaven.

In the Spring of 1963 a new academic accounting journal appeared. The well-named *Journal of Accounting Research* was jointly published by the Institute of Professional Accounting at the University of Chicago and the London School of Economics and Political Science at the University of London. Quantitatively oriented, it quickly achieved a high level of prestige among accounting academicians. This fact was not lost on the editors of the *Accounting Review*, the journal of the AAA.

The AAA's Committee on Educational Standards reconsidered the report of the AAA's Standards Rating Committee of 1954, and issued its report in 1963. It said that "Career accounting teachers should have doctoral degrees" and that research should be part of the requirements for promotion. The AAA's 1964 Committee on Doctoral Programs stressed the need for doctoral programs to prepare for a research career. By 1967-68 31 percent of accounting faculty had doctorates (still well below the average of 47 percent for all disciplines); by 1972-73 this figure had risen to 41 percent.[36]

Confusion

Since the quantitative techniques enjoying favor were management tools (in Bach's terminology), academic accountants who used those techniques claimed to be doing research in management accounting. It soon appeared as though management accounting was trying to take over the entire field of management. Accounting, management accounting researchers argued, is the area of providing information for use in management decisions. That included not only financial information, but *any* quantitative information (thereby swallowing up all mathematics, measurement, and statistics). And, since the field of accounting had always embraced a system of processing information, computer systems too were swallowed up by management accounting. The person who gathers information (the accountant) should help the person who is using it to learn how to use it properly, and therefore the whole area of decision science, human behavior, and even management itself belonged to management accounting. Management accounting, never had clear boundaries, but now it seemed to have no limits. It threatened to swallow the business school curriculum whole.

Bedford's and the AICPA's dream of an eternally expanding field of accounting was taking hold in the academic sphere as well as in public practice.

In 1965 Mautz, then president of the AAA, called attention to the pressing need for boundaries to accounting.

Accounting, as a field of professional practice and an organized discipline, needs to establish its limits. Whether one discusses accounting theory or accounting practice, there must be some limits to the topic; and unless these limits are clearly established, a degree of confusion is bound to result.

For example, there are those who talk in terms of accounting as the "measurement and communication of economic data." The question necessarily follows: Which data? ...Professor R.J. Chambers has suggested that our present definitions of accounting and our approach to accounting research has been unduly restrictive because of our preoccupation with the problems of accounting practice. He suggests: "The field shall not be limited to the ostensible products of the practice of accounting; it shall be considered as coextensive with all human action in its economic aspects." This is a stimulating suggestion and a rather large order, as well.[37]

In addition to Mautz's understated awe at the all-encompassing view of accounting, he also wondered whether the practice of management consulting by public accountants might be adding even more confusion. "How far can the profession extend its activities in the management services area before it loses its identity?"

Is the non-CPA employee or associate who is not engaged in accounting or auditing work a member of the profession of public accounting merely because he is employed by a public accounting firm? Is it possible that CPAs whose interests run to industrial engineering assignments or to marketing problems have departed from the ranks of public accounting and entered another profession? Does this mean that a public accounting firm may be actively engaged in more than one profession at a time? Or perhaps that it is engaged in a business as well as a profession? These are unpleasant questions, perhaps, but they require answers.[38]

It was no longer clear exactly what accounting was. Mautz summed up the confusion accountants faced:

> The business environment in which accounting exists is changing rapidly and even dramatically. Scientific management with its emphasis on operations research and the application of various quantitative methods in decision-making, the expansion of organization theory, a new interest in economic analysis, and innovations in methods of accumulating and processing business data all have significant implications for accounting. ...
>
> To some, these new developments appear to constitute a serious threat; these people see accounting as becoming obsolete. They are concerned lest certain combinations of data processing, quantitative methods, and perhaps operations research may ease accounting out of its role of supplying decision data. At the same time, the unpleasant thought that the accuracy and reliability of electronic data processing systems might make auditing unnecessary further shakes their confidence in the future of accounting.[39]

As a result of this shaken confidence, both professional and academic accountants were straddlers, standing with one foot in accounting and the other in management. They became increasingly confused. Many academic accountants were so preoccupied with keeping up with and doing research in every area of management that they lost interest in accounting education. The *Accounting Review* increasingly shoved its fewer accounting education articles to the rear of the journal (along with the book reviews), while the front part filled with more and more quantitative articles on "management accounting."

What Is Accounting and What Education Does It Need?

Much of the responsibility for improving accounting education was ironically left in the hands of the practitioners. The AICPA's committee on long-range planning took an interest in developing an understanding of the common body of knowledge required by accountants.[40] The growing confusion over what accounting was and what courses a student needed to qualify to sit for the CPA exam made the effort imperative, but it had been an important issue for some time. Back in 1956 the Perry Commission had pointed out that one of the characteristics of a profession was that it had a body of specialized knowledge, but it noted that no such body had been described for the accounting profession--nor did it go on to describe one.

In October of 1961 the governing council of the AICPA approved $50,000, contingent upon the receipt of a matching sum from a foundation, for a study to define the common body of knowledge for CPAs. One year later the Carnegie Corporation, after being approached by the Institute and reading the prospectus, granted the matching sum. The Carnegie Corporation wanted someone outside the field of accounting to do the work and wanted the results to be published without censorship by the Institute.

According to the prospectus, the study had three objectives:

> *First*, it will determine the knowledge which the CPA must have at the outset in order to provide the public with service of the minimum scope and quality which the public needs and has a right to expect from him at the start of his career. ...*Second*, it will define the knowledge and intellectual habits which the beginning CPA must have to be able to keep pace with the growth of general knowledge of the profession in the next generation and to work into one of the present or future specialties of the profession. ...*Third*, it will investigate the capabilities of the several types of educational institutions and processes--colleges and universities, in-training education and experience, and continuing adult education--for imparting the various kinds of required knowledge.[41]

In 1963 the Institute appointed a twelve-man Commission on the Common Body of Knowledge for CPAs to supervise the study. It was chaired by Elmer G. Beamer. Robert H. Roy, dean of the School of Engineering Science of Johns Hopkins University, was selected to be the study director, and James H. MacNeill, chairman of the department of accounting at Fordham University, was selected as associate director. Roy and MacNeill began their work on July 1, 1963.

The pair made their focus clear in their first report. They noted the role of public accountants in management consulting, and they noted in the schools the new mathematical and computer trends and "a transition to something called management accounting."[42] The two seemed to have no criticism of these directions.

After three years of work, Roy and MacNeill's common body of knowledge (CBOK) report was published in 1967. It was entitled *Horizons for a Profession: The Common Body of Knowledge for Certified Public Accountants*. The third of the objectives given in the prospectus--the objective of investigating the capabilities of the several types of educational institutions and processes--was largely ignored, except for a brief statement that continuing education should be used to upgrade CPAs' computer skills. A member of the overseeing Commission nicely summed up the approach of Roy and MacNeill:

> Some questions are interesting because they have quick answers--others because they do not. Some important problems of our contemporary world are of the first kind. They yield to solution after a few years of concentrated research effort. The problems of education seem to fall in the second class. ...
>
> The CBOK Study report concerns many as research --a badly misused word, borrowed by all of us who want to be sprinkled with the fallout of glamour associated with the natural sciences. ...This Study is by its very nature an evaluation, not a research project. It is based on some empirical description, and some deductive reasoning, but there is little explanatory theory.
>
> For example, to determine what CPA firms now do, questionnaires were sent to a large sample of public accounting firms. The data suffer a bit from the fact that it was not possible to give operational definitions to all the elements of work-description. But the result is a generalized description of practice and trends in practice.

A sample of educational programs in collegiate schools of business--past and present--was examined, and this afforded a rough description of changes in the pattern of business education. Decks of subject cards were mailed to a large select group of knowledgeable persons asking them to rank subject matter in order of importance. In my view this experiment, though interesting, was largely fruitless. The subject matter described in the cards lacked operational definition, and the term importance could not be operationally defined for the persons who participated in the card deck experiment. Within these limitations the effort afforded some evidence of current opinion as to the value of knowledge on particular topics. A great deal of thoughtful discussion with members of the profession was carried on by the Study directors. Many of the conclusions of the Study are distillations of these experiences in picking the minds of leaders in the profession. But none of this can really pretend to be an application of the scientific method.

The point is that anyone who expects provable conclusions from a study of this type is doomed to disappointment.[43]

Disappointment was forthcoming. As a distillation of currently accepted wisdom, the book was little more than an extended discussion listing all the things which it would be wonderful if accountants knew. The book recommended that a new CPA know accounting (concepts first, but also applications and methods and techniques--including the computer), the functional fields of business (finance, production, marketing, personnel relations and business management), the humanities (logic, ethics, and written and spoken English), economics (micro- and macro-), behavioral science (psychology and sociology), law, and mathematics, statistics, and probability. But the book never dealt with the hard choices that had to be made, the serious prioritizing of things, the allocation of scarce resources (i.e., time). In only one area was it at all controversial.

Dean Roy sees in the new ways of applying mathematical and statistical concepts to business decisions a

strong suggestion that a greater mathematical competence
is a must for the professional accountant. He is more
confident that this recommendation will be borne out by
the experience of the next 20 years than of any other
single recommendation in the report. On the other hand,
there was perhaps the least consensus among the
Commission members on this recommendation and its
emphasis in the report.[44]

Nor was the controversy over Roy's infatuation with mathematics
limited to his commissioners. Roy admitted (when he spoke about the
collection of opinion by means of the card deck experiment) that he
was going against prevailing opinion.

[I]n the main, the consensus of the card deck experiment
are [sic] consonant with the proposals of this report. We
have derived emphasis and support for the recommendations on communication skills from the first-place rank
given by so many to the subject card "Written and Oral
English." Conversely, we have gone contrary to consensus on subjects related to mathematics.[45]

Roy seems to have made a common mistake (such as occurred when
the Foundation Reports grouped accounting with mathematics and
statistics) by assuming that, since accountants work with numbers,
accounting is essentially a mathematical science. In fact, accounting is
essentially a communication art, in which definition is the greatest
challenge, and measurement (usually at a fairly non-complex level)
follows that definition.[46] Accounting rarely requires high levels of
mathematical skill, and it is not, therefore, obvious that a beginning
accountant needs sophisticated mathematical skills.

A Recommended Curriculum

Two moves were made to follow up on the CBOK Report. In
September of 1966 an *ad hoc* Committee on Education and
Experience Requirements was appointed by the AICPA to study its
policies on standards for admission to the profession. The Committee

was chaired by Elmer Beamer, who had also headed the Commission. MacNeill was also on the Beamer Committee. In addition, the AICPA, together with business schools throughout the country, sponsored a series of fifty-five seminars in 1967 and 1968. Representatives of 668 universities and colleges participated.[47]

In the seminars, it became obvious that there were two areas in which the CBOK study was not finding support. As MacNeill said, "If there is any part of *Horizons* that got people riled up it was our recommendations about mathematics, statistics, and probability."[48] Accounting academicians were simply not convinced that such large helpings of mathematics were needed. The second thing which bothered academicians was the generality of the Report.

> [A]cademicians were quite critical of the *Horizons* study because it did not give them more curriculum guidance, and they seemed to be unable to agree as to exactly how the common body of knowledge should be incorporated into the accounting curricula. An American Accounting Association committee to relate the recommendations of *Horizons for a Profession* to the accounting curriculum did not issue a report after two years of deliberation.[49]

The *Accounting Review* virtually ignored the CBOK Report. This effort by the AICPA to focus the attention of academic accountants upon the needs of public accounting was not nearly as successful as the Perry Report a decade earlier had been. It was obvious that the AICPA needed to take further steps if the study was to have the impact the Institute wanted.

At the end of 1968 the Beamer Committee suggested a model program, with course recommendations in terms of hours and generic terms, but stressing that "the course designation and hours are prepared only for possible curriculum guidance and *not* for legislative prescription." The Report also made the point that "our analysis of the recommendations [of the CBOK Report] leads us to conclude that the mastery of the body of knowledge which is commensurate with our public responsibility will require not less than five years of collegiate study."[50]

In the five-year program as recommended by the Beamer Committee, however, there would be no increase in liberal arts; they would remain at a total of 60 semester hours (equal to 50% of a four-year program). Not all of this 60 hours would be dedicated to what traditionalists would consider liberal arts, however. The Report recommended that 3 to 6 hours of elementary accounting be included in the liberal subject area (in keeping with MacNeill's belief that it belonged there). As the amount of liberal arts subjects did not increase under the Beamer approach, neither did the amount of accounting. Accounting would still amount to 30 hours (equal to 25% of a four-year program)--or 33-36 hours if one included elementary accounting. All of the recommended increase was to be in the general business area. It would increase from 30 to 54 hours (there were six hours of electives to complete the 150 hours).

The Beamer Committee recommendations were right in line with what Roy and MacNeill wanted. In the area of general education, the subject allocated the most time (12 hours) was "Mathematics (modern algebra, calculus, statistics and probability)" with "Communication" allocated 6-9 hours. Behavioral sciences and economics were each allocated 6 hours, but ethics and logic were not specified. In the area of general business, two subjects were allocated the most time: 9 hours to "Organization, group and individual behavior" and 9 more hours to "Quantitative applications in business (optimization models, statistics, sampling, Markov chains, statistical decision theory, queueing, PERT, simulation)." The areas which received 6 hours each were "Economics (intermediate theory and the monetary system)," "The social environment of business," "Business law," and "Finance." The functional areas of production and marketing, and business policy and "Written communication" received only 3 hours each. There were no surprises in the area of accounting. It was a business school dean's dream, with large dollops of all the latest fads.

A Controversial Trade-Off

At the time of these events, another set of related events was taking place. The CBOK Report had presented a story about the evolution of a profession--the same one invented by Kester in the 1930s--narrating that a true profession begins with apprenticeship and then outgrows it as it relies increasingly on higher (and higher and higher) education and finds little or no need for experience. Some

Neanderthals might struggle against the elimination of the experience requirement, but their efforts were doomed to failure. Roy and MacNeill psychoanalyzed these pathetic adversaries of progress:

> Actions taken to diminish the experience component of professional training always raise a hue and cry. Teachers of experience usually are senior faculty, who quite naturally resist discounts from the value of their instruction and the threat of intellectual obsolescence as well. By the same token, each profession epitomized by its leaders, elder statesmen, practitioners and professional societies, is more likely to esteem experience than new knowledge not possessed, not understood and not foreseen by the elders to be applicable. And, more subtly, to change the program *they* had seems to derogate its quality.
>
> Restraints such as these impede but never halt the evolution of each learned profession.[51]

The CBOK Report predicted such inevitable change in accounting for several reasons: the development of new methods of mathematics, statistics, and probability; the advent of the computer; the probability "that instruction in accounting itself increasingly will be augmented by representations of accounting procedures in the symbolic notation of mathematics"; and the fact that teaching would be at inductive and deductive levels (what was it before?). The Report neglected to clarify exactly how symbolic notation would do away with the need for experience.

In April of 1968 the AICPA's leadership, in the form of its planning committee, issued a report which dealt with the body of specialized knowledge CPAs should have and with the educational process for acquiring that knowledge. The committee had sent an earlier version of the report to about 700 interested people, and in that earlier version it proposed that the experience requirement for becoming a CPA be eliminated. That proposal was too controversial so it was eliminated from its final report.[52] The planning committee did, however, endorse a five-year program and encouraged practitioners to bring their influence to bear upon educators.

Not only were practitioners opposed to eliminating the experience requirement, so were the academicians. This was obvious in the seminars held to sell the CBOK to the academicians.

> The fact that the Common Body of Knowledge Study concentrates almost exclusively upon the formal educational process, however, continuously plagued the discussions. These difficulties stemmed in part from the fact that the Study fails to consider the nature and importance of practical experience and its relevance to the set of qualifications.[53]

When its first attacks failed, the AICPA sent the Beamer Committee in for another attack. The Beamer Committee article which emerged focused on the *choice* between higher education and experience.

> [A]ll participants [in the seminars which followed the CBOK Report] seemed to agree that the common body of knowledge could best be obtained from collegiate study. This question may then be asked: *If collegiate study can best provide the common body of knowledge needed by CPAs at the outset of their careers, is there a need for experience requirements?*[54]

Following this portrayal of the issue, all of the old arguments against requiring experience were trotted out. Against the argument that experience develops a sense of professionalism (as in appreciating the real-life issues in ethics and as in knowing one's own limits of competence) the counterargument was advanced that a person is ethical or unethical regardless of experience and that a new professional rarely overestimates his competence:

> The opposite is true--he is rarely stretched to the full extent of his abilities. The responsibilities of the young accountant employed by an accounting firm are limited by his superiors, whether he is certified or not. On the other hand, the young CPA starting his own practice, which he will rarely do without having served voluntarily on the staff of a CPA firm, will have a

> potpourri of small clients with simple problems to solve.
> Only through his own professional growth and
> reputation will the independent CPA practitioner attract
> more substantial clients with complex problems.[55]

So the argument was once again that no one is really going to go into
practice by themselves without experience, and anyway, if they do,
they will only be dealing with small businesses--and who cares about
them?[56]

The Beamer Committee's article clearly summarized the reasons
for requiring experience. Then it summarized the position against
requiring experience, and chose that position. It did no analysis of the
weaknesses of either position; it simply expressed a preference.
Against the argument that professional judgment can better be
developed through experience, for example, the article simply said,

> The fundamentals of professional judgement, materiality,
> and professional risk can be taught in the classroom. An
> awareness that professional accounting is an art and not a
> science is probably better developed through classroom
> instruction.[57]

Now it may or may not be true that professional judgment can
"probably" be better developed in the classroom, but the Committee
gave no proof of that, nor did it present any proof of the falsity of the
position that professional judgment is better learned by experience. It
simply chose, without apparent justification, to support one set of
arguments and reject the other.

Without explanation, the Committee chose to say, "There is
limited educational value to a relatively brief period of experiences."
Everything is of limited value, but the real question is how limited?
Contradicting itself, the Committee confessed that it could not tell:
"The value of experience cannot be measured in terms of time." If we
cannot measure value in terms of time, what does it mean that a brief
period of experiences has limited value? Throwing up their hands, the
Committee finally argued that nobody else can measure the value of a
period of experience either: "The success of efforts of the state boards
of accountancy to control the quality of experience is questionable."[58]

If the concern of the Committee were really with the issue of the value of experience, it could have focused on two possibilities. If experience has a unique value, assuming that it is gained under the right conditions, then efforts should be made to make certain that the right conditions prevail; perhaps some form of regulation should be required. If, on the other hand, experience has no unique value, then any requirement for experience should be dropped. Tellingly, the Committee did not choose either of these options. They framed the issue differently:

> In summary, the issue is this: Which does more today to inculcate a sense of professionalism--professional education, or experience acquired as a junior accountant to fill an experience requirement?[59]

An either/or approach is here assumed, rather than a both/and approach. We should have either an experience requirement or an additional education requirement, and, according to this approach, we should not have both (for the sake of efficiency?). The assumption is that both do the same thing, and thus the question is about which one does it better. But the assumption was never proven, and it is the point of contention. This trade-off approach lies behind all the Committee's arguments:

> Either the period of qualifying experience should be made meaningful, or the experience requirement recognized as ineffectual and replaced with a requirement yielding more significant benefits, which could be a fifth year of college.[60]

If the experience requirement is ineffectual, then nothing is required to replace it. If it contributes nothing, then simply eliminating the requirement "replaces" that contribution. But that is not what the Committee was after, as was obvious when it drove its point home in its conclusion:

> The current admission requirements of the profession now generally require at least five years--except in the "no experience" states--to fulfill. Since the trend is for

the experience requirement to be further reduced or watered down, the time is at hand for the profession to consider the advisability of replacing experience requirements with a requirement for a fifth year of college study. While some benefits, such as enhancement of professionalism and technical competence, may be obtained from the first year or two of good qualifying experience, a fifth year of college study offers greater benefits to the beginning certified public accountant and to the profession of public accounting as a whole.[61]

In summary, the Committee's argument appeared to be: we have five years anyway, so let's spend it on college instead of experience. The fact that the student would be spending money in that fifth year rather than making money was never mentioned. The whole point was obviously to persuade people to make a trade--asking people to let the accountants require a fifth year of college, and offering in exchange to give up the requirement of a year of experience.

In May 1969 the Beamer Committee's recommendations were adopted by AICPA Council as its official policy, replacing those passed in 1959. The CBOK Report was ratified, as was the notion that "college study should be in programs comparable to those" model programs created by the Beamer Committee. The proposals, however, were careful to note that "the accreditation of academic programs is the responsibility of the academic community," and "Educational programs must be flexible and adaptive and this is best achieved by entrusting their specific content to the academic community." The trade-off between the fifth year of college and the experience requirement was also adopted, with the wish that "The states should adopt this five-year requirement by 1975."[62]

At the beginning of the decade there had been no question that public accountants required both an adequate education and adequate experience before they could be trusted to practice public accounting on their own. Indeed, early in the decade, there had been a movement to shift more of the burden onto experience and out of formal education. In line with the Foundation Reports, formal education would handle the more conceptual items and practitioners would train people in techniques through various types of continuing education after they came to work. Yet, at the end of the decade, the AICPA leadership (in spite of widespread opposition among practitioners and academicians) was saying that the limited conceptual approach of college was enough to allow a person to practice on his own, so long as the total amount of time spent in college was five years. It is very hard not to conclude from this sequence of events that the leadership of the AICPA was willing to do whatever it would take to gain the additional prestige which would come from requiring five years of college education.

The Academicians Respond

The AICPA's hope of getting the states to accept the five-year accounting education requirement by 1975 was a pipe dream, apparently encouraged by the great success the profession had enjoyed during the 1960s in getting the states to require the four-year college education requirement.

> As of January 1, 1968, 27 of the 54 jurisdictions had enacted laws requiring that candidates for the CPA certificate possess a college degree (or its equivalent), 8 jurisdictions required two years of college or its equivalent, while 19 jurisdictions did not require any college education. Nevertheless, the Uniform Statistical Survey of CPA candidates for the November 1966 examinations reveals that 88% of the candidates sitting were college graduates, 5% had from two to four years of college and another 2% had attended college for less than two years.[63]

The leaders of the profession tried a hard sell on the academicians to accept the Beamer plan.[64] A series of 53 symposia, attended by faculty from 850 educational institutions, was sponsored in the fall and winter of 1970-1971 by one of the large public accounting firms. To short-circuit criticism of the plan, the symposia were directed towards a discussion of the implementation rather than an evaluation of the Beamer Report. The academicians, however, were resistant to this effort to overpower them and side-step the issues.

The symposium reports did not show an overwhelming enthusiasm for the CEER [Beamer] report recommendation that five years of college study are needed to obtain the common body of knowledge delineated by *Horizons for a Profession*. Forty reports noted some discussion of the five-year requirement, as many indicating approval of this recommendation as expressing reluctance to accept the need for it. Many reports expressing reluctance to accept the need for a five-year program nevertheless indicated that such a program might be desirable. The reasons for the reluctance of some discussants to accept the need for five years' study were the following:

* Evidence exists that additional education is not necessary for success in public accounting.
* The hiring practices of public accounting firms and business and governmental organizations do not place a very high premium on the fifth year of study.
* New teaching techniques and more efficient structuring of curriculums could streamline current four-year accounting programs, thus providing for the addition of materials formerly excluded.
* Perhaps some of the courses suggested in the five-year program could be more effectively presented as part of a firm's on-the-job training and/or continuing education courses.
* The five-year program suggested in the CEER report did not appear to differ significantly from what is being taught now in some four-year programs.
* The five-year program could present a significant financial burden to some students.
* In a period during which academic institutions already face serious financial problems, the five-year program could have the effect of intensifying their difficulties.
* Most four-year accounting majors have done well on the CPA examination.[65]

The fact that the AICPA had made the Beamer Report an official policy and that state societies of CPAs were already at work trying to change state accountancy laws stimulated the AAA to action as well. The AAA committee to study the Beamer Report surveyed accounting academicians, and reported on its findings and its own deliberations.

It began by pointing out that the AICPA's attempt to eliminate the experience requirement would only deepen the confusion about what public accounting (and education for public accounting) really was:

> The Beamer Committee discussions...make it clear that students leaving the university to go directly into industry, government or teaching would be encouraged to pass the CPA exam and receive the certificate. Thus, the separation of the CPA certificate from public practice would be complete.
>
> This raises two somewhat disturbing prospects. The Beamer Committee proposals, if enacted into law, would shift emphasis away from public practice to a very large degree and encourage the public to view the CPA certificate more as an academic badge of achievement of a certain level of proficiency in the common body of knowledge. At the same time, the Beamer Committee elected not to recommend that the CPA certificate and a license to practice be separated. Thus, the certificate would still constitute the license to practice, although it could be obtained with no particular commitment toward, nor experience in, the independent public practice area of accountancy.
>
> A second concern is with the ultimate effect that this might have upon the delineation of the common body of knowledge. ...If substantial numbers of accountants in industry, government, and education achieve the status of certified public accountant with no background in, commitment to, nor perhaps even interest in, the public practice area, then it seems inevitable that the common body will eventually evolve to be that body of knowledge common to the corporate controller, the

professor, the data processor, as well as the independent public accountant. ...

We believe that the designation "certified public accountant" should continue to be associated with the public practice facet of our profession in its continually expanding scope and that "CPA" should not be broadened to the all-inclusive concept to encompass accountants entering directly into industry, government, or education.[66]

The academic accountants did not want the CPA certificate to be something like an academic degree.[67] Moreover, they were not willing to take the whole responsibility in preparing a person to be a competent practicing public accountant.

The Beamer Committee recommendation that all experience requirements be eliminated for those candidates who have obtained the common body of knowledge is perhaps the most controversial of all their recommendations. Only fifty of the [accounting] department chairmen [that the Committee surveyed] indicated agreement with this recommendation, while seventy-six preferred one or more years of experience in addition to the common body of knowledge. Hundreds of interviews with practitioners indicate a similar widespread reluctance to eliminate all experience requirements. ...

It may be that the differences in points of view of the Beamer Committee and our AAA committee quite naturally led the two groups to different conclusions. The Beamer Committee was dominated by practitioners that were keenly aware of the profession's inability to develop and police meaningful experience requirements. Our committee, on the other hand, was dominated by educators who were acutely aware of the limitations of a classroom education and somewhat reluctant to have the academic community assume the entire responsibility for CPA preparation.[68]

The committee then addressed the five-year education requirement:

Trends in the discussions in the Haskins & Sells Symposia revealed the following concerns regarding the proposed five-year educational requirement:

1) The proposed programs were oriented to CPA examination preparation and the academic community should be "career preparing" not "examination preparing."

2) If the accounting curriculum becomes a five-year program, the decline in enrollments may be significant.

3) If the accounting major needs more formal education, he needs it in the communicative skills.

4) The four- and five-year "model programs" [outlined by the Beamer Committee] do not differ significantly. An educational institution might offer a program similar to the five-year program in four years.

5) The individual with superior ability might attain the required educational level in less than five years.

6) In order to go to a five-year program, the employers of accounting majors would need to require five years of college study. Many employers now discourage students from continuing their education for a fifth year before starting to work.

While the committee supports the general proposition that educational requirements should be increased for CPAs, we reject the notion that a prescribed time period is necessary to obtain the common body of knowledge. Why five years? Why not four years, or six or seven years? It would seem that time should not be the major constraint in measuring whether or not one has obtained the common body of knowledge.[69]

The academicians rejected the AICPA's deal. They did not want to give up the experience requirement, and they saw no educational need for a fifth year. Except with accounting department chairmen (among whom a majority believed that five years were needed to acquire the common body of knowledge), the notion of increasing educational requirements did not make sense to academicians.

It must have been frustrating to AICPA leaders to see that the academicians were missing their point. The academicians were focusing on the quality of education, but that was not the issue. To achieve status it is not the quality of the education but the time period that matters. A high-status person (and profession) is *more* educated than others. If most people are getting a four-year college education, then a person driven by a desire for prestige must get at least a five-year college education.

Notes

[1] "Report of the Committee on Management Accounting," *The Accounting Review*, April 1959, p. 207.

[2] Ibid, p. 210.

[3] Virgil Boyd and Dale Taylor, "The Magic Words--"Managerial Accounting," *The Accounting Review*, January 1961, pp. 110-111.

[4] E. Kennedy Cobb, "Current Status of Managerial Accounting As a Course of Study," *The Accounting Review*, January 1960, pp. 126-127.

[5] Paul E. Fertig, "Organization of An Accounting Program," *The Accounting Review*, April 1960, p. 192.

[6] "Report of the Committee on the Study of the Ford and Carnegie Foundation Reports," *The Accounting Review*, April 1961, p. 191.

[7] Ibid., pp. 192-193, 194, 195.

[8] Ibid., p. 195.

[9] William W. Werntz, "Accounting Education and the Ford and Carnegie Reports," *The Accounting Review*, April 1961, p. 187.

[10] Ibid., p. 186.

[11] James S. Lanham, "Problems of Professional Education in Accounting," *The Journal of Accountancy*, March 1960, pp. 72, 73.

12 William J. Vatter, "Education For Accountancy," *The Journal of Accountancy*, January 1964, p. 91.

13 Lawrence M. Walsh, "Accounting Education in Review," *The Accounting Review*, April 1960, p. 185.

14 Norton M. Bedford, "Education for Accounting as a Learned Profession," *The Journal of Accountancy*, December 1961, p. 38.

15 John L. Carey, "Higher Accreditation for CPAs," *The Journal of Accountancy*, March 1961, pp. 47, 48.

16 Ibid., p. 49.

17 Hershel M. Anderson and Fred B. Griffin, "The Accounting Curriculum and Postgraduate Achievement," *The Accounting Review*, October 1963, p. 818.

18 Walsh, p. 184.

19 Middle Atlantic Association of Colleges of Business Administration, "Statement of Policy Relative to a Fifth Year in the Accounting Curriculum," *The Accounting Review*, October 1961, p. 636.

20 Robert K. Mautz, "The Fifth Year--But Later," *The Journal of Accountancy*, February 1964, p. 89.

21 Ibid., p. 90.

22 Ibid.

23 Ibid., p. 91.

24 Ibid., p. 92.

25 Wilton T. Anderson, "Carnegie and Ford Reports on Education for CPAs," *The Journal of Accountancy*, February 1961, p. 89. See also C. Aubrey Smith, "An Experiment With a Five-year Professional Accounting Program," *The Journal of Accountancy*, May 1961, p. 87.

26 Philip E. Fess, "A New Breed of Public Accountant," *The Journal of Accountancy*, February 1963, p. 89.

27 Editorial, "Accountancy Education and Legislation," *The Journal of Accountancy*, March 1963, p. 33.

28 Glenn A. Welsch, "Is Accountancy an Academic Discipline?" *The Journal of Accountancy*, May 1966, 81-82.

29 G. Leland Bach, "Accounting Education for the 1980's," *The Journal of Accountancy*, September 1961, p. 51.

30 Ibid., p. 52.

31 Bedford, p. 36.

32 Ibid., p. 34.

33 R.K. Mautz, "Accounting as a Social Science," *The Accounting Review*, April 1963, p. 317.

34 Ibid., p. 319.

35 Ibid., pp. 320, 321.

36 Doyle Z. Williams, *Accounting Education: A Statistical Survey, 1972-73* (New York: American Institute of Certified Public Accountants, 1974), p. 17.

37 R.K. Mautz, "Challenges to the Accounting Profession," *The Accounting Review*, April 1965, pp. 305-306.

38 Ibid., pp. 306-307.

39 Ibid., pp. 309-310.

40 The people on the AICPA's long-range planning committee played an important role in the development of accounting education, even decades later, as well as in the development of the profession as a whole. A summary of the views of the 1956-1962 Committee on Long-Range Objectives is found in John L. Carey, ed., *The Accounting Profession: Where Is It Headed?* (New York: American Institute of CPAs, 1962). Additional insight into the Committee's views can be found in John L. Carey, *The CPA Plans for the Future* (New York: American Institute of CPAs, 1965).

41 Robert H. Roy and James H. MacNeill, *Horizons for a Profession: The Common Body of Knowledge for Certified Public Accountants* (New York: American Institute of Certified Public Accountants, 1967), p. 25.

42 Robert H. Roy and James H. MacNeill, "Study of the Common Body of Knowledge for CPAs: A Report of Plans and Progress," *The Journal of Accountancy*, December 1963, pp. 57, 58.

43 Charles E. Johnson, "The Many-Body Problem," *The Journal of Accountancy*, June 1967, pp. 76, 77.

44 Ibid., p. 79.

45 Roy and MacNeill, *Horizons*, p. 11.

46 The authors of *Horizons* sometimes seem to have some understanding of the nature of accounting, as when they make the following statement on p. 56: "Accounting is a man-made art and accounting research must be in the realm of ideas, not in the realm of nature, as in medicine and engineering. Thus the 'truth' in inventory valuation has never been discovered, nor will any 'solution' be found through research and discovery; there is no 'unknown' to be sought, nor any likelihood that the brain of some budding genius will

suddenly provide the long-awaited key to unlock the mystery. Accounting research must be philosophical or methodological, must revolve around such questions as fairness, utility, relevance, equity, questions to which there are no 'right' answers." In the light of these insights, it is hard to explain (except that their obsession with mathematics simply overpowered them again) the statement which occurs within a few pages (p. 61), that "some sort of 'marriage' between accounting and mathematics seems inevitable." Is it really helpful for mathematics and philosophy to be combined?

[47] A kind of official summary of these seminars appeared in an article by Doyle Z. Williams, "Reactions to 'Horizons for a Profession,'" *The Journal of Accountancy*, June 1969, pp. 81-84.

[48] James H. MacNeill, "A Readback on 'Horizons for a Profession,'" *The Journal of Accountancy*, April 1970, pp. 67-68.

[49] "Report of the Committee to Examine the 1969 Report of the AICPA Committee on Education & Experience Requirements for CPAs," *The Accounting Review*, Supplement 1972, p. 239.

[50] Committee on Education and Experience Requirements for CPAs, "Academic Preparation for Professional Accounting Careers," *The Journal of Accountancy*, December 1968, p. 57.

[51] Roy and MacNeill, *Horizons*, p. 4.

[52] Editorial, "On CPA Education and Experience," *The Journal of Accountancy*, April 1968, p. 25.

[53] Donald L. Madden and Lawrence C. Phillips, "An Evaluation of the Common Body of Knowledge Study and its Probable Impact Upon the Accounting Profession," *The Journal of Accountancy*, February 1968, pp. 87-88.

[54] William C. Bruschi, "Issues Surrounding Qualifying Experience Requirements," *The Journal of Accountancy*, March 1969, p. 47.

[55] Ibid., p. 50.

[56] This astoundingly flippant attitude is actually the attitude of the author of the article. He argued that the accounting profession should "step across the same threshold that the legal profession did in the 1930's when full reliance was placed upon formal education while clerkship requirements were generally abandoned." Then in a footnote he said: "Comparisons with medical internships are inappropriate. The neophyte lawyer or CPA starts his independent practice with small clients and grows with them. As these professionals develop in

competence, larger clients come to them. The doctor cannot begin his practice with the small child, not less important than an adult, nor with minor injuries and slight illnesses. His patients come to him with what they think are minor matters which he might have to diagnose as symptoms of serious illnesses." The clear implication is that small businesses, unlike small children, are unimportant--apparently because they might only involve the life savings and self-worth of just one family.

[57] Bruschi, p. 51.

[58] Ibid.

[59] Ibid., p. 50.

[60] Ibid., p. 53.

[61] Ibid., p. 54.

[62] *Report of the Committee on Education and Experience Requirements for CPAs* (New York: American Institute of Certified Public Accountants, March 1969), pp. 6-7.

[63] Planning Committee of the AICPA, "Education of Certified Public Accountants," *The Journal of Accountancy*, April 1968, pp. 48-49.

[64] Whether there was any organized resistance to the five-year requirement by smaller CPA firms, or whether the AICPA leadership would have cared if there were, is unclear. The "Big Eight" public accounting firms between 1966 and 1969 had 28 percent of their new hires possessing graduate degrees and they had the ability to pay for and train such graduates, while all the other public accounting firms relied upon people with undergraduate degrees for 97 percent of their new hires, according to William H. Gruber and Louis L. Logan, "The Education of Professional Accountants," *The Journal of Accountancy*, May 1971, p. 86.

[65] W. Thomas Porter, Jr., *Higher Education and the Accounting Profession: A Summary Report on the Haskins & Sells 75th Anniversary Symposiums* (a pamphlet, 1971), pp. 11-12.

[66] "Report of the Committee to Examine the 1969 Report of the AICPA Committee on Education & Experience Requirements for CPAs," *The Accounting Review*, Supplement 1972, pp. 242-243.

[67] This is an interesting contrast with the position taken by an AAA committee in the early 1950s.

[68] "Report of the Committee to Examine the 1969 Report of the AICPA Committee on Education & Experience Requirements for CPAs," pp. 243, 244.

[69] Ibid., p. 246.

Chapter 4

The Professional School Movement

Although the AICPA's undisguised bid for increased prestige may not have been defensible, it was understandable in view of the times. The accounting profession has always been beset by an inferiority complex, and the 1960s certainly aggravated the problem. On campus, not only was business education as a whole denigrated, but accounting was singled out for further disrespect. Furthermore, accounting education has always been strongest at the undergraduate level, and the whole of undergraduate business education lost considerable prestige (and resources) as the popularity of the Master of Business Administration (MBA) programs zoomed. As a result of the Foundation Reports, undergraduate accounting especially had contracted in terms of prestige and resources.

By the end of 1971 the situation was intolerable for some accountants. The proposal that accountants secede from business schools and establish their own separate professional schools of accounting was looking better and better. The venerable professor William A. Paton expressed the frustration well:

Professional accountants, including those in industry and governmental agencies, should take more notice of what has been happening to accounting programs in our schools of business administration. Triggered at least in part by the findings of the Gordon and Pierson reports on business education, and encouraged by a number of other factors and trends, there has been a continuing effort to subordinate and submerge the accounting courses in collegiate curricula.

...Instead of a strengthening and expanding of the work in accounting, we see weakening and curtailment in this area. Accompanying this development, and helping to explain it, is the fantastic growth--like the psalmist's green bay tree--of the programs in business policy, industrial relations, government in business, decision-making, social responsibility of management, and so on--fields that throw the door open to all sorts of baloney, and include little rigorous training in any subject matter that will be of help to the graduate in a professional career. Catch phrases such as "behavioral aspects," "human welfare," "cultural patterns," and the like fill the air.

Accounting is also being belittled by the substitution of new terms and labels for the present course offerings that retain some relation to the staples of earlier programs. In lieu of a solid array of *accounting* courses the student is offered work under such heads as "information analysis and systems," "management decision-making," "analysis, planning, and control," "human behavior and organization," "information function of management." In one well-known university, that had a strong "accounting" department some years ago, the word can no longer be found in any course title or anywhere else in the official announcements. ...

The developments referred to may well make a person who values accounting as good subject matter in higher education and as a high-caliber professional calling have grave doubts as to the future if accounting education continues to be controlled by the schools of business administration as now constituted. The plain fact is that accounting has not fared well in this association. ...Here we have a field that is fully comparable to law as a professional area, but isn't remotely in a class with law in academic prestige. As has often been suggested, it is a stroke of bad luck, and also somewhat of a reflection on accountants themselves, that college and university work in this field did not evolve in terms of "schools of accounting."[1]

So the movement toward professional schools of accounting, which had been effectively squelched by the Perry Commission in the late 1950s, began once again to build steam. And this time some very thoughtful accountants were on board. Professor John C. Burton was advocating it.[2] The eminent theoretician, Maurice Moonitz, advocated not necessarily the form of a professional school (which, for practical reasons, might not be achievable) but the substance of it when he argued that the accounting curriculum must be "professionalized" and largely autonomous accounting divisions created. He saw that those accounting academicians who were not really accountants would not be happy with such professionalization.

When we professionalize the curriculum, we will pay a price in the loss of some faculty and some students whose primary interest is not "professional." I refer to those whose concern is with stock market behavior (e.g., financial reports as predictors of the behavior of stocks and bonds), with employee motivation (e.g., budgets as devices to make employees work more efficiently), with economic issues to be resolved by studying accounting data (e.g., the national income accounts), etc. These areas are all worthy of attention; however, they do not fit the area of accounting, as it would be found in a professional school. The faculty and students interested in these areas will find a more congenial home in some other niche in the business school or in another part of the academic world.[3]

As can be inferred from Moonitz's remarks, the drive toward professional schools of accounting (or at least independent departments) was fueled in part by the desire to reduce the confusion about what accounting really was. Much of the self-designated "rigorous accounting research" was really research which more properly belonged in other academic fields, such as finance, personnel management, economics, and so on. This was a symptom of the downgrading of accounting by the business schools and resulted in accounting professors doing their research in more prestigious fields.

The Problem of Research

The fact that there was an increasing number of accounting professors who were not really interested in accounting was becoming a severe problem. At first glance, the issue seemed to be that of research vs. teaching, and research vs. practice--in fact, research vs. everything. Philip Fess, chairman of the AAA's Committee on CPA Examination, put it bluntly:

> The publish-or-perish doctrine is too prevalent to insure high quality research and, perhaps, to support a healthy academic environment. ...[T]oo often and at too many colleges, research is placed ahead of teaching. Some universities appear to be so wrapped up in research that they are little concerned with teaching and regard it only as a necessary evil.[4]

Fess suggested the creation of a new degree, which would be more than a master's but less than a Ph.D. and would be designed to "encourage more accounting teachers and to recognize the importance of teaching as a primary occupation." The counter-argument was not long in coming:

> Research emphasis in graduate education should be increased rather than, as Philip E. Fess suggests, supplanted. Good teaching, as well as good publication, requires acquisition of skills in verbalizing ideas. At the graduate level of preparation, we contend, teaching and

research are inseparable. Both require the ability to observe, synthesize and communicate knowledge. Both require an inquiring attitude and critical skills which enable the researcher to evaluate and utilize sources of information effectively. The suggestion of a non-research, "teaching" degree is inappropriate since it would lead to further dichotomizing of the two roles of teaching and research at a crucial time in the development of potential university faculty.[5]

The dichotomy was hard to avoid, for all that. For one writer the issue was simply that there were not adequate resources to do both good teaching and good research--either for individuals or for schools--and he lamented that undergraduate schools were being used as research mills.[6]

A reformist professor from UCLA, John Buckley, bluntly said, "What we have is a 'CPA' curriculum in disrepute!" He went on to argue that,

In part the decline of professional accounting education results from a schism within accounting academe itself. A state of cold war exists between avant garde and traditional faculty. Failure to influence professional accounting and/or accountants leads the avant garde to direct their attentions elsewhere, primarily toward management accounting, information systems and other "exotic" areas. Failure to understand the motives, objectives or methodologies of the avant garde leads the traditionalists to man their shrinking bastions in a last-ditch defense of the old empire. The inflexible posture of the traditionalists at some schools has led to the total abandonment of professional accounting education; at other schools the avant garde have left the accounting group to form coalitions with other disciplines or to form such independent areas as computing methods, information systems, planning and control, and so forth.

The schism is senseless and tragic. Each faction needs the other! ...The sacred cows must retire to pasture. Theoretical argument and not authoritarian

> pronouncement must prevail. Conceptual rather than mechanical exercise must be emphasized. ...On the other hand, the avant garde must come down from the heavens and mingle with mortal man. They must be concerned that their theories and highly abstracted models can benefit the real world of accounting. They must grapple with factual as opposed to utopian variables.[7]

Pulling the elite researchers down to earth so their work could have some real-world benefit seemed to be quite a problem.

The issue of the irrelevance of research often focused on the Accounting Principles Board (APB). The APB had been formed by the AICPA in April 1959 with the goal of placing accounting standards firmly upon the foundation of solid research and eliminating inconsistencies. In the speech that led to the formation of the APB, Alvin Jennings said, "Development of accounting principles should be regarded as in the nature of pure research."[8]

Research was done. Monographs were published. But the new age of accounting progress did not materialize. Research seemed to have little impact on practice standards and business pressures seemed to have an inordinate impact on practice. Mautz and Jack Gray came at it from the angle of sympathy for the work of the APB and asked what was lacking in accounting research.

> Although a number of studies have been completed and even more commissioned, one can discern no firm pattern indicating the kinds of evidence the Board wants and will accept as persuasive. ...[O]ur conclusion must be that the Board has acted contrary to research recommendations as often as it has moved to implement research results. ...We have no desire to describe the Board as composed of people who go their own way regardless of the evidence made available to them through accounting research studies and others.
>
> Given the caliber of Board personnel, one can only conclude that much accounting research has not been convincing to able, thoughtful, practical men of affairs concerned with pressing problems. This fact may be more of a criticism of accounting research than of the

Board. Why have Board members not been persuaded by the results of expensive and lengthy accounting studies? ...A superficial reply is that the research has not been convincing. But why isn't it convincing? One can scarcely avoid concluding that in many cases practitioners find the empirical evidence of their own experience more persuasive than the evidence cited by researchers in their studies. What is lacking in accounting research that makes its results so much less impressive than the results of research in other fields seem to be?

...Many accounting issues do not lend themselves to controlled experiments. Accounting includes a great variety of uncontrolled situations for each of which it seems possible to cite features that make it different from all the others. One answer, then, is that accounting is a very difficult subject in which to produce conclusive research findings. The kinds of evidence available to accountants are unlikely in many cases to be convincing in any ultimate sense.[9]

R.J. Chambers, the accounting theoretician from Australia, was not nearly so charitable with the APB members--or members of other AICPA or AAA committees--in his 1972 article entitled "The Anguish of Accountants." First Chambers critiqued the committee approach to coming up with truth:

I have elsewhere pointed out that seldom, if ever, has a material advance in knowledge been the work of a committee. ...Why are the products of research committees so unimpressive, unproductive, unenduring?

In the first place, too often the work assigned to a research committee is far more extensive than it is possible to carry out in a limited term. ...

Second, those who are invited to undertake assigned research tasks are in a sense pressed men. ...[F]ew indeed of the members of committees have been expert in the matters they have been invited to resolve. ...

Third, there seems to be a kind of deference to their sponsors on the part of committees. There is little evidence in their products of willingness to challenge the conventional wisdom. ...

Fourth,...To solve any problem it is necessary to hold the elements of the problem in sharp focus, while drawing successively on particular sets of ideas or experience which promise, even if only vaguely, to assist in its solution. ...It requires the concentrated attention of one mind. But a committee has not one mind.[10]

Chambers went on to discuss research itself. He contrasted the interests of a researcher, who is seeking to put all the factors together into a generalized solution, and the interests of a practitioner, who is seeking a solution in a specific circumstance. Chambers said it was unreasonable to expect strong research effort from practitioners, but then also went on to enumerate the faults of accounting research by academicians.

There is too great a tendency to rely on argument rather than evidence. ...

There is too great a tendency to be superficial. There are some who urge that, as accounting is information-processing, all information-processing should be the province of accounting and accountants. ...There are some who, sensing that accounting information is in the nature of financial measurement, blandly assert that all kinds of financial magnitudes are measures or measurements. ...

There is too great a tendency to "explore" accounting from other directions--economics, psychology, statistics--of which the explorer has too little acquaintance. ...

There is too great a tendency, on the part of academics, to flee from reaching conclusions. It almost seems to be regarded as unacademic to stand firmly in favor of some proposal and against all others. ...

Finally even among workers who show some diligence there is too little care given to the choice of a method of inquiry. There is an extensive range of research methods. But they are not all equally available or useful in all fields of inquiry. Experimentation is not available to astronomers or astro-physicists...political scientists, anthropologists, historians and economists. Nor to accounting researchers. Statistical methods are [only] useful in fields where the subjects of inquiry are in some important sense uniform. ...What seems to me to be the most fruitful method [for accounting research], which would supply the hard, empirical evidence of which there is such a serious shortage in the literature, has been almost entirely overlooked. It is the method of sustained observation of the consequences of particular practices, the intertemporal and international comparison of practices and their consequences. This is the method used by all researchers in fields where experimentation is impossible. ...No doubt the method has so few adherents because it is laborious and slow; perhaps also because it makes little or no use of sophisticated tools such as computers and statistics. But these are only drawbacks if we prefer instant prestige to enduring knowledge.[11]

Chambers advocated a division of responsibility among accountants: among academicians a division between researchers and teachers ("There should be a clear understanding that teaching is a distinctive and demanding function, no less respected and valued than research."), and a further division between academicians and practitioners ("The practicing arm of the profession...should vacate the field of research.").[12]

The practicing arm of the profession, however, did not vacate the field of research. Moreover, the public accountants continued to decide which research to ignore in their process of setting accounting standards through their Accounting Principles Board (APB). The bitterness this engendered was reflected in the lead article of the *Journal of Accountancy* in September 1973, which began:

Any practitioner or teacher in the field of accounting would find it difficult to assert that there is a congruence between research in his field and actual education and professional practice. ...In searching for an explanation for this behavior, schizophrenia occurred to me. However, that seemed overly harsh, as well as not providing an explanation for the prolonged presence of uncompromised differences without open warfare. Finally another explanation occurred to me;...contact is a necessary condition for the occurrence of conflicts, compromises or complementarities. Isolation prohibits all three relations.[13]

To illustrate the isolation of research from teaching and practice, the author gave an example of a case in which research had clearly shown that a certain accounting method was preferable, but in practice a different method was used and that was the method that was taught. Education mindlessly followed practice, and practice mindlessly followed education, *ad infinitum*. Research had no place in this circular chain of events. The writer suggested that the solution was that accounting methods based on research should be taught. But he pointed out one important impediment:

The influence of management upon accounting practices is too important to be neglected in this discussion. We noted above that practitioners add to their store of practices but that they rarely subtract from that store. If we inquire into the reasons for this, we find that managements desire additional practices and that managements have the power to get what they want. ...In this case they want enough flexibility to be able to realize and report the amount of income that suits their purposes. Thus some, if not most, accepted practices spring from managements' desire to serve their own ends. For this reason, some accepted practices are bad practices. I would hope that you would agree that it is not the duty of educators to codify and teach bad practices.[14]

So management was accused of being the cause of the crisis in accounting--the same management whom the business schools taught it was the duty of accountants to wholeheartedly serve. Management was said to be opposing the research findings and, whenever the APB tried to institute research findings in spite of the wishes of management, it faced considerable opposition. That opposition came, not only from management, but often from public accounting firms who took the side of management because, in the view of some, they were being paid by management and wanted its favor. In some instances even Congress opposed the theoretically preferable methods in order to allow management to account for things as it wished.

Finally the noble experiment of the APB collapsed. The APB was replaced in 1973 by the Financial Accounting Standards Board (FASB). While the APB had been an AICPA committee made up of CPAs mostly in public practice, the FASB was independent of the AICPA and deliberately included accountants directly employed by the companies affected by accounting standards. This was done in the hope that it would build a broader base of support and help in gaining acceptance for new standards. But it could also be accused of seeming a little like setting the foxes to guard the hen-house.

No such change would shake the growing impression among academicians that the whole business of setting accounting standards was a purely political process in which the search for truth (i.e., research) played no important part. Ironically, the debate about the value of research to teaching and practice was carried on in the pages of the practitioners' journal, the *Journal of Accountancy*, while the academicians' journal, the *Accounting Review*, remained aloof from such mundane matters. Finally in 1973 the *Accounting Review* carried an article which discussed the irrelevance of research to standard-setting.

> [I]f accounting presentations are to furnish useful information, accounting inquiry must be directed toward understanding human purposes, the information relevant to human purposes, and the communication of purposeful information among people. At the rule-making level, that means decisions made by authoritative accounting bodies such as the APB must be based on explanations and predictions of human behavior. And in that kind of decision-making, research has decided limitations.

[A]lthough their strength is in their rigor, research techniques are weak in their insensitivity to the subtleties of human experience that are predominantly important in human behavior. ...In fact, in any social issue (including accounting issues) complex enough to be interesting, systematic research generally fails at precisely the point that it encounters matters of real consequence.[15]

It was a misunderstanding about the way standard-setting works which had caused all the fuss:

That misconception is that the critical issues of accounting inquiry are essentially technical when they are actually political. ...In common with other essentially political activities, accounting rule-making must overcome as its chief obstacle not the inscrutability of nature, but rather the conflict between interest groups. For example, the defeats that the Accounting Principles Board encountered at the hands of conglomerates on the issue of business combinations, Congress on the investment credit matter, insurance companies on investment security valuation, and extractive industries on their reporting practices were not brought on by failures of the Board to comprehend and deal with the underlying accounting issues. The defeats arose instead from conflicts with other powerful interests, who acted to insure that they had strong voices in formulating accounting rules of consequence to them. In the face of conflict between competing interests, rationality as well as prudence lies not in seeking final answers, but rather in compromise--essentially a political process.[16]

The seeking of final answers--right answers--to accounting questions was causing all the trouble, according to this way of thinking. Research which was geared to finding the best way to communicate the underlying facts with consistency and integrity was the problem. The search for truth was at fault. Accounting was all politics, after all.

Such a focus on politics could not help but ultimately sever practice from research. In this view, research was the search for truth, but truth had little to do with the setting of standards for practice, so research had little to do with practice. If practice is essentially political and little concerned with truth, then whether research has any impact on practice has nothing to do with the true value of the research. In fact, any research which attempts to get practice to conform to some way of doing things is not really research but a part of the political game. So one type of research (branded "normative") which focused on accounting standards was considered not worthy of being called research, while much of the other type of research (quantitative) no longer had any reason to care about practicality.

The actual declaration of independence of the quantitative researchers from everybody else was published in the October 1973 issue of the *Accounting Review*. It was an article by Joel Demski entitled "The General Impossibility of Normative Accounting Standards." Essentially Demski said that no one set of information will necessarily best meet the needs of everyone or even always best meet the needs of any one person. In other words, you can't always please everyone. That is not a particularly profound conclusion (nor was it new), but it was couched not in elegant or even plain English but in extensive use of symbolic mathematical notation. It impressed a certain type of academician.

What quantitative, management accountants read into Demski's article was that the accounting standard-setting process was hopelessly and inevitably pointless--impossible, even--and that it did not deserve any further effort from them. What they failed to see was that Demski's proof proved too much. All attempts to find accounting information which could be used by any two people or by any one person at two different times and circumstances was hopeless. Demski himself said that his result "applies with equal force to so-called managerial and financial reporting areas. Allocation criteria, such as physical identification, facilities provided, and benefits received do not universally work, nor does a criterion of statistical correlation."[17] Demski had proven the impossibility of accounting, period--and not merely of accounting, but of the provision of any set of information with any general applicability, such as teaching, or research findings, etc. But Demski's work was not treated as it should have been, as an intellectual paradox similar to Zeno's paradoxes in philosophy, but rather as a giant horselaugh at the expense of the APB and "normative" research.

The educational implications of Demski's declaration were drawn out by one author:

> We are presented with proposals to disclose a variety of alternative accounting measurement, but we have no definitive method for evaluating these proposals. Given that any reasonable proposal could be relevant to the decisions of some subset of decision makers this simply means that no theoretical basis exists for excluding any of them from consideration in accounting courses. Yet we must perform some type of screening or otherwise students will have to spend their entire college career in accounting.
>
> What are some of the options? For our purposes, let me indicate but two feasible approaches. First, we could structure our courses around the present thinking of what is generally acceptable practice, including references to the policy statements of such political bodies as the SEC, (APB), FASB, CASB and others. This is more or less the approach followed in textbooks. ...Keep in mind that what is being suggested is that policy making bodies be allowed to do our screening as to what accounting proposals should be discussed within the financial accounting courses. ...
>
> Let me now turn to a second option. Rather than attempting to select which of many alternative proposals in accounting should be considered in our financial courses, we could adopt the strategy that the primary purpose of our courses, especially the advanced ones, is to teach students some operational methods for evaluating accounting proposals.[18]

The author did not make clear how a person could learn how to evaluate alternatives without there being any definite method for evaluating them. The only real alternative seemed to be to teach the official pronouncements (or, in management accounting, the most popular approaches), which effectively separated teaching from research--completing the total isolation of quantitative research from everything else.

The View from Public Accounting

Public accountants were not happy with the direction of quantitative research. By 1974 Mautz had left the academic world and had joined one of the large public accounting firms. The view was apparently different from that vantage point. Mautz's clarity of thought provides an instructive contrast between the two positions.

In the mid-sixties, while Mautz was still an academician, he light-heartedly pointed out the differences between academicians like himself and practitioners:

> First, we have essentially the same goals. We are all interested in the progress of accounting. You tend to talk in terms of establishing the practice of accounting as a "learned profession." We seek to secure for the subject matter of accounting the status of an "intellectual discipline" equal in prestige to the best of the sciences. Many of you covet the standing of such "prestige professions" as law and medicine; we envy the unassailable prestige of the physical sciences. Any frustration you may feel as the coveted goal appears just beyond your grasp cannot exceed our chagrin as we are continually reminded of our own rank in the "campus pecking order."
>
> ...Of most importance is a naive belief [by academicians] in the importance of truth and reason. Our members tend to be theorists, not pragmatists. Many of them have had no real experience with the kinds of pressures which you find a part of your normal working environment. They are likely to be unsympathetic to the very arguments you find most compelling. What will or will not work in what is still too competitive a profession is not only beyond their comprehension, it is outside their field of interest.

Our people tend to have a bias in favor of change. Note use of the word "change" rather than "progress." This contrasts sharply with the attitude of the practitioner, who tends to have a strong predilection in favor of continuity. Teachers are not much concerned about last year's engagement; we are not committed to consistency; we have no stake in the status quo. Change comes to us literally without cost and may even bring a premium. It represents something new and exciting for our students; we find it an opportunity, not a problem. And, it might even justify a new edition!

...What can you reasonably look forward to in the way of help from members of our organization?

You can expect criticism. Often it will seem unkind but it is seldom meant to be. We start with the assumption that any rational and courageous person is prepared either to defend his position or to abandon it. We joy in argument, in contests of ideas. ...

Finally, and this may well compensate for all the rest, you can expect a continuing supply of good graduates. ...But you should be aware that these graduates will be patterned after our own image; they will be critical, innovative and eager for change.[19]

Mautz, as a public accountant in 1974, was not so sanguine about the students who were coming out of the new educational approach.

The ability to argue persuasively for a "best" income ʒtermination model is a talent that will get him almost nowhere. ...The tendency at all levels, from the intermediate course on, to criticize conventional accounting for not giving more attention to economic value becomes, from the student's point of view, counter-productive. There are few scraps of knowledge of less value to a young accountant than an acquaintance with the arguments for current value accounting. Much better he should know how to reconcile a bank account. My intention is not to derogate theory construction and conceptual research. Research in accounting concepts is useful; it should go on; it should be given attention. But it is of little or no importance to beginning accountants. They have little opportunity to change the basic accounting model in business their first few years out of school. You may reply: "Ah, but we're preparing them for a career." Not by giving them a superficial understanding of esoteric concepts, you're not. Study of the avant-garde writers never prepared anyone for a career in accounting practice. Unless the young accountant knows a whole lot more than the disadvantages of historical cost and the advantages of realizable value, his career will be too brief to benefit from that study.

...Paralleling the emphasis on a conceptual approach [by academicians] is a strong lack of interest in teaching the analytical problems which helped many very successful practitioners to come to a better understanding of accounting, to develop the ability to separate important from unimportant data, to understand and master quantitative data, and to seek out the essence of an issue. The intellectual discipline required to pursue a difficult problem from beginning to end is far more similar to abilities called for in accounting practice than is a facility in arguing abstract accounting theory.[20]

In a veiled threat Mautz said that if the accounting firms were unable to use accounting graduates without extensive technical training after they were hired, then the firms might as well not worry about hiring accounting graduates and hire graduates from any major area.

Mautz noted that the problem arose because among academicians there was little concern about gaining practical experience and that applied research (as compared to theoretical research) was languishing. And, he added,

...I can't help asking, "For goodness sake, what has happened to THE ACCOUNTING REVIEW?" Most of us, and here I include academic types as well as practitioners, find this foreign language magazine almost impossible to read. ...I cite this as an illustration of how

> far apart academic and applied accounting have become.
> Ask the next ten practitioners you meet whether they
> find THE ACCOUNTING REVIEW stimulating, interesting,
> and helpful. Ask them when they last read it.[21]

Mautz apparently did not understand that the quantitative researchers
wanted the *Accounting Review* exactly the way it was--intimidating,
filled with jargon, difficult to understand, in short, a mystery that
only the initiated could pretend to appreciate. In fact, the article
which immediately followed Mautz's article was entitled "Perceptions
of Journal Quality" and presented the results of a survey of accounting
professors to determine which accounting journal had the highest
status. The *Accounting Review* was second only to the thoroughly
quantitative *Journal of Accounting Research*. Status belonged to
quantitative research.

Public accountants felt a strong need to recapture higher
education from the pressures which were pulling it away from them.
The attempt by accounting academicians to achieve status in the
business schools was seen as the problem, and the divorce of
accounting from the business schools was more and more seen as the
solution.

For the third time within six years a series of seminars on
accounting education was held, sponsored by the AICPA and AAA
jointly. A total of 48 seminars was held from November 1972 through
May 1973. Four primary topics were discussed: the status of
accounting, the role of accounting, *Horizons for a Profession* and the
Beamer Report, and professional schools of accounting.

A summary of the seminars noted that there was concern about
the status of accounting education and its submergence into the
business school, and there was a suggestion that, if it was submerged,
it might be because it had lost its uniqueness. Discussion of the role
of accounting revealed that there was a mixture of ideas about what
accounting was and what it should be doing. Not a five-year but "a
four-year program was the favorite among seminar participants."[22]

Less than half of the seminars discussed professional schools of
accounting, though at some it was the primary topic. There was little
support for separate schools of accounting. "Some discussants were
concerned that the public prestige that would accompany a separate
professional school of accounting was a primary motivational factor

behind this movement." Also, "A primary reason given against the establishment of professional schools of accounting was the assumed isolation that would occur in subject matter if such a school were operated apart from a school of business administration."[23] Costs were mentioned as an argument against professional schools. An accounting division within the business school was a compromise which appeared to find some favor.

In July 1973, the AICPA Board of Directors directly addressed the problem and stated its position by adopting the following policy resolution:

> The Institute recognizes that during the last several years the professional dimension of accounting as an academic discipline has suffered a decline in most schools--a decline which is of great concern to accountants. The Institute views this as contrary to public interest which requires that strong professional programs be generally available at universities throughout the United States.
>
> The Institute strongly endorses any action which provides such strong professional programs. As one way, and perhaps the preferable way, of achieving an increased emphasis on the professional dimension of the discipline, the Institute endorses and encourages the establishment of schools of professional accounting at qualified and receptive colleges and universities.[24]

With the AICPA now committed clearly to the professional school approach, the ball was rolling. Support for the movement grew.

An article in the October 1973 *Journal of Accountancy* explained to practitioners how research was the key to an academician's success in terms of both promotion and prestige, and that this research was

> assessed by individuals often unfamiliar with the discipline in question; a provost may have a background in philosophy and make judgments about research in accounting. Therefore, the academician who has the option of researching a topic which may appear of a vocational, or practical, nature and such an erudite topic as the "Psycho-linguistical Analysis of Alternative

Methods of Accounting" may easily conclude that the latter is "superior," due to the nonprofessional orientation of his peer evaluators.[25]

The authors explained that any curricular changes in accounting would have to be accepted by the entire faculty of the business school, among whom the accountants were a minority. The only accounting which could be taught and researched in such a political environment was accounting which was acceptable to non-accountants. The authors stopped short of advocating professional schools, but they did say that autonomy of the accounting program was necessary--the autonomy to establish its own reward structure and develop its own curriculum.

Not everyone was so reticent about wanting professional schools. The lead article in the *Journal of Accountancy* in September 1974 went all the way and strongly advocated that the present generation of accountants leave schools of accountancy as its legacy to the next generation.[26]

On March 1, 1974, a one-day symposium on professional schools of accountancy was sponsored by one of the large public accounting firms, and a proceedings book entitled *Schools of Accountancy: A Look at the Issues* was published. Here was a thoughtful and favorable consideration of the issue by a group which included, among others, both Mautz and Burton.

John Burton, then chief accountant of the Securities and Exchange Commission, believed that accountants could be better educated in a professional school than in a business school. The common argument against professional schools was that these schools would be too narrow and that, in order to be interdisciplinary, accounting should stay in the business school. Burton advocated the interdisciplinary approach but noted that business schools themselves were not adequately interdisciplinary and that, if accountants handcuffed themselves to the business schools, they could not be adequately interdisciplinary either. For example, Burton pointed out that one area in need of attention by accountants was communication, but business schools did not meet that need. He noted that, though business schools have studies of the behavioral sciences, such studies were pointed in a direction different from the needs of accountants. Similarly, accountants needed more knowledge of law than a business school commonly provides.[27]

Burton pointed out one more need that made public accountants different from others in the business school:

> Finally, one important aspect that is needed is what I call attitude training. Lawyers get attitude training very early in their academic experience. ...Business schools tend to emphasize an approach geared substantially to profit maximization in a competitive environment.
>
> Accountants, on the other hand, need a different approach. They need what might be called the dispassionate professional approach. Alone among the professions, the accountant achieves his social purpose by being independent of his client rather than serving the client's interest to the exclusion of others or following his own profit-maximizing interest. ...I think this is something that needs emphasis which a business school is less likely to give than a professional school of accounting.[28]

As another speaker at the symposium pointed out, accounting professors are a minority in a school of business, and their concerns are not going to be appreciated by many in the school. The same speaker noted that there was a serious lack of applied research in the present research efforts of accounting academicians, and that a school of accounting could remedy that.

Guy Trump, AICPA vice president for education and regulation, narrated his journey away from being opposed to schools of accounting. He noted that he had always been unimpressed with the argument for schools of accounting based on prestige on the campus. He said that he had recently been converted, however, because he had become distressed by

> the clear shift in too many schools of business to the position that their objective is the preparation of managers, decision makers, if you please, and that within their objectives there is no place for the preparation of accounting professionals. If this is an attitude which becomes more widely held than it is today, I think it leaves the profession little alternative.[29]

In the discussion that followed, he pointed out that "the percentage of accounting faculty possessing CPA certificates has declined in the last five years" and that research interests had moved away from professional concerns.[30]

A Renewed Focus on Education

Many academicians were also dissatisfied with the direction of accounting education.[31] In particular, they did not appreciate the way the *Accounting Review* ignored the issues involved in the teaching of accounting. The advisory committee of the AAA's director of education in 1971

> felt that there was no significant opportunity available for the publication of articles dealing with accounting matters, including education research, except in the teaching notes section of the *Accounting Review*...and that this "second class" status for education articles inhibited educators not only from writing about accounting education matters but also inhibited research in accounting education.[32]

In an effort to provide such an opportunity, the director of education proposed to the executive committee of the AAA that a fifth issue of the quarterly *Accounting Review* be published annually dealing with accounting education. It was hoped that this would eventually lead to a separate *Journal of Accounting Education*. The proposal was at first viewed favorably, but later, for reasons not entirely clear, the editor of the *Accounting Review* opposed it and it was rejected. An alternative proposal to publish a book containing accounting education articles was, however, found acceptable.

The book, containing the work of six editors and of 80 educators and practitioners in over 600 pages, appeared in 1974. It was entitled *Accounting Education: Problems and Prospects*. It was more a sampling of what was going on rather than a systematic coverage of the field. One section dealt with current forces for change in accounting education. Other sections dealt with (1) what the accounting educator needs to know about learning; (2) instructional innovations of the previous fifteen years such as modular concepts, self-paced and programmed instruction, computer and multi-media approaches, games and simulations, etc.; (3) evaluation of student and teacher performance; and (4) empirical research in accounting education.

In the section on current forces in accounting education, a number of the writers expressed concern that academicians were not meeting the needs of practitioners. Instead, they believed, the demands of practitioners that graduates possess "skill in applying accounting knowledge immediately upon entry into the field are being ignored by more and more accounting educators and programs of accounting education." One writer noted that

> The business faculty prefers that coverage of accounting reveal the use of accounting but not its structure; much, perhaps, as typing courses concentrate on the use of a typewriter rather than on its construction. As a result, only a fraction of the total educational function in the accounting profession is performed at institutions of higher education. The writer has been told that one of the "Big Eight" accounting firms annually spends a greater sum on in-house education than the sixty biggest departments of accounting in the United States combined! No other major profession relies so little on institutions of higher education in terms of relative resource commitments.[33]

But it was Mautz who most eloquently expressed the frustration, in his article entitled "The Over-Intellectualization of Accounting Education." With his considerable academic experience, he launched a devastating indictment against accounting academicians. He first reviewed the history of the pampered academician, beginning with the fact that the postwar shortage of accounting teachers and the strong demand for accounting graduates put the academician in a very favorable position. Also, "During this period, the so-called search for excellence by academic administrators put a high premium upon the services of those teachers who also published." It was young research-oriented graduates with no accounting experience who were hired most and came to dominate the schools. And practitioners dared not complain.

> These circumstances combined to provide those in academic positions with a degree of freedom not previously experienced. There was almost no interference with the individual's choice of what he would teach or how he would spend his research efforts. Changes in curricula, whether brought about by formal or informal means, became almost the sole prerogative of those doing the teaching, and some very young educators with little experience beyond their own undergraduate and graduate courses assumed positions of substantial importance in curriculum development. In some cases, the faculties of expanding universities were staffed almost completely with very young and inexperienced people. In other cases, by sheer weight of numbers, recent additions to the faculty outvoted their more experienced seniors.
>
> During this period, accounting faculty members have enjoyed an enviable position of status and prestige. There has been an almost total absence of criticism of educational content and processes by practitioners, many of whom have been led to believe that the great developments since they left school have rendered their education largely obsolete. Thus, for practitioners to criticize academic programs not only would be interference with academic freedom but might also be an embarrassing display of ignorance. At the same time there has been no absence of criticism of practice by educators who, by and large, have far less acquaintance with the world of the practitioner than that individual has with the world in which the professor reigns supreme.[34]

What did academicians having such an advantage do with that advantage? They did as they pleased, according to Mautz. They put what benefited them (i.e., research) first, and the needs of the students last.

To conserve their own time and energies, whether done deliberately or unintentionally, many professors brought to their classes the same issues with which they were working in their efforts to improve their publication records, regardless of the relevance of such issues to their students' educational and career goals. More than one class of elementary accounting students has been overwhelmed by material from a doctoral candidate's thesis when both the students' interests and their needs would have been better served by some less esoteric topic.

The total impact of this tendency is evidenced by a great concern in accounting curricula with topics which are only peripheral to accounting. ...We have introduced into the curriculum heavy doses of mathematics, statistics, and behavioral science, sometimes without any serious effort to justify those injections in terms of the actual needs of the student.[35]

Mautz then explained where the tension was occurring in education for professional accounting.

A profession implies practice, service to clients. It implies doing, not merely discussing. It implies helping clients to meet problems. It implies something far more than an intellectual interest in accounting theory. ...[A] way of viewing intellectualization vs. professionalism is to recognize that there are essentially two ways in which accounting might be presented in a university curriculum. One possibility is to present it as an organized discipline based on certain essential concepts which lead to principles, procedures, techniques, and standards, and which concepts themselves are influenced by unavoidable postulates. By concentrating on a clarification of the current status of these elements of the system and by testing the elements against rules of logic, internal consistency, and observations of the real world, our understanding of these elements can be improved and progress can be made toward better descriptions of what the system should be. This is basically the intellectualization approach.

A second possibility is more operational than theoretical in approach, more professional than intellectual. It emphasizes what accountants do, whatever the nature of their employment. Questions such as the following receive attention: What problems does an accountant face? What tools does he have to work with? How might he best approach different kinds of problems? What should he watch for? To whom is he responsible? When is he in difficulty? What makes some situations differ from others?

Intellectualization reflects emphasis on the construction of theory. Professionalization stresses quality performance of important tasks. Of course, some attention to both is needed. In the early days of accounting education, a how-to-do-it approach prevailed and theory received little, if any, attention. In the last two decades, the balance has swung just about as far as it can the other way. Relatively little time is now spent on how to do it. Considerably more time is spent on how it ought to be done, with all the reasons why an educator thinks so.[36]

To counter that, Mautz gave his view of what a balanced professional accounting education would include:

1. A thorough grounding in the current state of the accounting art. This should be a balanced presentation, one that includes adequate attention to both the technical and the conceptual aspects of accounting. It is important that the graduate know what current practice includes. He should also know why it exists in the form that it does, i.e., what the reasons are, historical and otherwise, that accounting has developed as it has to its present state. Beyond this, he should also have a realistic comprehension of accounting's strengths and weaknesses. And this too must be a balanced presentation so that the student has pride in the profession he is joining,

yet knows there is much opportunity and need for additional progress.

2. He should have a thorough introduction to professional responsibilities and obligations ...The social, legal, and professional responsibilities imposed by the various aspects of accounting practice should be presented in such a way that the student looks forward to measuring up to them. ...

3. The purpose, nature, and role of regulatory bodies should be a topic of considerable importance and attention. ...

4. The student should be given a sufficient historical perspective of the evolving role of the profession so that he can fit current developments into long-term trends. Perhaps no other kind of knowledge will permit him to look forward to future demands and obligations quite as well as a sound understanding of how accounting came to be where it now is.

5. The nature of professional institutions, organizations, and methods of operation are essential knowledge for the professional who would participate effectively in the advancement of his profession. ...

6. Finally, the student should have an awareness of research trends and the potential of research for influencing the development of accounting and accounting practice. ...[I]f he is to take an active part in the advancement of his subject, he must at least know what is going on in it and be able to distinguish recommendations based upon sound research from those which represent little more than someone airing his private and unsupported views.[37]

Mautz had spelled out the primary concerns and elements of a professional accounting education.

Standards for Professional Programs

In July 1974 the AICPA created a 12-member Board on Standards for Programs and Schools of Professional Accounting, consisting of representatives from the AICPA, the AAA, the American Assembly of Collegiate Schools of Business (AACSB), and the National Association of State Boards of Accountancy (NASBA). Its charge was to

> identify those standards that, when satisfied by a school, would justify its recognition by the accounting profession. Particularly, attention should be given to the criteria for the school's curriculum which would be appropriate for a professional program in accounting.[38]

This "recognition" obviously implied accreditation. In fact the Institute asked the Board to prepare a proposal for accreditation of accounting programs, and asked the AAA and the AACSB (the accrediting agency for schools of business) to join with it in forming an agency to accredit professional accounting education programs. The AACSB was reluctant to see a rival accrediting agency formed, and the AAA disagreed with the Institute position that only five-year programs should be accredited. The AAA wanted to accredit four-year and MBA programs with accounting concentrations as well.[39]

With both of these major players balking, the AICPA threatened to establish its own accrediting agency. In October 1976 the AICPA Council overturned the Beamer recommendation that accreditation should be handled by the academic community and resolved that the AICPA should encourage the development of programs of professional accounting and should participate in their accreditation. That was enough to pull the AAA back into the game, but it conditioned its re-entry on allowing other accounting organizations to participate, allowing the accrediting agency to set the standards (though the AICPA "expected" it to "follow fairly closely" the discussion draft on standards which the Board on Standards had released in 1976), and allowing more than one type of program to be accredited (though, again, the AICPA was looking only at "collegiate schools of professional accounting"[40]). The AAA feared that the AICPA was interested only in accrediting programs designed to prepare students to enter public accounting. The Institute agreed to underwrite most of the start-up costs of an accreditation agency.

A "committee of six" was formed in 1976 to move toward accreditation. It was made up of three each from the AICPA and the AAA, and had co-chairmen--one from each organization. It also invited representatives from the National Association of Accountants (NAA), the Financial Executives Institute (FEI),[41] and the Association of Government Accountants (AGA) to meet with it.

> The formation of the committee of six became an immediate concern of the AACSB, which met with AICPA representatives and later sent an official response to the AICPA about its proposed educational standards. The AACSB opposed the autonomy of programs and schools of accounting and concluded that the proposed separate accreditation was undesirable and unnecessary. Later, the AACSB rejected a joint effort with the AICPA. In the meantime, the president of the AAA...urged the committee of six to investigate the possibility of a cooperative effort with the AACSB. At an exploratory meeting, it was generally agreed that the AICPA and the AAA would jointly sponsor an accounting accreditation agency that would set its own standards in consultation with the AACSB.[42]

In May 1977 the Board on Standards for Programs and Schools of Professional Accounting issued its final report. The most significant change from its earlier draft was a softening of its language deriding undergraduate education. Dropped were statements such as: an adequate level of quality for entry-level professional accountants "cannot be achieved within the traditional baccalaureate program" and "four-year programs of study are considered inadequate and will not be accredited." Though the harsh language disappeared, however, the point was still there: "professional" education involved post-graduate education. The AICPA was more committed than it had ever been to gaining for itself the prestige which would come from requiring five years of higher education.

There would be two years of "preprofessional preparation" and "not less than three years of progressively more advanced professional-level study. "[43] Spelling things out carefully, the report suggested

> The curriculum should be conceived as a unit and should cover all those aspects of business and governmental activities that relate to the economic and social forces that influence and interface with accountancy. ...The preprofessional program shall provide for a broad general education in the humanities and sciences, including a knowledge and understanding of topics relevant to accounting such as communications, the behavioral sciences, quantitative methods, economics, and an introduction to computer science. ...The foundation is intended to provide--
> * Understanding of the content and processes of scientific thought and systematic approaches to problem solving.
> * Facility in the use of mathematics and statistics to measure and express economic events.
> * Ability to communicate effectively orally and in writing.
> * Appreciation of the institutions and forces--legal, financial, economic, political, and sociological-- that influence and interface with accountancy.[44]

The accounting curriculum would include the traditional subjects of financial, managerial, and governmental accounting, tax, auditing, and systems, as well as "organization of the profession," ethics, and the "environment of accounting" (dealing with institutions and "the impact of regulatory agencies and professional bodies on current and emerging accounting issues"). The curriculum would also stress realism.

> Certain of the courses dealing with the discipline of accountancy should consist of cases and/or problems reflecting actual business situations that require analytical problem solving and utilization of the body of knowledge acquired in the earlier segments of the study program. ...During the professional program, an

integrative approach should be developed within the curriculum. Cases and other teaching methodologies should interrelate accounting and/or auditing decisions in a setting that requires assessment of realistic environmental influences, understanding of the implications and significance of the decisions, and utilization of a variety of tools, skills, and knowledge obtained from other segments of the program.[45]

To achieve this the faculty should be practical people, who could teach practically. At least 50 percent should have an appropriate earned doctorate, but at least 60 percent should have the CPA certificate. Also, "Not less than 60 percent of the full-time faculty should have relevant professional accounting experience to bring to the classroom." Again, "School administrators and faculty should be encouraged to bring to the campus qualified, practicing accountants to complement the full-time faculty."

The focus on research should be adjusted, too.

In establishing and applying criteria for evaluating faculty performance, the quality of teaching is of primary importance. ...In evaluating research, equal value shall be given to theoretical, applied, and educational-oriented studies.[46]

The standards focused on what were considered the essential conditions for a professional program. The first of these, of course, was "knowledge and methodology." The other two were "identity" and "autonomy." Regarding identity the report said,

The profession's pride in its identity is an important motivating factor that assures successful completion of the process of education. Such identity should allow suitable visibility both within and outside the academic setting. ...The success of the educational process for accountancy demands a separate "identity" for the program.[47]

Regarding autonomy, the standards went on to require:

> [T]he accounting administrator and the accounting faculty should have authority to--
> * Administer the accounting program.
> * Select, retain, compensate, promote, and award tenure to faculty.
> * Develop curricular policy including methods of instruction.
> * Establish academic standards for admission, retention, advancement, and graduation of students.
> * Develop, submit, and administer, within university guidelines, the budget of the accounting unit.
>
> To assure that the proper academic environment is created and maintained, there must be an effective evaluation and accreditation process for professional schools or programs of accounting.[48]

This type of power in the hands of accounting educators was intolerable to the business school deans who made up the AACSB. They were unwilling to relinquish their authority over accounting programs. Those programs were the crown jewels of the business schools. They were the only truly professional programs in those schools and generally the most rigorous and popular. It was certain that the deans would not idly sit by and watch them slip out of their hands.

Nevertheless, accounting educators proceeded to pursue their dream of independence. The *Accounting Review*, though it could not bring itself to publish a thoughtful discussion article on the issues, did publish a series of surveys on the attitudes of people involved. One revealed that over 60 percent of educators and CPAs believed five years of schooling was needed, but over 60 percent of industrial accountants and controllers disagreed. All considered the master's degree more essential than a doctorate and only the academicians agreed that 50 percent of the faculty should have doctorates. All agreed on the importance of practical experience, and considered it more important than either the doctoral degree or the CPA certificate.[49]

Two other studies included business school deans among those surveyed. One of them reported concern by deans that there would be decreased interaction among the disciplines if accountants formed their own professional schools; accounting chairs, on the other hand, did not see this as a problem. The deans' dismissal of accounting schools was obvious: accounting chairs believed autonomy over accounting curriculum would increase, while deans did not; chairs believed autonomy over faculty staffing would increase while deans did not; chairs believed relations with accounting practitioners would improve while deans did not; deans strongly disagreed with the idea that schools of accounting would halt the decline of accounting as an academic discipline.[50]

The other study including deans also showed that academic isolation was a crucial factor in the minds of deans and non-accounting faculty. Both considered such an event likely if separate accounting schools were formed. While isolation was considered a crucial factor by accounting faculty (but not chairs) and practitioners, they did not consider it likely. The deans and non-accounting faculty also believed that harmful duplication would occur, while accounting chairs doubted it. Both accounting chairs and faculty saw better courses resulting, more control over student quality, and more funds for the accounting programs. Accounting practitioners saw many of the same advantages that academicians saw but they also saw more prestige and more practitioner input into accounting education. In general, deans and non-accounting faculty were opposed to schools of accountancy while accounting academicians and practitioners favored them.[51]

The Schools of Accounting Movement

Schools of accounting continued to form, whether the deans liked it or not. The first appeared in 1973 at the C.W. Post Center of Long Island University. It was followed by the University of Denver in 1975. Two more were born in 1976, at Brigham Young University and Louisiana Tech University, and three more in 1977, at the Universities of Florida, Georgia, and Missouri-Columbia. In 1978 two more arrived, at the University of Alabama and San Diego State University. Seven universities flooded the roster in 1979: Mississippi and Mississippi State and Southern Mississippi, DePaul, Golden Gate,

Southern California, and Oklahoma State. Eleven more schools would join the movement during the following four years.

In October 1976 the first national conference on "professionalization of the accountancy curriculum" was held in Kansas City, hosted by the School of Accountancy of the University of Missouri-Columbia. Participants included representatives of 23 universities that had or were planning to have schools of accountancy, and 21 representatives of accounting organizations. Kermit D. Larson of the University of Texas gave voice to the fears of many and then attempted to allay those fears.

> If I thought that accounting schools were bound to generate a domination of accounting education by practitioners, or if I thought accounting schools would generate a reversion toward emphasizing procedural skills at the expense of our efforts to mold a more conceptually based curriculum, or if I thought accounting schools would de-emphasize the interdisciplinary character of accounting and fail to emphasize the importance of basic disciplines in education, then I would also assume the role of skeptic or antagonist.[52]

Larson sketched out a dream of the brave new world of accounting education, in which the fate of accounting would be in the hands of accountants. They would even control the liberal arts and sciences and bend them to their will. The new approach would

> specify much more completely and integrate much more carefully the background course work, the generally relevant, and the specifically relevant subject matter from related disciplines such as law, philosophy, mathematics, statistics, economics, psychology, sociology and political science. ...The underlying intent of this objective is to dare to lay hands upon the content of the liberal education, and to partially constrain it so that an increased percentage of it will have either general or even specific relevance to the professional competence areas of accounting.[53]

The schools, he assured, would form among students a culture in which they would become immersed in the joy of accounting:

> [I]n the right organization, the distinction between courses and extracurricular programs...would be minimized. I would envision, for example, student competition involving accounting practice cases such as those that are discussed at the seminars for faculty that some of the CPA firms sponsor. First year students would listen, second year students would argue the alternatives, and third year students would critique the presentations and play devil's advocate. I would envision regular student convocations, at which professional representatives would draw students into the critical issues of the day.[54]

The political, ethical, and legal dimensions of accounting practice would move to the forefront in education.

In Larson's dream, the new schools would also serve practitioners well. Research would be to "provide information and direction in the resolution of significant problems that confront accounting practice" as well as to develop the curriculum. The schools' programs would train students in a specialty. Accounting schools would even "establish a set of professional development programs that will serve to fulfill the responsibility of a professionally oriented school to make a substantive contribution toward continuing education." There had been an increasing focus on continuing professional education (CPE) by practitioners since Iowa had required CPE of licensed CPAs in 1969 and other states had followed its lead.

The dream of accounting schools animated the conference. At the conference's concluding luncheon, the participants decided that a strong national organization of schools of accounting was needed. In December 1977, another meeting was held in New York City and the Federation of Schools of Accountancy (FSA) was formed. The FSA had 21 charter members, including most of those schools which already had schools of accountancy as well as others who intended to form them. The FSA was committed to promoting the formation of schools of accountancy, whether within or outside the schools of business.

Support for the movement came from everywhere--even un-expected places. For example, the Subcommittee on Reports, Accounting and Management of the Committee on Governmental Affairs of the United States Senate (the Metcalf Committee) observed:

> [T]he establishment of professional schools of account-ing within universities provides an atmosphere which encourages development of professional responsibility and independence.[55]

In 1978 the AICPA-formed Commission on Auditor's Responsibilities (the Cohen Commission) also gave considerable attention to accounting education. It said that the public accounting profession had not been able to rely upon formal education to the same extent other professions had.

> Formal accounting education does not provide students with a sense of professional identity. A program of learning imbedded in a school that views its mission primarily as educating the student for business management provides little opportunity to expose students to the customs, traditions, philosophical issues, and pragmatic approach of the practice of the profession.[56]

The Commission called attention to the schism between academic and practicing accountants, noting that the research efforts of academicians had been directed toward managerial accounting or financial analysis with a mathematical emphasis, and not toward auditing or the current problems of immediate concern to practitioners. Most Ph.D.s came into teaching with no business experience, and had little interest in the accounting profession. The Commission favored separate schools as a solution but, recognizing the practical difficulties involved, recommended as an intermediate step "the creation of graduate professional accounting schools of clearly identifiable programs within the framework of existing schools of business."

There was some intelligent opposition to the accounting schools movement also. At a 1977 conference entitled "Accounting

Education: New Horizons For the Profession," a stimulating discussion took place involving discussants from Canada and Australia and from the medical and legal professions, and a business school dean as well; these "outsiders" were not impressed with all the sacred cows of the American accounting education establishment, and they were not shy about saying so.

K. Fred Skousen, director of the school of accountancy at Brigham Young University, presented the AICPA party line.[57] There were numerous interesting responses to his position. Most usefully, a member of the medical profession had some warnings from his experience.

> In my opinion, the deficiency in the medical education process is that the medical school is the gatekeeper for physicians. Numerous tests have shown that those whose scores are high on admission criteria do not necessarily make the best practicing physicians. ...On the other hand, the accounting profession is for the most part open to those who work and study. ...In the accounting profession, an individual can switch from a career in one field (such as engineering) to the appropriate accounting courses and enter into the accounting profession. The ease of transfer into the accounting profession and the fact that an individual can switch careers at almost any time for a reasonably low cost to him and to society provides the opportunity for a large number of perspectives to be synthesized into the accounting profession. In my opinion, this diversity of perspectives offers an extremely valuable power and information base that can be lost if the accounting department's (or school's) screening committees ever become the gatekeepers to the profession. ...There are those who would argue that the move by the accounting profession toward more strict requirements for entry into the accounting curriculum and screening at the earlier stages is *not* an attempt to limit the profession; rather it is an attempt to professionalize accounting education. I would disagree. History in the medical profession has shown that control begets control, first by the profession, now

by the federal government. ...The accounting profession should be proud of the fact that there is a diversity of opinion among its practitioners.... By leaving the [CPA] examination external to graduation from an accounting program, the accounting profession will permit a diversity of individuals, all equally competent but with different perspectives, to provide input into the profession. ...In my opinion, it seems that the profession should carefully consider any approach toward accrediting or developing accounting schools so they become an elitist group.[58]

This warning had a strong effect upon the participants at the conference, as can be seen in their later discussions where it was repeatedly asserted that alternative programs should be endorsed, leaving it to the marketplace to decide which program was more desirable. A great number of participants opposed the concept of schools as gatekeepers.

The AICPA Is Outmaneuvered

The AICPA continued to press its campaign for accreditation of professional programs. In 1978 the committee of six was firming up accreditation standards. It proposed that (1) an accrediting agency be established and called the Accounting Accreditation Council (AAC), (2) it be funded by organizations represented on the council, (3) it only accredit programs leading to graduate (master's level) degrees in accounting, and (4) it normally limit accreditation to schools which had AACSB accreditation.

The committee's co-chairmen reported their progress in the March issue of the *Journal of Accountancy*. Herbert Miller, AICPA co-chair, reported that the NAA (the association of management accountants) supported the proposed accrediting agency. He also reported that, although two AAA committees supported it, "many accounting educators still remain unenthusiastic about accreditation."[59]

Miller was pleased that the AACSB had recently demonstrated a willingness "to participate and cooperate in the accounting accreditation process" because he saw the possibility of efficiency, in that needless duplication might be avoided through a marginal "add-on" to an already existing accreditation structure. He also interpreted AACSB support as "reducing the opposition of deans and business school faculties to current efforts...."[60]

Sidney Davidson, AAA co-chair, carefully expressed his support for the resolution which the AAA executive committee had passed when the committee of six was being formed. He noted that, when the AAA agreed to join with the AICPA in the accreditation project, its executive committee cautioned:

> [T]o protect the diversity in education which we consider important, accreditation should not be confined to any one type of program.[61]

Davidson pointed out that the committee of six's decision to accredit only master's programs violated that resolution. He warned that "there is an ever-present danger of limiting accreditation to CPA preparation." He had been at the "New Horizons" conference and supported the view which had found favor there.

> I have a general preference for a free market system of evaluation: that is, let there be an evaluation by a free choice of students, faculty and employers. However, it is clear that market forces operate with a time lag, sometimes a substantial one, between the adoption of a policy and its eventual effects. ...I've suggested that the benefit [of accreditation] would be a more prompt improvement in accounting programs. What are the costs and dangers of accreditation?
>
> ...The real danger is that accreditation standards will stifle diversity and creativity in accounting programs. Standards must be flexible and permit innovation. They should represent floors rather than ceilings. Dr. Kenneth Young, who is president of the council on postsecondary education, pointed out some of the problems in accreditation recently. He said, "Accreditation never has been able to define 'quality' of education except in terms of specific criteria (percent of Ph.D.'s in the faculty,

number of books in the library) and the validity of these criteria never has been established."

...Another main danger of accreditation in my view is that it may turn out to be a means of bringing about a monopoly path of entry to various professional callings. The plain fact is that we need more highly talented people in accounting. Talent may be developed more quickly and more effectively in accredited programs, but such programs are not the only reservoir of talent. We must always keep the lines open for the people who have prepared through other educational programs.[62]

The committee of six, however, had made its decision. It was consulting with legal council on the AAC's charter and bylaws, when suddenly the AACSB, in a surprise move in the spring of 1978, announced that it would start accrediting accounting programs and invited the AAA and AICPA to participate in its process. The move infuriated representatives of the AICPA,[63] but they meekly capitulated. They halted their own accreditation efforts. The events were reported in the *Journal of Accountancy*:

The committee of six responded promptly to the new AACSB position by suggesting that the proposed accounting accreditation planning committee (AAPC) of the AACSB include two accounting educators (nominated by the AAA), two accountants in public practice (nominated by the AICPA), two accountants from commerce and industry (one nominated by NAA and the other by FEI) and two or three deans. Subsequently, the AACSB accepted the committee of six's membership proposal for the AAPC; members were nominated by the constituent organizations; and the body began its deliberations.

In the meantime, the committee of six disbanded, and the AICPA and AAA have established the Accounting Accreditation Council on a standby basis. It may be needed if any accounting programs at AACSB non-accredited schools should eventually apply for accreditation or in the unfortunate event the AACSB's efforts to establish standards and an accreditation process should prove unsuccessful.[64]

A news article announcing the take-over by the AACSB said it all: "Final authority for the accreditation plan, which will apply to graduate and undergraduate programs in AACSB-accredited schools, will rest with the AACSB accreditation council."[65] Victory had been snatched out of the AICPA's grasp. While the AICPA had busied itself with defeating the AAA's opposition, the AACSB had come around from the rear and sent it into a rout. The most significant thing about the AACSB proposal, to the AICPA, was that it covered not just five-year professional accounting programs, but both undergraduate and MBA programs with concentrations in accounting as well. In October 1979 the AACSB proposed accreditation standards for these three programs. In an apparent effort to placate the AICPA, the AACSB agreed to call only five-year programs "professional accounting programs." In 1980 the proposed standards were approved by the AACSB. The AICPA petulantly refused to provide financial support for anything but the accreditation of master's of accounting programs.

The accreditation standards required that a minimum percentage of faculty have professional certification (such as the CPA certificate) and show "recent relevant experience." In the curriculum, greater emphasis would be placed on "the environment and organization of the profession, its ethics and responsibilities and the impact of governmental and private-sector organizations on current and emerging issues."[66] These were goals that the AICPA had sought in the accreditation struggle, but the essential fact was that accreditation was in the hands of the business school deans. The standards of business school deans would prevail, including the demand for prestige quantitative research from faculty. The AICPA, along with the academicians who had allied themselves with it, had been flanked.

> The AACSB's accreditation of the three types of accounting programs was in effect a deliberate move to hinder the AICPA's desire to encourage the establishment of separate schools of professional accounting. ...[I]mplicit in the decision by the AICPA (1980) to finally capitulate to the AACSB's accreditation

proposals, "was the virtual abandonment of an AICPA
drive for the establishment of separate schools of
professional accounting, which were strongly opposed
within the AACSB." ...[67]

Furthermore, after all this struggle, in the opinion of accounting
department chairs, accreditation was not likely to improve accounting
education. They did not believe it would result in increased
importance given to teaching but they did see that demand for Ph.D.s
would greatly increase and aggravate the shortages already present.[68]
Added to this was controversy over the requirement that academicians
have up-to-date relevant practical experience--thereby making it even
more difficult to find qualified faculty.

While the conquest of accreditation by the AACSB and the retreat
of the AICPA did not kill the school of accountancy movement, it
certainly crippled it. The AICPA's abandonment of the school of
accountancy movement strongly suggests that its real concern was the
status of CPAs rather than improvement of accounting education. The
following statement, made by proponents of schools of accountancy,
likely captures the real heart of the issue for the AICPA and the
reason it had pushed for schools of accountancy:

> If accountants are to claim the prestige and status that
> physicians and attorneys enjoy, it is essential that they be
> perceived as well-educated. In our opinion, this requires
> a move towards post-baccalaureate education, similar to
> that required in the other recognized professions.[69]

The usefulness of the schools of accountancy movement to the AICPA
centered on requiring a five-year program of all accounting students.
When the AACSB allowed four-year programs to be accredited, the
five-year school of accountancy became only one option among
others. A student could graduate from an accredited program in
accounting after only four years. Thus the primary usefulness of the
five-year school of accountancy movement was lost, as far as the
AICPA was concerned.

Notes

[1] William A. Paton, "Accounting's Educational Eclipse," *The Journal of Accountancy*, December 1971, pp. 35, 36. See also some earlier comments by Paton in W.A. Paton, "Some Reflections on Education and Professoring," *The Accounting Review*, January 1967, pp. 11-12.

[2] John C. Burton, "An Educator Views the Public Accounting Profession," *The Journal of Accountancy*, September 1971, p. 47.

[3] Maurice Moonitz, "The Beamer Committee Report--A Golden Opportunity for Accounting Education," *The Journal of Accountancy*, August 1973, p. 67. In *Horizons* Roy and MacNeill pointed to Moonitz's work as a model for the future of research in accounting (p. 61).

[4] Philip E. Fess, "Teaching and/or Research: A Time for Evaluation," *The Journal of Accountancy*, March 1968, p. 85.

[5] John W. Kennelly and John H. Smith, "More on Research and Teaching," *The Journal of Accountancy*, July 1969, p. 87.

[6] Lawrence C. Lockley, "Some Comments Regarding University Education," *The Journal of Accountancy*, May 1969, pp. 96-97.

[7] John W. Buckley, "A Perspective on Professional Accounting Education," *The Journal of Accountancy*, August 1970, pp. 43-44.

[8] Alvin Jennings, "Present-Day Challenges in Financial Reporting," *The Journal of Accountancy*, January 1958, p. 32.

[9] R.K. Mautz and Jack Gray, "Some Thoughts on Research Needs in Accounting," *The Journal of Accountancy*, September 1970, p. 55. See also Mautz's earlier comments on the APB in "Challenges to the Accounting Profession," *The Accounting Review*, April 1965, pp. 299-311. Another article reflecting disappointment with the APB already in 1965 is by Patrick S. Kemp, "The Authority of the Accounting Principles Board," *The Accounting Review*, October 1965, pp. 782-787.

[10] R.J. Chambers, "The Anguish of Accountants," *The Journal of Accountancy*, March 1972, pp. 69-70.

[11] Ibid., pp. 71, 72.

[12] Ibid., p. 73.

13 Robert R. Sterling, "Accounting Research, Education and Practice," *The Journal of Accountancy*, September 1973, pp. 44-45.

14 Ibid., pp. 51, 52.

15 Dale L. Gerboth, "Research, Intuition, and Politics in Accounting Inquiry," *The Accounting Review*, July 1973, p. 476.

16 Ibid., pp. 478, 479.

17 Joel S. Demski, "The General Impossibility of Normative Accounting Standards," *The Accounting Review*, October 1973, p. 721.

18 Nicholas Dopuch, "Models for Financial Accounting vs. Models for Management Accounting: Can (Should) They Be Different?" *Researching the Accounting Curriculum: Strategies for Change*, edited by William L. Ferrara (The American Accounting Association, 1975), pp. 108, 109.

19 Robert K. Mautz, "The Practitioner and the Professor," *The Journal of Accountancy*, October 1965, pp. 64, 65.

20 R.K. Mautz, "Where Do We Go From Here?" *The Accounting Review*, April 1974, pp. 355, 356-357.

21 Ibid., p. 356.

22 William G. Shenkir, ed., *The Future of Accounting Education: A Summary Report on the Seminars Sponsored by the American Accounting Association and the American Institute of Certified Public Accountants* (New York: American Institute of Certified Public Accountants, 1974), pp. 8-9.

23 Ibid., p. 10.

24 Guy Trump, "Attributes of a New (Public) Accountant," *Accounting Education: Problems and Prospects*, edited by James Don Edwards (American Accounting Association, 1974), pp. 62-63.

25 Paul J. Aslanian and John T. Duff, "Why Accounting Teachers Are So Academic," *The Journal of Accountancy*, October 1973, p. 50.

26 Edward L. Summers, "Accounting Education's New Horizons," *The Journal of Accountancy*, September 1974, p. 56.

27 John C. Burton, "The Need for Professional Accounting Education," *Schools of Accountancy: A Look at the Issues*, edited by Allen H. Bizzell and Kermit D. Larson (New York: American Institute of Certified Public Accountants, 1975), pp. 5, 6.

28 Ibid., pp. 6, 7.

29 Guy Trump, "Comments by...", *Schools of Accountancy*, edited by Bizzell and Larson, p. 37.

30 Ibid., p. 43.

31 In the war-torn landscape of the early 1970s, a significant effort was made to improve the quality of accounting education. In 1968 Price Waterhouse, one of the "Big Eight" public accounting firms, financed a study group to examine the introductory accounting curriculum. That group, headed by Gerhard Mueller and Robert Sprouse, worked for three years and issued its report, *A New Introduction to Accounting*, in 1971. It specified eight modules and thirty-six topics covering the first year of accounting, but its most innovative features were in the long-neglected area of financial accounting (only one of the eight modules dealt with managerial accounting). A task force developed instructor lecture notes and student materials for the modules for the first course (not the whole first year), and the materials were used for the first time in the Fall of 1970 at the University of Washington and the University of Texas. The introductory accounting course had been receiving special attention for decades, and the Foundation Reports had focused on them as needing improvement. Numerous suggestions for improvement had been made, and many of them stressed the need to get away from the mechanics of debits and credits. An article by Warren Reininga in 1965 suggested an innovative approach to elementary accounting which eliminated debits and credits ("An Approach to Elementary Accounting," *The Accounting Review*, January 1965, pp. 211-214). At the same time articles which advocated teaching the broader aspects of accounting appeared. The work by Mueller and Sprouse discussed accounting in terms of broader economic concepts, looked at alternative accounting theories, and showed that it was possible to teach accounting without the use of debits and credits. The textbook which came out of this work (authored by Mueller, Robert May, and Thomas Williams, and first published in 1975) relegated the debit and credit terminology to an appendix. For the first time since the second world war , at least, accounting educators had a textbook which approached the beginning financial accounting course in a truly conceptual way.

32 Harold Q. Langenderfer, "Foreword," *Accounting Education: Problems and Prospects*, edited by James Don Edwards (American Accounting Association, 1974), p. ix.

[33] Edward L. Summers, "The Professional School in Accounting Education," *Accounting Education: Problems and Prospects*, edited by James Don Edwards (American Accounting Association, 1974), p. 79.

[34] Robert K. Mautz, "The Over-Intellectualization of Accounting Education," *Accounting Education: Problems and Prospects*, edited by James Don Edwards (American Accounting Association, 1974), p. 31.

[35] Ibid., p. 32.

[36] Ibid., pp. 33, 34.

[37] Ibid., pp. 35-36.

[38] Board on Standards for Programs and Schools of Professional Accounting, *Final Report* (New York: American Institute of Certified Public Accountants, 1977), p. 1.

[39] Robert Bloom, Araya Debessay, and William Markell, "The Development of Schools of Accounting and the Underlying Issues," *Journal of Accounting Education*, Spring 1986, pp. 16-17.

[40] "AAA and AICPA to Consponsor Accreditation," *The Journal of Accountancy*, October 1976, p. 38.

[41] The NAA and the FEI are primarily organizations of management accountants in private industry.

[42] Harold Q. Langenderfer, "Accounting Education's History-- A 100-Year Search for Identity," *The Journal of Accountancy*, May 1987, pp. 318-320.

[43] Board on Standards, p. 7.

[44] Ibid., pp. 7-8.

[45] Ibid., p. 9.

[46] Ibid., p. 10.

[47] Ibid., p. 4.

[48] Ibid., p. 4.

[49] J. David Spiceland, Vincent C. Brenner, and Bart P. Hartman, "Standards for Programs and Schools of Professional Accounting: Accounting Group Perceptions," *The Accounting Review*, January 1980, pp. 134-143.

[50] Wayne G. Bremser, Vincent C. Brenner, and Paul E. Dascher, "The Feasibility of Professional Schools: An Empirical Study," *The Accounting Review*, April 1977, pp. 465-473.

51 Frank R. Rayburn and E.H. Bonfield, "Schools of Accountancy: Attitudes and Attitude Structure," *The Accounting Review*, July 1979, pp. 753-754.

52 Kermit D. Larson, "Schools of Accountancy: What Should Be Their Objectives?" *Proceedings of the First National Conference on Professionalization of the Accounting Curriculum*, edited by Joseph A. Silvoso and Raymond C. Dockweiler (Columbia, Missouri: University of Missouri, 1977), p. 22.

53 Ibid., pp. 24, 25.

54 Ibid., p. 27.

55 Quoted by Doyle Z. Williams, "Schools of Accounting: Anatomy of a Movement," *Issues in Accounting Education*, 1984, p. 17.

56 "Summary of the Conclusions and Recommendations of the Commission on Auditors' Responsibilities," *The Journal of Accountancy*, April 1978, p. 99.

57 An adaptation of his paper was printed in the *Journal of Accountancy* within months (i.e., in the July 1977 issue); he had also had a lengthy article announcing the establishment of the BYU school of accountancy in the November 1976 issue.

58 Irwin M. Jarett, "Discussion of 'What We Can Learn from Other Countries and Other Professions,'" *Accounting Education: New Horizons For the Profession; Proceedings of the Arthur Young Professors' Roundtable, March 31 - April 1, 1977*, edited by Donald H. Skadden (Reston, Virginia: The Council of Arthur Young Professors, 1977), pp. 53, 54.

59 Herbert E. Miller, "Accreditation: Two Views; Where Such Education Standard Setting Is Headed," *The Journal of Accountancy*, March 1978, p. 57.

60 Ibid., p. 60.

61 Sidney Davidson, "Accreditation: Two Views; A Plea for Flexibility," *The Journal of Accountancy*, March 1978, p. 61.

62 Ibid., pp. 63, 64.

63 Bloom, et al, p. 17.

64 David B. Pearson, "Will Accreditation Improve the Quality of Education?" *The Journal of Accountancy*, April 1979, p. 56.

65 "AACSB Approves Proposal for Accrediting Accounting Programs," *The Journal of Accountancy*, July 1978, pp. 13-16.

66 "AACSB Council Adopts Rules to Accredit Accounting Programs," *The Journal of Accountancy*, August 1980, p. 13.

67 Bloom, et al, p. 18.

68 David R. Campbell and Robert W. Williamson, "Accreditation of Accounting Programs: Administrators' Perceptions of Proposed AACSB Standards," *Issues in Accounting Education*, 1983, pp. 68-69.

69 Bloom, et al., p. 24.

Chapter 5

The Battle for the
Five-Year Requirement

Although the AICPA lost the battle of separate schools of accounting, it was determined not to lose the war. There were other ways of achieving its goal of increased prestige for CPAs and it quickly turned its attention to one of these.

In the early 1970s the AICPA and a multitude of seminars had failed to convince educators that five-year programs were necessary. The AICPA's accreditation effort also failed to achieve that objective. But it still had one big gun: the licensure requirement. While it is the state legislatures which set standards for CPA licensure, they look to the leadership of the profession (the AICPA and its affiliated state societies) for guidance. The AICPA determined to work harder for state legislation requiring that all who wanted to take the CPA exam have at least five years of collegiate education.

They had already achieved some success in this area. In 1977, Hawaii became the first state to require five years of higher education (in the process dropping its experience requirement). Colorado followed also in 1977. The push was on in other states as well.

In 1975 Florida and Utah came under siege by the proponents of the five-year requirement. The Florida effort took center stage. Florida's board of accountancy and its CPA society joined to draft a law which would require five years of higher education plus two more years of experience, and it would separate certification from licensing. The bill was introduced in 1976 but failed; it failed again in 1977. In 1979, however, with sunset laws requiring that some sort of legislation be passed for accounting regulation, a compromise bill was passed which required five years of education (including at least 36 hours of accounting beyond the elementary courses) but no experience--beginning August 1, 1983. In Utah, which did not even require a four-year degree for public accounting, the CPA society, supported by Brigham Young School of Accountancy faculty, submitted a bill in 1978 which would require five years of education and separation of certification and licensing. It failed, but a compromise bill, dropping CPE requirements, was passed in 1981--to go into effect in 1986. In 1981 the Texas board of accountancy resolved that it would work toward bringing the five-year requirement to Texas.

There were set-backs, however, even during these early years. Hawaii moved away from the strict AICPA position. It allowed students to sit for the CPA exam after four years, even though five years of education were required for licensure. It also reinstated the two-year experience requirement.[1]

An unsuccessful attempt was made to bring New York into the fold in 1977. The board of accountancy proposed a five-year program which included 36 hours of accounting. Academicians strongly opposed the requirement in hearings held in 1977 and again in 1979. They argued: (1) that the proposal would disqualify both graduates of four-year programs as well as MBA programs, and 85 percent of new public accounting employees were then coming from those two sources, (2) that there was no proof that greater exposure to accounting courses would improve CPA exam scores nor would the five-year program attract better students, (3) that the quality issue was being handled through the development of accounting accreditation standards, and (4) that the additional requirements would be an extra barrier to entry into the profession--which was contrary to the efforts to increase competition which the Federal Trade Commission was making at the time, and was also not fair to the poor and minorities who would be less able to overcome such barriers.

The AICPA nevertheless supported the proposed additional requirements because: (1) "business practices have become more complex," (2) "increased responsibilities have been imposed on CPAs," (3) "the scope of services of CPAs has been expanded," (4) "rule-making bodies have responded with a proliferation of accounting and auditing pronouncements," (5) "more exposure to the behavioral sciences" is required, and (6) "technological changes have occurred, most notably the development and widespread application of the computer" which required increased knowledge of mathematics. An attempt was made in the AICPA's journal to rebut the academicians' concern that the five-year requirement would limit access to the profession. The argument was made that all change has costs, and that accounting should not be any more accessible to the poor and minorities than medicine or law, or else it would be considered merely a "second-class profession" filled with "second-class citizens." Once again, status was the ultimate argument.[2]

Making the 150-Hour Requirement Official

Realizing that the struggle to get the states to require the five-year program was going to be longer and harder than it had hoped, the AICPA in 1976 appointed the Task Force on the Report of the Committee on Education and Experience Requirements for CPAs "to determine if the curriculum requirements set forth in...the Beamer Report...continue to be appropriate...."[3] It was chaired by Wayne J. Albers. It is unclear which events, in the little more than six years that had passed since the Beamer Report, were thought by the AICPA leadership to potentially indicate a need for significant changes. Not surprisingly, the Albers Report in 1978 was in substantial agreement with the Beamer Report. Its most significant action was to begin calling the five-year requirement a "150-hour" requirement. It recommended that the 150-hour program lead to a master's degree rather than a bachelor's.

The Albers Report also recommended curricular adjustments. The general education requirements (including elementary accounting) were essentially unchanged but the general business requirements were cut drastically from the 54 hours the Beamer Committee had recommended to 36-39 hours. The legal and social environment of business was cut from 12 to 9 hours; organization, group, and individual behavior was cut from 9 to 3-6 hours; quantitative applications were cut from 9 to 6 hours; and production or operational systems and business policy were both completely eliminated. The accounting requirements were increased from 30 to 39 (so that they actually exceeded the amount given to general business), with financial accounting going from 9 to 15 hours, and tax from 3 to 6 hours. All of this marked a significant reversal of the CBOK Report's push toward more general business courses.

The Federation of Schools of Accountancy followed in 1979 with their recommendation that an accounting program be not less than 150 hours and that it contain a curriculum remarkably like that found in the Albers Report.[4] In 1980 the board of directors of the National Association of State Boards of Accountancy resolved that "Accounting laws should provide that the education requirement will ultimately be a baccalaureate degree plus additional study to equal a total of 150 hours...."[5]

In September of 1981 the AICPA gathered together its followers (the FSA and the NASBA) and the AAA to form an "independent study group gathering information for formulating strategies to promote the 150-hour education requirement for entry into the CPA profession."[6] The goal of the Commission on Professional Accounting Education, as it was called, was to gather evidence to support the 150-hour requirement and to formulate a strategy to implement it. After eighteen months of study, the nine-member Commission (chaired by Wayne Albers) released two reports in July of 1983. The first presented arguments and evidence for requiring a five-year program; the second presented strategies for generating profession-wide support and getting laws enacted.

The unsurprising conclusions of the Commission were:

> 1. Due to significantly increased knowledge require-
> ments and to a changing accounting profession and
> environment, a baccalaureate accounting program is no
> longer an adequate education for entry into the CPA
> profession. The result is a compelling need to move

forward with the implementation of a postbaccalaureate education requirement.

2. Significant benefits will accrue to society, CPA firms, and individuals entering the profession if a postbaccalaureate education is required.

3. Additional education costs and transitional problems associated with implementing a postbaccalaureate education requirement must be addressed in the implementation process. With careful planning, the effects of these problems can be minimized, thus assuring maximum net benefits.

4. Legislative intervention is appropriate and necessary to accomplish the timely establishment of a post-baccalaureate education as a prerequisite for entry into the CPA profession.[7]

The Commission recommended that the AICPA "should provide the leadership to accomplish legislative enactment of a postbaccalaureate education requirement in all states." It also recommended that a special body be formed to develop and implement a national strategy to get the laws passed, designating key states for top priority and using state societies of CPAs and state boards of accountancy as key organizations in the attack.

The AICPA had its official mandate and, as advised, immediately set up a committee to develop and implement a national strategy. The committee was originally chaired by Robert Ellyson and later by Doyle Williams, dean of the school of accounting at the University of Southern California. The evolutionary processes of the market had failed to bring about demand for five years of higher education, so the AICPA dedicated itself to forcing the five-year program in through legislation.[8] As early as 1981, it had authorized $50,00 a year for the purpose, and now it set up an on-going machinery for the task. At the beginning of 1984 the AICPA exposed a "model accountancy bill" requiring post-baccalaureate education, which it suggested that all states adopt.

Setbacks

Although the campaign to enact five-year legislation in all states picked up steam, the task was not an easy one. Colorado had repealed its law requiring 150-hours in a sunset review in 1981. Florida's law took effect in late 1983, but the accountants' fears that there would be a drop in the supply of recruits and that salaries might increase to unmanageable levels were both soon realized. A total of 2,300 first-time candidates sat for the November 1983 CPA exam in Florida (the last exam at which four-year graduates would be eligible for licensing); in May 1984, the next time the exam was offered, there were only 13. Of course, the 1983 figure was swollen by students who wanted to get in under the wire, and the next set of graduates would take an additional year to emerge. Although 1984 was a dreadful year for recruiters, supply recovered in a couple of years. Still, starting salaries rose far above the national average and stayed there--as much as 10 to 20 percent above. And with all the additional cost, did the quality of recruits improve? The first-time pass rate on the CPA exam rose from 15 to 35 percent, but Florida CPAs were not convinced that graduates had significantly better analytical and communication skills.[9]

Florida CPAs and students found various ways to circumvent the 150-hour obstacle. Many students were hired after four years and then required to complete the fifth year on a part-time basis. Some left Florida to work in other states (one Florida educator reported: "what happens is that a lot of recruiters from the State of Georgia, specifically Atlanta, are coming down to hire the best 4-year graduates..."[10]). Some Florida CPAs looked for students from out of state. A few hired experienced CPAs from other states, although this was not feasible in many cases because out-of-state CPAs did not usually meet Florida's educational requirements.

In 1984 Hawaii eased its five-year requirement, offering an alternate route. Holders of bachelor's degrees could be licenced if they gained four and one-half years of experience instead of the two years required of someone with 150 hours of education.

In Utah there had been constant battle since the 150 hour requirement was passed in 1981. Bills for repeal were introduced annually. Finally, in 1986, the defenders of the law gave up and accepted a compromise. Students with a bachelor's degree plus a year of experience could sit for the exam; they could then obtain a license after three more years of experience. Proponents of the five-year requirement hoped that the cost would prove so high it would discourage anyone from avoiding the five-year program.

The AICPA's cause was not helped by studies that concluded that a master's degree in accounting did not help a student perform better on the CPA exam. One of them showed that, once students had accumulated 30 undergraduate hours of accounting, graduate study added very little to exam scores.[11] Another concluded that, when the effects of differences in personal characteristics were eliminated, postbaccalaureate education "does not consistently improve Exam performance."[12] Its authors went on to argue:

> The effect of PBE [i.e., postbaccalaureate education] on technical competence can also be shown in the hiring practices of CPA firms. If CPA firms perceive PBE candidates to be technically more competent, the profession's demand for PBE candidates should increase. However, since 1976-77, the peak hiring year for PBE candidates, the profession's demand for PBE candidates has decreased 35 percent while the demand for non-PBE candidates has increased 45 percent.[13]

Practitioners were simply not convinced that five years of college education was necessary. A survey of small CPA practitioners in the mid-1970s revealed their belief that, though they favored a very practical education, the "four-year undergraduate program is adequate."[14]

The State of Academia

It was not practitioners, however, who had in the past been the strong line of resistance against the efforts of the AICPA leadership. It had been the academicians who had met the charge of the champions of increased education. In the early 1940s and the early 1960s and the early 1970s, it had been the academicians who had turned back the assaults of the AICPA. Their arguments had essentially been, first, that additional education was unnecessary from a practical sense and, second, that additional education unnecessarily restricted entry into the profession, through additional costs in time and money. If the first part of the argument was an issue of efficiency, the second part of the argument was an issue of morality. The academicians had acted as the conscience of the profession. But there were forces at work which were weakening their ability to continue in that role.

The Cohen Commission in the 1970s identified the forces which were weakening the academic community and making it unable to effectively oppose unethical conduct within the profession.

> One of the roles of the academic arm of a profession is to serve as the profession's conscience. In the past, the academic community failed to provide the intellectual leadership and criticism that might have stimulated corrective action. It appears that the relative estrangement of the two professional communities made it easier for that failure to occur.[15]

The schism between the academicians and practitioners had occurred largely as a result of efforts by academicians to achieve increased status within the broader academic community during the 1960s. This had resulted in a move to quantitative research among status-seeking academicians. It had also resulted in an increasingly cynical belief among those academicians that standards of quality are merely things which are concocted in a purely political process.

That schism and its results were not healed but were actua. aggravated in the late 1970s. A pair of celebrated articles by Ross Watts and Jerold Zimmerman appeared in the *Accounting Review* in 1978 and 1979. Watts and Zimmerman embraced the philosophy of positivism, a philosophy long since weighed and found wanting among many intellectual leaders in other areas of academia. Positivism may be characterized as an imperialistic empiricism. It believes that empirical reality is the only reality.

This "positive" approach stands in direct opposition to a "normative" approach. For positivism, only "what is" matters, and "what should be" does not matter at all--at least not in research. The essense of the theory is that "what is" for business is economic self-interest only. Watts and Zimmerman said,

> [W]e assume that individuals act to maximize their own utility. In doing so, they are resourceful and innovative. The obvious implication of this assumption is that management lobbies on accounting standards based on its own self-interest. ...We assume that management's utility is a positive function of the expected compensation in future periods (or wealth) and a negative function of the dispersion of future compensation (or wealth).[16]

That many business people presumably act entirely in their own economic self-interest is, of course, no great revelation. But the theory went far beyond that. It said that all managers always act in their own economic self-interest, and that such self-interest would explain all of their actions, as future empirical research would prove. Moreover, it subtly implied (as do some economic theories) that such complete self-interest is normal and acceptable (i.e., should be accepted) and is justified as the mechanism by which the invisible hand of a free market works.

In their second article, Watts and Zimmerman fiercely attacked normative notions:

> The literature we commonly call financial accounting theory is predominantly prescriptive. Most writers are concerned with what the contents of published financial statements should be; that is, how firms should account. Yet, it is generally concluded that financial accounting theory has had little substantive, direct impact on accounting practice or policy formulation despite half a century of research. ...Our objective in this paper is to begin building a theory of the determinants of accounting theory. This theory is intended to be a positive theory, that is, a theory capable of explaining the factors determining the extant accounting literature, predicting how research will change as the underlying factors change, and explaining the role of theories in the determination of accounting standards. It is *not* norm-

> ative or prescriptive. ...Understanding why accounting
> theories are as they are requires a theory of the political
> process. We model that process as competition among
> individuals for the use of the coercive power of
> government to achieve wealth transfers.[17]

It was a dark view of human nature which the pair offered. Standards
of behavior in accounting are the result only of a political game
played by people motivated only by love of money, according to this
view. An agent (someone supposed to be acting in someone else's
interest) could only really be controlled by making sure that it is in
the agent's economic self-interest to act properly. Trust could only be
placed in a person's love of money, and seemingly endless contractual
provisions and laws and enforcements are necessary.

The pure epistemological relativism heralded by Demski in the
early 1970s had taken its natural course toward pure moral relativism
by the late 1970s.

Many quantitative researchers found "truth" in the notion of
Watts and Zimmerman (at least so far as it reflected their own
motivations, apparently). Research in economic incentives, under the
name of testing "agency theory," became popular with quantitative
researchers. Soon the approach was extended beyond management as
agents, to public accountants as agents. The assumption was that
public accountants should be expected to act only in their own
economic self-interest, and it was naive and unrealistic to expect
anything else. For such a mind-set, the efforts of the AICPA to
increase the status of the profession, and thereby increase the ability
of professionals to command higher fees, was not at all surprising nor
anything to get excited about. The political games of the AICPA did
not appear to adversely affect the economic well-being of such
academicians, so how could it be of anything but academic interest to
them? Indeed, it was possible that requiring another full year of
education for all accounting students could actually economically
benefit established academicians.

By the early 1980s, quantitative research had largely conquered
accounting academia. It had a deadening effect on accounting
education. Discussion of the great issues affecting accounting
education did not appear in the prestige journals. An extremely rare
event occurred when, in 1983, the *Accounting Review* published a

discussion article on the five-year education requirement. The author was allowed to express the opinion that the issue should be left up to the market to decide, and he thought the five-year requirement was a bad idea because it provided little additional benefit at considerable additional cost. Before he was allowed to express this opinion, however, the author had to meet the standards for incoherence prevailing among the prestige journals. He explained the reason for the five-year movement thusly:

> In an environment characterized by information asymmetry, the high-productivity types [of education suppliers] have an economic incentive to identify themselves. ...The effectiveness of a signal as a discriminator of quality classes rests on a critical signal characteristic. The cost of the signal must dissuade low-productivity types from falsely providing the signal (adverse selection). In other words, there must be a negative correlation between the cost of the signal and the unobservable quality characteristic. Two types of signaling satisfy this criterion, contingent contracts and exogenously costly signals.... Contingent contracts require the labor supplier to self-select into quality classes that are bound by employment contracts. These contracts provide for an employer-induced penalty on those individuals who overstate their quality by selecting the wrong quality class. ...A problem develops, however, when the suppliers do not possess perfect information about their own skills, but have some residual uncertainty. ...If contingent contracting produces excessive risk sharing, the suppliers may then choose exogenously costly signals as an alternative information medium. This type of signal does not require employer action to be effective, but relies on the cost structure of the signal itself....[18]

Prestige research journals were simply not interested in the major issues of accounting education--except, apparently, when a writer was able to display an astounding facility with jargon when writing about it.

Communication within the academic community had largely come to a halt. A survey published in 1983 regarding readership of the *Accounting Review* showed that accounting practitioners simply did not read it and accounting educators who did read it considered its typical main article to be "boring, abstract, irrelevant, meaningless, not readable, inappropriate, vague, trivial, unrewarding, and useless, but of high quality."[19] "Quality," according to some of the comments, appears to have something to do with the conferral of prestige. The perceptions of teachers, naturally, were somewhat more negative than the perceptions of researchers. There was a clear desire for more relevant and less mathematical articles.

Accounting academicians wanting intelligent discussion of educational issues were wandering a barren land. The AICPA lost interest in the substance of accounting education as it focused solely on the five-year program. The AICPA's *Journal of Accountancy* had carried a regular education department, which had been a useful outlet for ideas on education, but the department was dropped in 1976, and by the 1980s the journal's attention to education had been reduced to little more than brief news articles.

There was some involvement by the AAA with educational issues in the late 1970s because large public accounting firms were contributing large amounts of money for academic research, in order to prove that they were truly concerned about quality education. In 1979 the AAA published a 234-page report on a survey of "leading accounting educators and practitioners" about what accounting topics they thought were most important in a curriculum.[20] Also published in 1979 was a monograph in which it was argued that the views of the Swiss psychologist, Jean Piaget, on the development of thinking skills should be applicable to accounting education.[21] In 1980, two more monographs were published. There was a review of innovative teaching methods, such as the use of modules, computers, case studies, simulations, and so on.[22] There was also a report on a survey of accounting practitioners and academicians about what communication skills were important, how important they were in terms of effects, and what was being done and could be done in education to improve those skills.[23] Apparently, that was when the money dried up. The impact of this brief period of education research was slight.

Some accounting educators were becoming more and more starved for discussion of accounting education. They finally received some satisfaction in 1983 when Ralph L. Benke, Jr., at James Madison University, began publishing a semi-annual journal called the *Journal of Accounting Education*. In response, the AAA, seeing that its policy of ignoring accounting education had given rise to competition, brought out a journal of its own titled *Issues in Accounting Education*. When it began in 1983 it was published only annually, but in 1986 it became semi-annual. Those who cared about accounting education had now at last some ways to communicate with each other.

Getting the AAA into Line

Academicians, starved and weak, were just beginning to find their way out of the desert. But what was important from the AICPA's view was that they had still not fallen into line behind the AICPA in its campaign for the five-year program. Nor, for that matter, had practitioners. A high-ranking partner in one of the Big Eight public accounting firms still held to the most venerable position of the practitioner: the real education of accountants began when they began the job, and a good four-year college education was plenty good enough to prepare them for that.

> Most of the baccalaureate students perform very well at the entry level. However, it is at this level that what I call their clinical education begins. Much of the knowledge they obtained from books and course work takes on new meaning when applied in the field.... The top accounting students enter the profession generally well prepared with technical knowledge. However, the degree of conceptual knowledge and communication skills they possess varies depending, in part, on the strength of the university programs they attended.[24]

The fact is that the AICPA and its followers were waging a lonely battle. A survey of CPA practitioners in the early 1980s revealed that 65 percent preferred a four- rather than a five-year program. Among accounting educators, 35 percent favored a four-year program, 44 percent a five-year program, while 21 percent were undecided.[25] While the AAA leadership favored five years of education, it did not believe that a fifth year should be required. The AACSB flatly opposed a mandatory five-year program.[26] Although the AICPA leadership could apparently ignore the practitioners it supposedly represented, it desperately needed to get academicians to support legislation if it were to have any hope of implementing a national five-year program.

In 1984 the AAA executive committee led by Doyle Williams appointed the Committee on the Future Structure, Content, and Scope of Accounting Education, chaired by Norton Bedford of the University of Illinois. Bedford had been a member of the AICPA's long-range planning committee in the late 1950s and early 1960s, and the Bedford Report which came out in early 1986 had the musty smell of that by-gone era, without any freshening from the events that had occurred in the intervening quarter-century. Indeed, the impression it gave was that it was written in 1961 and perfumed with two references to two reports on higher education from the early 1980s and with the scattered insertion of terms used in those reports. The idea which had caused all the confusion in the 1960s--the notion of accounting as an all-inclusive information system function--was still present and pre-eminent:

> This Committee foresees the continuing emergence of an accounting profession that will provide information for economic and social decisions, using sophisticated measurement and communication technologies applied to a substantially enlarged scope of phenomena. ...Accountants must know how to design and diagnose comprehensive information systems for all types and sizes of organizations. ...Accounting should be viewed as a broad economic information development and distribution process, based on the design, implementation, and operation of multiple types of information systems....[27]

The appeal for change in education was based on change in the profession, but when the Report moved beyond stirring generalization, the examples of the tasks the profession was performing sounded very much like the ones they had been performing for decades. Vague generalizations were all the Report relied upon for its validity; no references were made to studies showing accounting education to be inadequate in practice nor were references made to anything at all. Claims were merely asserted. Likewise, suggestions for improvement seemed to come from nowhere; there were no references to studies showing that these suggestions would improve accounting education. The Report was an extended editorial--a discussion piece of some interest. William Shenkir, a member of the Committee, said, "The recommendations are intended and are purposely written to be very general, in hopes that they will provide more of a policy direction for accounting faculties."[28]

The Bedford Committee included two members who were also members of the AICPA's Future Issues Committee, a committee formed in 1982 that favored expansion of the services and products of public accounting. These two, according to Shenkir, "brought to the committee all of the work that had been done by that body over the last several years. So the Report's overall conclusions certainly were influenced by that future issues study."[29] In every sense of the term, the Report was redundant and Shenkir himself admitted that there was nothing new in it.

As a piece of scholarly work the Bedford Report was not impressive, but the impact it had upon the academic community was impressive. It was a semi-official AAA report, and it contained the one specific statement the AICPA needed to turn the tide with academicians:

> Specialized professional accounting education should be offered only at the graduate level. Thus, a complete curriculum covering all three levels of education [i.e., general education, general professional accounting education, and specialized professional accounting education] will normally take a minimum of five years.[30]

Of course, the Report only said that five years was needed *for the sake of specialization*. The AICPA expressed disappointment over that.[31] Its primary concern was not specialization, but the five-year requirement. Still, after all, the words "five years" were there, and if the Report only justified the five years in terms of specialization, it served the Institute's immediate needs. If specialization were necessary, then five years were necessary.

When explaining their Report, Bedford and Shenkir suggested that general education should take *two to four years*, while general accounting education should take two years, and specialized accounting education should take one year.[32] Here was the possibility that accounting could gradually increase the general education requirements, just as legal education had, until accounting required three years of post-graduate education, just as law does. At any rate, the fact that the Bedford Report advocated comprehensive change in accounting education and spoke favorably of a five-year program, was enough for the AICPA to hail the Report as a significant achievement for accounting education. The change process can be steered, after all.

The Bedford Report sparked discussion in the educational community and, if the points were not really new, they were at least being voiced again. A conference in April of 1986, for example, discussed the issues the Report had once again raised. One presenter said that four years were enough and accreditation was a bad idea because it fostered uniformity; it was better to let the market decide. Another attacked the market arguments, saying that the market should not be relied upon when the safety of the public was at stake. Another argued that the research doctorate was not appropriate for everyone, and a teaching doctorate should also be offered and be considered acceptable; respondents pointed out that most doctoral students prefer to teach, so, if they were not forced to do research instead, many good researchers would never develop their talents. Much discussion centered around letting the market decide rather than forcing a five-year program on students, and most discussants appeared to prefer the market approach. One educator made the following trenchant comment:

> I've heard practitioners talk a lot about wanting students who are able to analyze problems that they have not seen before and make reasonable judgments about those problems. And after arguing with them a great deal about what kind of student they want, I discovered that many are looking at the 5-year program really as a MBA

equivalent in the following sense. They would prefer to hire MBAs who are from good MBA programs with accounting concentrations and have liberal arts background as an undergraduate. But they can't afford them because those people go for at least 150% of what accountants pay. They're not going to pay...what the good MBA students get now.[33]

The AICPA Breaks through the Defenses

While the academicians argued, the AICPA pressed its assault. The AICPA's Special Committee on Standards of Professional Conduct for Certified Public Accountants, appointed in October 1983 and chaired by George Anderson, issued its report in the Spring of 1986. Its last three paragraphs contain the extent of the Committee's comments with regard to higher education. They read:

> The expanding scope of services and the expanding body of knowledge that CPAs must master require that the Institute take action to assure that the profession will have an adequate supply of entrants with a sound educational base to meet future demands.
>
> The Institute has vigorously promoted the 150-hour postbaccalaureate education program as a basic requirement for entering the profession. Progress toward that goal has been slow; only three jurisdictions (Florida, Hawaii, and Utah) have adopted such programs as requirements, and only a few other jurisdictions have taken positive steps toward the goal. The prospect of its becoming a national requirement on a timely basis is highly uncertain without more positive and direct action by the Institute to make its policy an educational reality.
>
> Therefore, the committee recommends that the Institute take appropriate action before the year 2000 to adopt the 150-hour postbaccalaureate education requirement as a condition for membership in the Institute for those qualifying for entry into the profession after that year. Such a commitment by the Institute would send a

forceful signal not only to the licensing bodies but also
to the institutions of higher education concerned with
developing acceptable education programs. Such a commitment by the Institute would enable those institutions
to mobilize the necessary resources to establish the
required programs and to develop the required facilities
and faculties for that purpose.[34]

Using this report as its mustering site, the AICPA in 1987 launched
its greatest offensive. Like many aggressors, however, it portrayed its
offense as a defense.

The profession had just endured two years of Congressional
investigation arising from the accusation that auditors had failed to
warn investors of impending bank failures in the early 1980s. In a
survey of its members, the AICPA found that 80 percent believed that
"the reported extent of substandard audits warrants professional
action," that "the threat of government regulation is likely," and that
"greater self-regulation was the best response to the threat of
government regulation."[35] The fear of practitioners that the
government might impose unwanted rules provided an opportunity for
the AICPA to promote the five-year education requirement as at least
a partial solution to the problem.

Six recommendations of the Anderson Committee were packaged
as proposed amendments to the Institute's by-laws. The last of the six
was that anyone becoming a member of the AICPA after the year
2000 must have 150 hours of higher education. In 1987 the AICPA,
celebrating its centennial with the theme, "A Century of Progress in
Accounting," publicized the six proposals as a fitting symbol of that
progress. It said the proposals were "for the members and by the
members" in "the pursuit of excellence" and it urged the members to
"vote excellence."

The vote was scheduled for November. The October issue of the
Journal of Accountancy strongly urged members to vote for all of the
proposals. Its discussion of the 150-hour requirement was the briefest
of the six. The AICPA's August newsletter described the sixth
proposal obliquely as "Expanded educational requirements for future
candidates for AICPA membership." As the last and most briefly
discussed proposal, it seemed almost hidden.

AICPA members were given the option of voting for each proposal individually or they could vote for all of them together by checking only one box. Most took the easy way and checked the single box. In February of 1988 the AICPA announced that all the proposals had been overwhelmingly approved.

Five dissident AICPA members brought suit over the "tainted ballot" on the grounds that the ballot itself had favored approval of the proposals.[36] More than three years later the AICPA was forced to settle with the dissidents. From then on, when there was more than one item to be voted on, each item would be voted on separately. Also, both pro and con sides would be presented, rather than just the pro side as on the 1988 ballot. Furthermore, the AICPA was forced to join in establishing a fund to finance the study of ethics in business.[37]

After the vote, some academicians also grumbled over the sneak attack of voting for all proposals at once. Moreover, the National Conference of CPA Practitioners (representing smaller practitioners) opposed the 150-hour requirement, claiming that "a year of practical experience in an accounting firm is superior for an accountant's development to another academic year."[38] The organization was also influential in soliciting funds for the dissidents' suit.

But the lines had been broken. It was a brilliant and daring, if deceitful, strategic move, and the AICPA war machine was now rolling over everything in its path. In the summer of 1988, the AAA executive committee capitulated and became collaborators with the AICPA in working for the 150-hour requirement. At the same time the executive committee empowered itself for the first time "to speak on behalf of the AAA on 'academically relevant matters.'"[39]

In a mopping-up action in February of 1988, the AICPA issued a revision of the Albers Report of a decade earlier. The point of that exercise was simply to restate the AICPA's 150-hour policy; no significant changes were made to it. The only changes were in the "illustrative program" which suggested that general education be 60-80 hours (rather than just the 60 in the old Albers Report), that general business education be 35-50 hours (rather than 36-39), and that accounting education be *reduced* to 25-40 (rather than 39). The revised Albers Report did not specify hours for specific subjects, as the old Report had, but it was clear that, from the AICPA's perspective, the five-year program was not really for the purpose of increasing accounting specialization much (if any) beyond the approximately 30 hours required in an undergraduate program.

The AICPA 150-hour requirement was only a requirement for membership in the AICPA. A CPA need not be a member of the AICPA in order to practice.[40] It is the state legislatures and boards of accountancy who determine the educational requirements for CPAs to practice in their states. If the states would not require 150 hours, the AICPA requirement would result only in the drying up and blowing away of the AICPA (unless, as it obviously would do, it voted to change its entrance requirement). This distinction between an AICPA membership requirement and a state practice requirement, however, was deliberately obscured. The 150-hour requirement was presented in terms of a "done deal" and state legislatures and boards of accountancy were pressured to get on board, because the train was leaving the station.

The states began to get on board. In 1987 Tennessee passed a law requiring 150 hours to go into effect April 14, 1993. In the spring of 1989 150-hour requirements were passed by Alabama (effective January 1, 1995), Montana (effective July 1, 1997), and West Virginia (effective July 1, 2000) in the first year in which such laws were proposed in those states. Texas failed to pass the law in 1987 because of the opposition of a group of university professors, but passed in the spring of 1989 a law requiring 150 hours and no less than 42 hours in accounting, to go into effect after August 31, 1997. In 1990 came Kansas (effective June 30, 1997), Kentucky (effective January 1, 2000), Mississippi (effective February 1, 1995), Louisiana (effective December 31, 1996), and Arkansas (effective January 1, 1998). In 1991 came Nebraska (effective January 1, 1998), Georgia (effective January 1, 1998), South Carolina (effective July 1, 1997), Alaska (effective September 1, 1997), and Illinois (effective January 1, 2001). In 1992, South Dakota (effective January 1, 1998), Indiana (effective January 1, 2000), Ohio (effective January 1, 2000), Iowa (effective January 1, 2001), Connecticut (effective January 1, 2000), and Rhode Island (effective July 1, 1999) required 150 hours, and in 1993 Wyoming (effective January 1, 2000), North Dakota (effective January 1, 2000), Idaho (effective July 1, 2000), Maryland (effective July 1, 1999), Missouri (effective July 1, 1999), and Nevada (effective January 1, 2001) passed the requirement. By the summer of

1993, 30 states had passed laws which would require 150 hours of education to practice as CPAs in their states.

Resistance to the requirement was beginning to build, however. In 1992, California refused to pass the requirement. Also, the Rev. Jesse Jackson, president and founder of the National Rainbow Coalition, urged the AICPA to withdraw its support for the 150-hour law, saying that such a law "will greatly impede the potential for African-American and other minority students to successfully pursue careers in the field of accounting."[41] By the spring of 1993 fifteen states had rejected the law, and Florida was the only state to have fully implemented an undiluted 150-hour requirement.[42] The Coalition Against Restrictive Entry into the CPA Profession (CARE CPA) had formed to lobby legislatures and was running advertisements publicizing the following facts:

> Experience in Florida, the only state where the model law is currently implemented, reveals that because of the law's restrictive nature, **first-time** applicants for the CPA Exam have **decreased 56%** from 1,862 in 1980 (four years before the implementation of the law) to 824 in 1991. This occurred despite a 33% increase in the state population over the same period.
>
> In addition, Hawaii saw a **47% reduction in total** exam candidates from 764 in 1977 (two years before implementation) to 404 in 1981. As a result, in 1981 the Hawaii legislature amended the law to include a four-year degree track where students could substitute additional work experience for the fifth year of college. Currently, about 90% of those passing the CPA Exam in Hawaii opt for the four-year track.[43]

The Coalition pointed out that the model law of the AICPA required no additional accounting courses (and that the AICPA preferred that additional courses be in the liberal arts). The deduction followed: if there were no additional accounting courses and there were 50% fewer students, many accounting professors would lose their jobs and many smaller colleges would stop offering accounting.

Whether there would be fewer accounting courses was not clear, however.[44] State legislatures and boards of accountancy have to have some good reasons to require additional education of accounting students, and the best reason is that those students should learn more accounting. Some of the states were requiring additional accounting education in the laws they passed. Florida and Utah were requiring 36 hours of accounting beyond the elementary accounting courses, for example. Other states did not require much accounting; Hawaii, for example required only 18 hours in accounting. These varying requirements mean that someone who could practice in one state might not be able to practice in another--even if both states required 150 hours. The issue of reciprocity would become a nightmare. The AICPA is desperately attempting to achieve uniformity among the states, but has not yet been noticably successful.

It is not yet certain that the 150-hour requirement will stick, even though over half the states have passed it. Legislatures can repeal laws and the AICPA can vote to change its membership requirement--particularly if the requirement proves too hurtful to students and to the CPA firms who need to hire those students.

The danger that the profession might have trouble attracting students is exacerbated by the reluctance of CPA firms to pay five-year graduates any more than they paid four-year graduates. In discussing the issues it faced with the 150-hour requirement, one of the largest firms said:

> Another potential effect on the firm may be pressures to increase starting compensation, since traditionally, accounting students with advanced degrees receive higher starting salaries than those with bachelor's degrees. Our belief is that increased compensation to individuals should result from the increased value (i.e., expanded personal and technical skills and abilities) they bring to the firm; it should not result solely from the fact that they took a longer academic program or received an additional degree. In the long run, we believe better-qualified students will command higher salaries and those salaries, in turn, will attract the highest caliber students to the profession.[45]

How students will respond to the message that a longer academic program is necessary but that a longer academic program should not of itself command additional compensation is problematic.

A major partner in one of the largest accounting firms was asked if the profession could attract the best and brightest; his response was:

> There's clearly a risk that we won't be able to. And we're worried about whether high school kids will go into accounting or into medicine or engineering instead.
>
> The 150-hour rule makes it tougher for us to get there. I'm personally not a proponent of 150 hours. I'd rather find the time once they join us to educate them. Let us decide what they need, and we'll give them the continuing education.
>
> We can do it better than the universities. We'd like our people to be broad-based worldly people. Business is global and we need people that can understand a global stage. We'll give them the accounting, we'll give them the audit and tax skills, because we can do that better.
>
> I'm disappointed at the trend. It hasn't affected us yet, but we're going to try to be ahead of the curve on this.[46]

In spite of it all, the AICPA sounds confident that its war has resulted in victory. Already in the summer of 1989, the new AICPA vice president for education pronounced the debate ended:

> The issue of postbaccalaureate education to become CPAs has been debated since the 1950s, with a great deal of discussion during the 1970s. But now, since the Institute's membership referendum last year, the issue has been settled. This overwhelmingly favorable vote has set aside the debates and convinced everybody that the 150-hour requirement will happen.[47]

The Response of the Academicians

With its 1988 vote, the AICPA seemed to have silenced debate. Small practitioners had little opportunity to express themselves. Academicians had a bit more freedom of expression, but they appeared to be overpowered by the practitioners for the first time in decades. In spite of their long-standing opposition to requiring (rather than simply encouraging) a five-year education, hardly a peep was heard from them.

The AICPA designed seminars for academicians to discuss the 150-hour rule. As it did in the 1970s, it instructed seminar leaders to side-step the issue of *whether* there should be a 150-hour rule and to focus on *how to* implement the 150-hour rule. This approach had not worked against the academicians of the 1970s, but it appeared to be successful against the more malleable academicians of the 1980s and 1990s. Academicians, along with many small practitioners, resigned themselves to the apparent fact that the AICPA had won, and they worked busily on how to best do the AICPA's bidding. They did this by focusing uncritically on the Bedford Report.

In 1989 the AAA published in book form the reports of three committees which had been formed to carry on the work that the Bedford Committee had inspired. The three reports were from the Professorial Environment Committee, which gathered numerous statistics and data on the professorate; the Changes in Accounting Education Committee, which gathered numerous statistics and data on trends in accounting education; and the Follow-Up Committee on the Future Structure, Content, and Scope of Accounting Education, which dealt with main issues. Actually, there were two follow-up committees, one "following up" on the other. The purpose of the committees was apparently to gather evidence to support the opinion piece the Bedford Committee had turned out.

The first follow-up committee, in reporting on its investigation through survey and discussion, noted that Bedford's ideas were now popular and

> Strong support apparently exists for changing the scope
> of accounting education from the traditional transaction
> model to that of a broad economic information

developmental model. However, evidence suggests that this change will be difficult to achieve.[48]

The committee also noted:

> It appears that the academicians and practitioners agree that a more structured approach to the selection of liberal arts and sciences courses is advisable, that more general business knowledge is desirable, that a broad base of general professional accounting education is essential, and that specialized professional accounting areas should be a part of a student's education. Combining all of these elements of an education, the academicians and practitioners conclude that a minimum of five years of education is required.[49]

The committee did note that although support for the five-year program was not universal, a majority now supported it. The committee recommended that the AAA should take a firm stand on the need for a five-year program, and so did the second follow-up committee. Doubtless it was these committee recommendations which caused the AAA to reverse itself and begin supporting the five-year requirement. The second follow-up committee also recommended that the AAA executive council assume a leadership role and become a "powerful champion" of restructuring.

Part of the restructuring, they thought, should involve the role of teaching:

1. Doctoral programs should require a seminar in teaching methodology.
2. All existing faculty members should participate in a workshop on teaching methodology.
3. Outstanding teaching should be recognized in the same way as outstanding research and publishing.[50]

The pious wishes of the committee to improve accounting education through improved teaching had little to do with reality, however. A report on a survey of accounting faculty and business school deans noted that emphasis on research had risen significantly in promotion and tenure decisions over the preceding twenty years, while emphasis on teaching had declined significantly. The future seemed to hold more of the same.

> At doctorate-granting institutions, faculty expect a small decline in the importance assigned to teaching while deans expect a modest increase. At nondoctorate-granting institutions, both faculty and deans anticipate a decrease in the emphasis placed on teaching; the faculty anticipate the magnitude of the decline to be greater than do the deans.
>
> As to research, faculty and deans at both types of institutions expect a marked increase in emphasis by 1995. Faculty at nondoctorate-granting institutions, however, expect significantly more emphasis on research than do those at doctorate-granting institutions.[51]

A later study bore out these expectations. It found that deans and accounting program heads in AACSB-accredited schools place more emphasis on research and less on teaching than do administrators associated with non-accredited programs.[52]

The Big Eight Bring Money

Some of the AAA's second follow-up committee recommendations and comments were influenced by another important event which took place in 1989. In April, the "Big Eight" public accounting firms (which were much larger than any second-tier firms) issued a 15-page "white paper" report entitled *Perspectives on Education: Capabilities for Success in the Accounting Profession*. Never before had they acted in such a unified way on accounting education and, as the employers who dominated public accounting, their words dominated the discussion. But it was not just their words which caught everyone's attention; they promised up to $4 million over five years "to support the development of stimulating and relevant curricula."

The paper applauded the Bedford Report and its follow-up committees. It was issued because:

The accounting profession faces a unique convergence of forces, which creates a critical need to re-examine the educational process.

* The profession is changing, expanding and, as a result, becoming increasingly complex.
* Declining enrollments in accounting programs indicate that the profession is becoming less attractive to students.
* Implementation of the AICPA requirement of 150 hours of education for membership by the year 2000 must be addressed.[53]

The paper made no effort to argue the rightness of the 150-hour requirement; instead, it took the high road of focusing on educational quality rather than quantity. It was particularly concerned with curriculum but did not focus "on specific course content or the number of hours in the curriculum, but on the capabilities needed by the profession that should be developed through the educational process." It listed the skills necessary for public accounting as communication skills, intellectual skills, and interpersonal skills. It also detailed the knowledge needed for public accounting. First was general knowledge, which covered the following factors:

* An understanding of the flow of events in history and the different cultures in today's world.
* The ability to interact with diverse groups of people and at the highest levels of intellectual exchange.
* A sense of the breadth of ideas, issues and contrasting economic, political and social forces in the world.
* Experience in making value judgments.

The general education component of university education should...leave the student excited about, and prepared for, lifelong learning.[54]

With respect to organizational and business knowledge, the paper said,

> To understand their clients' and their own work environments, public accountants must have an understanding of the economic, social, cultural and psychological forces that affect organizations. They must also understand the basic internal workings of organizations and be able to apply this knowledge to specific examples. This requires an understanding of interpersonal and group dynamics.
>
> Given the rapid pace of change in the business world, public accountants must understand the methods for creating and managing change in organizations. The professional environment is also characterized by rapidly increasing dependence on technological support. No understanding of organizations could be complete without attention to the current and future roles of information technology in client organizations and accounting practice.[55]

With regard to accounting and auditing knowledge, the paper said,

> Post-secondary education should provide a strong fundamental understanding of accounting and auditing. This includes the history of the accounting profession and accounting thought, as well as the content, concepts, structure and meaning of reporting for organizational operations both for internal and external use. A companion area includes the methods for gathering, summarizing and analyzing financial data. Entering practitioners must also understand the meaning and application of, as well as the methodology for, attest services.
>
> Accounting knowledge cannot focus solely on the construction of data. The ability to apply decision rules embodied in the accounting model is only a part of the

goal. Accountants must be able to use the data, exercise judgments, evaluate risks and solve real-world problems.

Passing the CPA examination should not be the goal of accounting education. The focus should be on developing analytical and conceptual thinking--versus memorizing rapidly expanding professional standards.[56]

The paper's most far-reaching recommendation was to form a coordinating committee (which would include representatives from the AICPA, AAA, AACSB, NASBA, FEI, NAA, and the "big eight" firms) "to guide the academic community in re-engineering the curriculum." The AAA should take the leadership role in this committee, according to the paper.

The Accounting Education Change Commission

At its April 1989 meeting the AAA executive committee authorized the organization of an Accounting Education Change Commission. The 16-member Commission, operating under the oversight of the AAA but given significant autonomy, was chaired by Doyle Williams and also had a full-time executive director. The Commission was charged to

* Act as a forum for the identification, examination, and discussion of issues related to academic preparation of future accounting professionals.
* Provide a focal point for learning, assimilating, and synthesizing the interests, concerns, and priorities of the various parties at interest with respect to higher education in accounting and prospective changes thereto.
* Serve as a catalyst to bring about demonstrable improvements in the education of accountants through curriculum restructuring, alternative education processes, development of new and different education materials, different utilization

of faculty resources, and new and different ways of
educating future accounting faculty.[57]

It was also to distribute grants, exercise oversight over the grants, and
disseminate the results of the grants. With four million dollars in its
pocket, the Commission quickly became the focal point of accounting
education thought.

The first meeting of the Commission was held September 8,
1989.

> The commission agreed that changes in accounting
> education will not come easily. Among the impediments
> to change identified by the commission are university
> constraints, professional examinations, accreditation,
> faculty standards/reward structures, recruiting practices,
> institutional inertia, publishers, and the focus of Ph.D.
> programs. The commission will attempt to break down
> impediments without jeopardizing the positive influences
> of many of these same items.[58]

By mid-November the Commission had issued a request for
proposals. It specified that its grants would be for *implementing*
changes, not for studying them, and proposals for comprehensive
changes in the curriculum were preferred to those addressing only
portions of the curriculum.

In early 1990, the Commission announced grants to five
universities totalling nearly one million dollars. Brigham Young
University was conducting a survey to learn what competencies were
important, and planned to redesign its curriculum according to what it
learned. It learned that many of the competencies "deal with students
understanding how to find, organize, and use information to address
complex reporting and recording problems."[59] Accounting content in
courses would be used to instill the desired competencies rather than
as an end in itself. Courses would also feature interactive learning
tools and case-oriented teaching.

Kansas State's proposal was primarily concerned with sequencing
logically (i.e., simple to complex) the content of the accounting
curriculum. The University of Massachusetts at Amherst proposed to
do three things: develop a networked classroom which employed an

actual company's data base for hands-on learning; develop an accounting survey course stressing concepts and social effects; and develop a communications module emphasizing both written and oral communications.

The University of North Texas proposed to integrate the business and accounting curriculum with the liberal arts, by using its existing "classic learning core" (using the learning themes of virtue, civility, and reason, and adding one called accountability), having accounting faculty attend the regular meetings of the faculty who teach that core, and continuing the themes into the accounting courses (and the early accounting courses would have a user orientation rather than a preparer orientation, so that non-accounting students could profit from them). North Texas also planned to structure business and accounting courses together in related clusters. The proposal of Rutgers University likewise was concerned with integrating business and accounting subjects, this time in the MBA program. Topics of different disciplines would be broken down into basic units and then brought together in a coherent framework; this was called an "information/decision module focus." Rutgers also proposed a pervasive socialization process with an initial "unfreezing" period, followed by a "change" period, and ending in a "refreezing" period.

When the Change Commission announced the winners, it also announced a second round with proposals due December 1, 1990. In January 1991, these winners were announced.

Arizona State plans a major revision of its accounting core courses. The goal is to create an environment in which students are active participants in learning and where they develop the ability and motivation for life-long learning. A laboratory science model of instruction will be used to provide an information systems foundation for upper-division accounting courses.

Chicago focuses on a user orientation in an MBA curriculum. Its program is aimed at highly sophisticated users of accounting information. It will emphasize the use of information, but will also have enough technical content that users develop a full understanding of the conventions underlying the preparation of internal and external accounting reports.

In a joint project, Illinois and Notre Dame will develop a curriculum designed to make students become critical thinkers and to take an active role in the learning process. Using a contracting framework, the program will integrate the accounting curriculum with general education requirements and with general business courses. The faculty will design a system to incorporate both technological features of the practice environment and research findings into classroom materials.

North Carolina A&T will emphasize the enhancement of professional awareness, the development of problem-solving skills, the improvement of communication, interpersonal, and leadership skills, and the promotion of computer-reliance. A highlight of their project is a program to establish student-mentor relationships.

The McIntire School at the University of Virginia will shift its focus from the narrow objective of preparing students for the CPA exam to the broader objective of producing graduates who have the capabilities that are necessary for ultimate success as an accounting professional. Through the use of cases, accounting classes will explore a limited number of topics in depth, so that students can develop a thorough understanding of the principles involved. This will allow an emphasis on developing basic capabilities and communication and interpersonal skills.[60]

It is clear from the summary that the schools involved have mastered the jargon required to receive grants from the Commission, but it remains to be seen whether any real changes will result from this heavy investment of funds (though it is refreshing to see that at least one school will finally stop being a CPA-exam mill and will become interested in principles of accounting). Furthermore, the Commission has spent the bulk of its money, and it remains to be seen what impact it can have without that carrot.

It has tried to keep the issues alive. It established task forces to target specific issues. Its Regulatory Issues and Professional Examinations task force, for example, has used its influence to support two positions for state accountancy laws: that accounting requirements be met by either 24 hours of undergraduate or 15 hours of graduate-level accounting courses (rather than 24 hours regardless), and that students not be allowed to take the CPA exam during their last term in school (thereby disrupting their academic studies). The Commission's Faculty Incentives task force publicized a statement urging a higher priority for teaching, and drafted an issues statement on evaluating and rewarding effective teaching which was issued in 1993. The Accreditation task force attempted to persuade the AACSB that Ph.D. programs should have training in teaching and that the AACSB's idea of exempting the undergraduate introductory accounting course from accounting accreditation was a mistake and would result in lowered quality in that course.

The AECC has maintained a high level of visibility. Its original executive director, Gary Sundem, was elected president of the AAA for the 1992-1993 year. Commission members have participated in numerous presentations and articles. Williams, chairman of the AECC, has begun trying to ascribe mystical qualities to the popular teaching innovations by calling them "the new age accounting curriculum." In 1992 the AECC issued a position statement on the first course in accounting, stressing its importance and objectives. It also issued an issues statement on the importance of two-year colleges for accounting education, and it made curriculum-development grants to two community colleges.

In 1993 the Big Six (formerly the Big Eight) accounting firms announced that they were contributing another one million dollars to the AECC in order to allow it to follow up its previous work. No more grants would be made, but there would be the dissemination of results of previous grants. The money would also allow the AECC to work with the AAA on faculty and program development, for which purpose the AAA also received a half-million dollars from the Big Six. It was presumed that the AECC would wind down its work by the fall of 1996, and its work would be taken over by the AAA.

Onward (and Upward?)

What the end of all such efforts will be cannot be told. There is an apparently wide-spread interest in improving accounting education. This is certainly not all due to the efforts of the AECC. Before the AECC came into existence, for example, a book was published which revolutionized the thinking of accounting academicians about management accounting. In 1987 Thomas Johnson and Robert Kaplan said that management accounting as taught by university professors was irrelevant and even harmful to real businesses. They identified what they believed were the causes and the results of the problem.

> We believe the academics were led astray by a simplified model of firm behavior. ...Sixty years of literature emerged advocating the separation of costs into fixed and variable components for making good product decisions and for controlling costs. This literature, very persuasive when illustrated in the simple one-product settings used by academic economists and accountants, never fully addressed the question of where fixed costs came from and how these costs needed to be covered by each of the products in the corporations' repertoire. Nor did the academic researchers attempt to implement their ideas in the environment of actual organizations, with hundreds or thousands of products and with complex, multistage production processes. Thus, the academic literature concentrated on increasingly elegant and sophisticated approaches to analyzing cost for single-product, single-process firms while actual organizations attempted to manage with antiquated systems in settings that had little relationship to the simplified model researchers assumed for analytic and teaching convenience.[61]

This book was a wake-up call to academicians in managerial accounting, the field in which "rigorous" research had supposedly begun and flourished. It was a call to return to reality, and it generated an impressive movement toward "activity-based costing."

Johnson and Kaplan's critique of academic accounting, combined with the work of the AECC, produced a climate in which intelligent discussion of the broad vision of accounting education was once again respectable. A particularly impressive discussion of the issues by Stephen Zeff was published in 1989. He first identified the weaknesses in accounting education.

> Beginning with the textbook for the first financial accounting course and continuing through the intermediate and advanced accounting textbooks, the subject [of accounting] is offered as if a tedious catalogue of practice were being inputted into computer memory. Accounting is not presented as an *interesting* subject that figures importantly in the calculations of managers, investors and creditors, and government policy makers but instead as a collection of rules that are to be memorized in an uncritical, almost unthinking way. Typically, a problem facing the profession's practitioners is asserted (not argued), the official solution is exposited, journal entries and sample financial statements illustrating the official solution are presented, and the students are then put through the hoops of numerical problems that test their capacity to apply the official solution to hypothetical situations. Authors do not ask why the problem arose, why the official solution was preferred over alternatives (and what were the alternatives?), and whether the official solution spawned any further problems. More often than not, at least in the textbooks, the official solution is not even subjected to evaluation or criticism.[62]

Zeff identified as the causes of this sad situation (1) a concern with getting students to pass the practice- and rule-oriented CPA exam and (2) "a climate of conformity in the United States which encourages the belief that current accounting standards constitute the final word on the subject."[63] Zeff accused accounting educators of abdicating their leadership position to the standard-setters, and called for them to decide what should be taught rather than letting the CPA exam writers and standard-setters determine the content. He listed the qualities he considered essential to a good accounting education.

Above all, a historical perspective is essential. When learning a subject, a student's natural curiosity turns to the origins of thought and practice. In this way, one proceeds from the simpler to the complex, from the past to the present, establishing relevance and stimulating interest in the phenomena under study. Yet one is unable to find a single financial accounting textbook--introductory, intermediate, or advanced--that purports to explain the historical source of present-day accounting thought or practice. ...

Another desirable quality is the interpolation of nonaccounting factors that have influenced the development of accounting practice. This quality is related to that of historical perspective, but it focuses on contemporary influences. Standard setters are acutely sensitive to the fact that their agenda of issues, as well as the roll call of possible solutions to accounting problems, is buffeted by the diverse and changing self-interests of managers, government policy makers, and auditing firms. Yet I suspect that the vast majority of accounting teachers seldom refer to these motivations and their effects on accounting practice. ...It is as if the impact of its environment were irrelevant to the teaching of accounting--hardly the hallmark of a subject in the liberal tradition.

Still another desirable quality would be a recognition of the impact of accounting on the economy and on society. ...

A further desirable quality is elaboration of the international dimension of accounting. ...

Finally, it is desirable in any field of liberal learning that students be equipped with a critical faculty for evaluating alternatives and making decisions.... A curriculum that dwells on current practice, without instilling a critical faculty, is more suited to the preparation of technicians than professionals.[64]

In the same issue of the journal in which Zeff's article was published, however, was an article which seemed to hope that such visionary articles as Zeff's would disappear; the authors of that article rejoiced in the fact that there were proportionately more empirical articles appearing in accounting education research and they called for an even larger proportion.

Even the AICPA's *Journal of Accountancy* devoted a main article to educational issues in 1992--an event almost unheard of for a decade or more. The point/counterpoint article examined the question: "Do Academic Traditions Undermine Teaching?" As articles had done many years before, it focused on the effect of research requirements on curriculum development. The author of the "Yes" answer to the question was a CPA who was shocked to learn "that faculty members at many institutions would be committing academic suicide to devote substantial time and effort to a major curriculum project." The author of the "No" answer was a professor who spelled out the main issue:

> The standards of performance for the members of the accounting faculty need to be reasonably consistent with the performance standards for faculty members in the areas of finance, marketing, strategy and so on if accounting is to maintain its relative stature in the university system.[65]

The issues have not changed, but they are being discussed again.

Accounting educators seem to be in the mood for change. The word change is heavy in the air throughout the land. On the strength of that word, Bill Clinton was elected U.S. president in 1992. But there are various types and levels of change. There is the possibility of bad change as well as good change. There is the possiblity of talking about good change but never doing it. There is the possiblity of making superficial changes for show, but not solving the real problems. And there is the possibility of making real improvements. The type and level of change which will actually occur in accounting education is not yet apparent.

Notes

[1]   American Institute of Certified Public Accountants, *Issue Brief: Implementation of the 150-hour Education Requirement for*

Certification and Licensure (New York: American Institute of Certified Public Accountants, January 1990), p. 4.

2   Michael Schiff, "The Business School Establishment Versus the Accounting Profession," *The Journal of Accountancy*, April 1980, pp. 84-89.

3   Task Force on the Report of the Committee on Education and Experience Requirements for CPAs, "Education Requirements for Entry into the Accounting Profession: A Statement of AICPA Policies," *The Journal of Accountancy*, March 1979, p. 121.

4   Curriculum Committees of the Federation of Schools of Accountancy, 1978 and 1979, *Curriculum Recommendations of Federation of Schools of Accountancy* (Federation of Schools of Accountancy, 1979), p. 2.

5   Williams, p. 28.

6   "Council Focuses on Education Requirement," *The Journal of Accountancy*, November 1981, p. 3.

7   The Commission on Professional Accounting Education, *A Postbaccalaureate Education Requirement for the CPA Profession* (New York: The Commission on Professional Accounting Education, July 1983), pp. 5-6.

8   Robert C. Ellyson, A. Tom Nelson, and James H. MacNeill, "Educating Tomorrow's CPAs," *The Journal of Accountancy*, October 1985, pp. 95-102.

9   Stephen M. Cowherd, "150-Hour Rule: its Repercussions," *Accounting Today*, March 6, 1989, pp. 1, 26.

10   "Roundtable Discussion," *Future of Accounting Education*, edited by Teddy L. Coe and Barbara D. Merino (Denton, Texas: North Texas State University, 1987), p. 85.

11   W. Marcus Dunn and Thomas W. Hall, "An Empirical Analysis of the Relationships Between CPA Examination Candidate Attributes and Candidate Performance," *The Accounting Review*, October 1984, p. 681. See also discussion in article cited in the following footnote.

12   W. Marcus Dunn and Thomas W. Hall, "Postbaccalaureate Education and CPA Examination Performance," *CPA 86*, February/March 1986, p. 39.

13   Ibid., p. 41.

14   Norton M. Bedford, "Small Practitioners' Views of Accounting Programs and Schools," *Accounting Education: New*

Horizons For the Profession; Proceedings of the Arthur Young Professors' Roundtable, March 31 - April 1, 1977, edited by Donald H. Skadden (Reston, Virginia: The Council of Arthur Young Professors, 1977), pp. 88, 89.

[15] "Summary of the Conclusions and Recommendations of the Commission on Auditors' Responsibilities," *The Journal of Accountancy*, April 1978, p. 99.

[16] Ross L. Watts and Jerold L. Zimmerman, "Toward a Positive Theory of the Determination of Accounting Standards," *The Accounting Review*, January 1978, pp. 113, 114.

[17] Ross L. Watts and Jerold L. Zimmerman, "The Demand for and Supply of Accounting Theories: The Market for Excuses," *The Accounting Review*, April 1979, pp. 273-274, 275.

[18] James M. Reeve, "The Five-Year Accounting Program as a Quality Signal," *The Accounting Review*, July 1983, p. 641.

[19] Bikramjit S. Garcha, Gordon B. Harwood, and Roger H. Hermanson, "A Study of the Readership of the Accounting Review," *Journal of Accounting Education*, Fall 1983, p. 31.

[20] Richard E. Flaherty, *The Core of the Curriculum for Accounting Majors* (Sarasota, Florida: American Accounting Association, 1979).

[21] George E. Shute, *Accounting Students and Abstract Reasoning: An Exploratory Study* (Sarasota, Florida: American Accounting Association, 1979).

[22] Beatrice Gross and Ronald Gross, *A Review of Innovative Approaches to College Teaching* (Sarasota, Florida: American Accounting Association, 1980).

[23] Robert W. Ingram and Charles R. Frazier, *Developing Communication Skills for the Accounting Profession* (Sarasota, Florida: American Accounting Association, 1980).

[24] Donald R. Sloan, "The Education of the Professional Accountant," *The Journal of Accountancy*, March 1983, p. 58.

[25] Robert W. Lentilhon and Anthony T. Krzystofik, "Education, Preparation and Examination of the CPA," *The Journal of Accountancy*, June 1984, p. 129. Another study at about that time also showed that practitioners "seemed to favor having the post-graduate educational requirements taught (at least in part) through continuing educational programs as opposed to being taught entirely at the pre-entry level (i.e., a fifth-year requirement)."(p. 322) The

study showed that practitioners were not generally in favor of the fifth-year requirement, except for Florida practitioners who did strongly favor it--and the question was raised whether Florida passed the law because practitioners favored it or practitioners favored it because Florida had passed it. The study was by Donald F. Arnold and Thomas J. Geiselhart, "Practitioners' Views on Five-Year Educational Requirements for CPAs," *The Accounting Review*, April 1984, pp. 314-324. Another survey showed most managing partners favoring the five-year requirement, most presidents of state CPA societies opposing it, and educators and chairs of state boards of accountancy were split about evenly; practitioners also preferred to retain an experience requirement. The survey was by Robert H. Mills, "Views on Education and Experience Requirements," *The Journal of Accountancy*, October 1985, pp. 106-114.

[26] "AACSB Restructures Standards Group, Votes Against Postbaccalaureate Education Requirement for CPAs," *The Journal of Accountancy*, October 1984, pp. 20, 22.

[27] The American Accounting Association Committee on the Future Structure, Content, and Scope of Accounting Education, "Future Accounting Education: Preparing for the Expanding Profession," *Issues in Accounting Education*, Spring 1986, pp. 171, 174, 185.

[28] William G. Shenkir, "Comments on the AAA Committee Report," *Future of Accounting Education*, edited by Teddy L. Coe and Barbara D. Merino (Denton, Texas: North Texas State University, 1987), p. 75.

[29] Ibid.

[30] Ibid., p. 186.

[31] "AICPA Responds to AAA Report on Future Accounting Education," *The Journal of Accountancy*, October 1986, p. 26.

[32] Norton M. Bedford and William G. Shenkir, "Reorienting Accounting Education," *The Journal of Accountancy*, August 1987, p. 91.

[33] "Roundtable Discussion," pp. 84-85.

[34] Special Committee on Standards of Professional Conduct for Certified Public Accountants, *Restructuring Professional Standards to Achieve Professional Excellence In a Changing Environment* (New York: American Institute of Certified Public Accountants, 1986), p. 65.

[35] Rholan E. Larson, "For the Members, By the Members," *The Journal of Accountancy*, October 1987, p. 118.

[36] "Institute Facing 1990 Trial In Suit over Code Balloting," *Accounting Today*, July 31, 1989, p. 2.

[37] "AICPA Scraps Ballot Method," *Accounting Today*, December 23, 1991, pp. 1, 33.

[38] "Group Fights 150-hour Rule for Education," *Accounting Today*, June 5, 1989, p. 6.

[39] "AAA Supports AICPA 150-Hour Requirement," *The Journal of Accountancy*, November 1988, p. 102.

[40] There is presently an exception to this. To be a member of the SEC Practice Section (or the Private Companies Practice Section) of the AICPA, all partners of a member firm must be members of the AICPA. Such present rules could change, of course.

[41] "Jackson Rips 150-Hour Law," *Accounting Today*, June 8, 1992, p. 1.

[42] "Maine Spurns 150-Hour Law," *Accounting Today*, April 15, 1993, p. 3.

[43] Coalition Against Restrictive Entry into the CPA Profession, "How The 150 Hour Law Will Cost Accounting Professors Their Jobs," *New Accountant*, February 1993, p. 15.

[44] An interesting discussion of this issue is found in: Richard J. Schmidt, "Accounting Curriculum Responses to the 150-Hour Requirement," Journal of Accounting Education, Spring 1993, pp. 15-41.

[45] Ernst & Young, *Update on Developments in Accounting Education: October 1992,* p. 16.

[46] "Q&A: Louis Salvatore," *Accounting Today*, September 7, 1992, p. 32.

[47] Rick Elam quoted by Stephen H. Collins, "Meeting the New 150-Hour Standard," *The Journal of Accountancy*, August 1989, p. 57.

[48] "Report of the Follow-Up Committee on the Future Structure, Content, and Scope of Accounting Education, 1986-87," *Reorienting Accounting Education: Reports on the Environment, Professoriate, and Curriculum of Accounting*, edited by Joseph J. Schultz, Jr. (Saratoga, Florida: American Accounting Association, 1989), p. 183.

[49] Ibid., p. 186.

50 Ibid., p. 187.

51 Joseph J. Schultz, Jr., Janet A. Meade, and Inder Khurana, "The Changing Roles of Teaching, Research, and Service in the Promotion and Tenure Decisions for Accounting Faculty," *Issues in Accounting Education*, Spring 1989, pp. 114-115.

52 C. Douglas Poe and Ralph E. Viator, "AACSB Accounting Accreditation and Administrators' Attitudes Toward Criteria for the Evaluation of Faculty," *Issues in Accounting Education*, Spring 1990, p. 76.

53 *Perspectives on Education: Capabilities for Success in the Accounting Profession* (New York: Arthur Andersen & Co., Arthur Young, Coopers & Lybrand, Deloitte Haskens & Sells, Ernst & Whinney, Peat Marwick Main & Co., Price Waterhouse, and Touch Ross, 1989), p. 1.

54 Ibid., pp. 7-8.

55 Ibid., p. 8.

56 Ibid.

57 Gerhard G. Mueller and John K. Simmons, "Change in Accounting Education," *Issues in Accounting Education*, Fall 1989, pp. 248-249.

58 "Accounting Education Change Commission Meets," *Accounting Education News*, October 1989, p. 4.

59 *A Proposal for a New Order of Accounting Education* (Brigham Young University, January 1990), pp. 11-12. If the BYU proposal sounds a bit vague, one must remember that BYU was a leader in the fight to establish schools of accounting and in making Utah one of the first three states to require 150 hours of higher education.

60 "AECC Awards Grants," *Accounting Education News*, March 1991, p. 7.

61 H. Thomas Johnson and Robert Kaplan, *Relevance Lost: The Rise and Fall of Management Accounting* (Boston: Harvard Business School Press, 1987), pp. 14-15. See also p. 177.

62 Stephen A. Zeff, "Does Accounting Belong in the University Curriculum?" *Issues in Accounting Education*, Spring 1989, pp. 203-204.

63 Ibid., p. 207.

64 Ibid., pp. 204-206.

65   A. Marvin Strait and Ivan Bull, "Do Academic Traditions Undermine Teaching?" *The Journal of Accountancy*, September 1992, p. 72.

Bibliography

"AAA and AICPA to Consponsor Accreditation." *The Journal of Accountancy* (October 1976): 38.

"AAA Supports AICPA 150-Hour Requirement." *The Journal of Accountancy* (November 1988): 102-106.

"AACSB Approves Proposal for Accrediting Accounting Programs." *The Journal of Accountancy* (July 1978): 14-16.

"AACSB Council Adopts Rules to Accredit Accounting Programs." *The Journal of Accountancy* (August 1980): 10-13.

"AACSB Restructures Standards Group, Votes against Postbaccalaureate Education Requirement for CPAs." *The Journal of Accountancy* (October 1984): 20-22.

"Accountancy Education and Legislation." *The Journal of Accountancy* (March 1963): 33-34.

"Accounting Education Change Commission Meets." *Accounting Education News* (October 1989): 4-5.

"Accounting Education for Nontechnical Students." *The Journal of Accountancy* (May 1946): p. 359-360.

"Accounting Education." *The Journal of Accountancy* (September 1945): 161-163.

"Accounting Teachers Evaluate the Uniform CPA Examination." *The Journal of Accountancy* (March 1949): 253-256.

"Advanced Education in Accounting." *The Journal of Accountancy* (January 1951): 67-68.

"AECC Awards Grants." *Accounting Education News* (March 1991): 7, 25.

"AICPA Responds to AAA Report on Future Accounting Education." *The Journal of Accountancy* (October 1986): 26-27.

"AICPA Scraps Ballot Method," *Accounting Today*, December 23, 1991, pp. 1, 33.

"Are CPA Examinations Too Hard?" *The Journal of Accountancy* (June 1947): 457-459.

"Council Focuses on Education Requirement." *The Journal of Accountancy* (November 1981): 3.

"Developments in Accounting Education." *The Journal of Accountancy* (October 1950): 355-356.

"Education and Experience for CPAs: The Report to Council of the American Institute of CPAs by the Special Committee on the Report of the Commission on Standards of Education and Experience for CPAs." *The Journal of Accountancy* (June 1959): 67-71.

"Educational Background of Certified Public Accountants." *The Journal of Accountancy* (July 1949): 4-5.

"Group Fights 150-hour Rule for Education." *Accounting Today*, June 5, 1989, p. 6.

"Institute Facing 1990 Trial in Suit over Code Balloting." *Accounting Today*, July 31, 1989, p. 2.

"Jackson Rips 150-Hour Law." *Accounting Today*, June 8, 1992, p. 1.

"Maine Spurns 150-Hour Law." *Accounting Today*, April 15, 1993, p. 3.

"On CPA Education and Experience." *The Journal of Accountancy* (April 1968): 25-26.

"Professional Education in Accounting." *The Journal of Accountancy* (October 1950): 280-281.

A Proposal for a New Order of Accounting Education. Brigham Young University, January 1990.

"Q&A: Louis Salvatore." *Accounting Today,* September 7, 1992, p. 32.

Report of the Commission on Standards of Education and Experience for Certified Public Accountants. University of Michigan, 1956.

"A Report of the Committee on Auditing Education." *The Accounting Review* (July 1954): 465-471.

Report of the Committee on Education and Experience Requirements for CPAs. New York: American Institute of Certified Public Accountants, March 1969.

"Report of the Committee on Management Accounting." *The Accounting Review* (April 1959): 207-209.

"Report of the Committee on Professional Education in Accounting." *The Accounting Review* (April 1959): 195-199.

"Report of the Committee on the Study of the Ford and Carnegie Foundation Reports." *The Accounting Review* (April 1961): 191-196.

"Report of the Committee to Examine the 1969 Report of the AICPA Committee on Education & Experience Requirements for CPAs." *The Accounting Review* (Supplement 1972): 237-257.

"Report of the Follow-Up Committee on the Future Structure, Content, and Scope of Accounting Education, 1986-87." In *Reorienting Accounting Education: Reports on the Environment, Professoriate, and Curriculum of Accounting*, pp. 183-206. Edited by Joseph J. Schultz, Jr. Saratoga, Florida: American Accounting Association, 1989.

"Roundtable Discussion." In *Future of Accounting Education*, pp. 79-106. Edited by Teddy L. Coe and Barbara D. Merino. Denton, Texas: North Texas State University, 1987.

"Summary of the Conclusions and Recommendations of the Commission on Auditors' Responsibilities." *The Journal of Accountancy* (April 1978): 92-102.

"Undergraduate Curriculum Study: Report of the Task Committee on Standards of Accounting Instruction." *The Accounting Review* (January 1956): 36-42.

Accounting Education Change Commission. "AECC Urges Priority for Teaching in Higher Education." *Issues in Accounting Education* (Fall 1990): 330-331.

Accounting Education Change Commission. "Objectives of Education for Accountants: Position Statement Number One." *Issues in Accounting Education* (Fall 1990): 307-312.

Allen, C.E. "The Growth of Accounting Instruction since 1900." *The Accounting Review* (June 1927): 150-166.

The American Accounting Association Committee on the Future Structure, Content, and Scope of Accounting Education. "Future Accounting Education: Preparing for the Expanding Profession." *Issues in Accounting Education* (Spring 1986): 168-195.

American Institute of Certified Public Accountants. *Issue Brief: Implementation of the 150-hour Education Requirement for Certification and Licensure.* New York: American Institute of Certified Public Accountants, January 1990.

Anderson, G. Lester. "Professional Education: Present Status and Continuing Problems." In *Education for the Professions: The Sixty-first Yearbook of the National Society for the Study of Education, Part II*, pp. 20-21. Edited by Nelson B. Henry. Chicago: University of Chicago Press, 1962.

Anderson, Hershel M., and Griffin, Fred B. "The Accounting Curriculum and Postgraduate Achievement." *The Accounting Review* (October 1963): 813-818.

Anderson, Wilton T. "Carnegie and Ford Reports on Education for CPAs." *The Journal of Accountancy* (February 1961): 86-89.

Arnold, Donald F., and Geiselhart, Thomas J. "Practitioners' Views on Five-Year Educational Requirements for CPAs." *The Accounting Review* (April 1984): 314-324.

Arthur Andersen & Co., Arthur Young, Coopers & Lybrand, Deloitte Haskins & Sells, Ernst & Whinney, Peat Marwick Main & Co., Price Waterhouse, and Touche Ross. *Perspectives on Education: Capabilities for Success in the Accounting Profession.* April 1989.

Ashburne, Jim G. "The Five-Year Professional Accounting Program." *The Accounting Review* (January 1958): 106-110.

Aslanian, Paul J., and Duff, John T. "Why Accounting Teachers Are So Academic." *The Journal of Accountancy* (October 1973): 47-53.

Bach, G. Leland. "Accounting Education for the 1980's." *The Journal of Accountancy* (September 1961): 50-54.

Baldwin, Rosecrans. "A Practitioner's Plea for More Training in Written English." *The Accounting Review* (July 1956): 358-362.

Bedford, Norton M. "Education for Accounting as a Learned Profession." *The Journal of Accountancy* (December 1961): 33-41.

_____. "Small Practitioners' Views of Accounting Programs and Schools." In *Accounting Education: New Horizons for the Profession; Proceedings of the Arthur Young Professors' Roundtable, March 31 - April 1, 1977*, pp. 88-89. Edited by Donald H. Skaddon. Reston, Virginia: The Council of Arthur Young Professors, 1977.

Bedford, Norton M., and Shenkir, William G. "Reorienting Accounting Education." *The Journal of Accountancy* (August 1987): 84-91.

Belser, F.C. "How the Universities Can Aid the Accounting Profession." *The Journal of Accountancy* (October 1927): 37-42.

Bennett, R.J. "Educational Training of an Accountant." *The Journal of Accountancy* (January 1912): 182-195.

Bloom, Robert; Debessay, Araya; and Markell, William. "The Development of Schools of Accounting and the Underlying Issues." *Journal of Accounting Education* (Spring 1986): 7-29.

Board on Standards for Programs and Schools of Professional Accounting. *Final Report*. New York: American Institute of Certified Public Accountants, 1977.

Boedecker, Karl A. "The Correlation of Accounting Instruction With Instruction in Other Business Fields." *The Accounting Review* (January 1951): 70-76.

Bossard, James, and Dewhurst, Frederic. *University Education for Business: A Study of Existing Needs and Practices.* Philadelphia: University of Pennsylvania Press, 1931.

Bowers, Russell. "Curriculum Building for Prospective Industrial Accountants." *The Accounting Review* (January 1953): 58-63.

Boyd, Ralph L. "A Suggested Program for College Training in Accountancy." *The Accounting Review* (January 1946): 51-56.

Boyd, Virgil, and Taylor, Dale. "The Magic Words--"Managerial Accounting." *The Accounting Review* (January 1961): 105-111.

Bremser, Wayne G.; Brenner, Vincent C.; and Dascher, Paul E. "The Feasibility of Professional Schools: An Empirical Study." *The Accounting Review* (April 1977): 465-473.

Bruschi, William C. "Issues Surrounding Qualifying Experience Requirements." *The Journal of Accountancy* (March 1969): 47-54.

Buckley, John W. "A Perspective on Professional Accounting Education." *The Journal of Accountancy* (August 1970): 41-47.

Burton, John C. "An Educator Views the Public Accounting Profession." *The Journal of Accountancy* (September 1971): 47-53.

_____. "The Need for Professional Accounting Education." In *Schools of Accountancy: A Look at the Issues*, pp. 3-7. Edited by Allen H. Bizzell and Kermit D. Larson. New York: American Institute of Certified Public Accountants, 1975.

Butts, R. Freeman, and Cremin, Lawrence A. *A History of Education in American Culture.* New York: Holt, Rinehart and Winston, 1953.

Campbell, David R., and Williamson, Robert W. "Accreditation of Accounting Programs: Administrators' Perceptions of Proposed AACSB Standards." *Issues in Accounting Education* (1983): 60-70.

Cannon, Arthur M. "Education and the CPA Standards Report." *The Journal of Accountancy* (January 1957): 33-40.

Carey, John L. "Toward Higher Educational Standards." Editorial in *The Journal of Accountancy* (December 1937): 403-405.

_____. "Higher Accreditation for CPAs." *The Journal of Accountancy* (March 1961): 47-53.

_____. *The CPA Plans for the Future.* New York: American Institute of CPAs, 1965.

_____. *The Rise of the Accounting Profession: From Technician to Professional, 1896-1936.* New York: American Institute of Certified Public Accountants, 1969.

_____. *The Rise of the Accounting Profession: To Responsibility and Authority, 1937-1969.* New York: AICPA, 1970.

_____, ed. *The Accounting Profession: Where Is It Headed?* New York: American Institute of CPAs, 1962.

Carroll, Gay. "Some Challenges to Accounting." *The Accounting Review* (January 1951): 9-18.

Chambers, R.J. "The Anguish of Accountants." *The Journal of Accountancy* (March 1972): 68-74.

Claire, Richard S. "Training for the Public Accounting Profession." *The Accounting Review* (April 1944): 150-159.

Coalition Against Restrictive Entry into the CPA Profession. "How the 150 Hour Law Will Cost Accounting Professors Their Jobs." Advertisement in *New Accountant*, February 1993, p. 15.

Cobb, E. Kennedy. "Current Status of Managerial Accounting as a Course of Study." *The Accounting Review* (January 1960): 125-129.

Collins, Stephen H. "Meeting the New 150-Hour Standard." *The Journal of Accountancy* (August 1989): 55-57.

The Commission on Professional Accounting Education. *A Postbaccalaureate Education Requirement for the CPA Profession.* New York: The Commission on Professional Accounting Education, July 1983.

Committee on Education and Experience Requirements for CPAs. "Academic Preparation for Professional Accounting Careers." *The Journal of Accountancy* (December 1968): 57-63.

Cowherd, Stephen M. "150-Hour Rule: its Repercussions." *Accounting Today*, March 6, 1989, pp. 1, 26.

Cox, Robert G. "Accounting." In Frank C. Pierson and Others, *The Education of American Businessmen: A Study of University-College Programs in Business Administration*, pp. 355-391. New York: McGraw-Hill Book Company, Inc., 1959.

Curriculum Committees of the Federation of Schools of Accountancy, 1978 and 1979. *Curriculum Recommendations of Federation of Schools of Accountancy.* Federation of Schools of Accountancy, 1979.

Davidson, Sidney. "Accreditation: Two Views; A Plea for Flexibility." *The Journal of Accountancy* (March 1978): 61-65.

Deinzer, Harvey T. "Specialization or Integration as the Objective of Graduate Accounting Instruction." *The Accounting Review* (April 1953): 249-257.

Demski, Joel S. "The General Impossibility of Normative Accounting Standards." *The Accounting Review* (October 1973): pp. 718-723.

Dopuch, Nicholas. "Models for Financial Accounting vs. Models for Management Accounting: Can (Should) They Be Different?" In *Researching the Accounting Curriculum: Strategies for Change*, pp. 103-122. Edited by William L. Ferrara. The American Accounting Association, 1975.

Duncan, John C. "Some Scientific and Educational Problems of the Accountancy Profession." *The Journal of Accountancy* (October 1914): 260-275.

Dunn, W. Marcus, and Hall, Thomas W. "An Empirical Analysis of the Relationships Between CPA Examination Candidate Attributes and Candidate Performance." *The Accounting Review* (October 1984): 674-689.

_____. "Postbaccalaureate Education and CPA Examination Performance." *CPA 86* (February/March 1986): 39-40.

Ellyson, Robert C.; Nelson, A. Tom; and MacNeill, James H. "Educating Tomorrow's CPAs." *The Journal of Accountancy* (October 1985): 95-102.

Ernst & Young. *Update on Developments in Accounting Education: October 1992.*

Fertig, Paul E. "Organization of an Accounting Program." *The Accounting Review* (April 1960): 190-196.

Fess, Philip E. "A New Breed of Public Accountant." *The Journal of Accountancy* (February 1963): 89-90.

_____. "Teaching and/or Research: A Time for Evaluation." *The Journal of Accountancy* (March 1968): 84-87.

Fetters, Michael L.; Hoopes, James; and Tropp, Martin. "Integrating Concepts from Accounting, American History and English Literature: A Cluster Course Approach." *Journal of Accounting Education* (Spring 1989): 69-82.

Firmin, Peter A. "The Five-Year Accounting Program--With Due and Deliberate Speed." *The Accounting Review* (October 1959): 591-602.

Flaherty, Richard E. *The Core of the Curriculum for Accounting Majors.* Sarasota, Florida: American Accounting Association, 1979.

Foster, L.O. "Accounting in the Liberal Arts Curriculum." *The Accounting Review* (March 1933): 22-25.

Fulmer, William E., and Cargile, Barney R. "Ethical Perceptions of Accounting Students: Does Exposure to a Code of Professional Ethics Help?" *Issues in Accounting Education* (Fall 1987): 207-219.

Garcha, Bikramjit S.; Harwood, Gordon B.; and Hermanson, Roger H. "A Study of the Readership of the Accounting Review." *Journal of Accounting Education* (Fall 1983):

Gerboth, Dale L. "Research, Intuition, and Politics in Accounting Inquiry." *The Accounting Review* (July 1973): 475-482.

Gilman, Stephen. "Is College the Only Way?" *The Accounting Review* (June 1937): 105-111.

Gordon, Robert Aaron, and Howell, James Edwin. *Higher Education for Business.* New York: Columbia University Press, 1959.

Graham, Willard J. "How Can the Colleges Serve the Profession?" *The Journal of Accountancy* (February 1956): 45-50.

Greer, Howard C. "The Present Status of Accounting Teaching." *The Accounting Review* (May 1933): 62-67.

Gross, Beatrice, and Gross, Ronald. *A Review of Innovative Approaches to College Teaching.* Sarasota, Florida: American Accounting Association, 1980.

Gruber, William H., and Logan, Louis L. "The Education of Professional Accountants." *The Journal of Accountancy* (May 1971): 85-88.

Gruneberg, Curt. "Is Accountancy a Field of Science?" *The Accounting Review* (April 1950): 161-162.

Gutek, Gerald L. *Education in the United States: An Historical Perspective.* Englewood Cliffs, N.J.: Prentice-Hall, 1986.

Hatch, Nathan O., ed. *The Professions in American History.* University of Notre Dame Press, 1988.

Haynes, Benjamin R., and Jackson, Harry P. *A History of Business Education in the United States.* Cincinnati: South-Western Publishing Co., 1935.

Horn, Frederick E. "Managerial Emphasis in Elementary Accounting." *The Accounting Review* (July 1951): 305-312.

Howard, Stanley E. "Accounting Instruction in the Liberal Curriculum." *The Accounting Review* (June 1930): 146-149.

_____. "Accounting in a Liberal Arts Curriculum." *The Accounting Review* (June 1936): 149-154.

Ingram, Robert W., and Frazier, Charles R. *Developing Communication Skills for the Accounting Profession.* Sarasota, Florida: American Accounting Association, 1980.

Jarett, Irwin M. "Discussion of 'What We Can Learn from Other Countries and Other Professions.'" In *Accounting Education: New Horizons for the Profession; Proceedings of the Arthur Young Professors' Roundtable, March 31 - April 1, 1977*, pp. 43-54. Edited by Donald H. Skadden. Reston, Virginia: The Council of Arthur Young Professors, 1977.

Johnson, Charles E. "The Many-Body Problem." *The Journal of Accountancy* (June 1967): 76-80.

Johnson, H. Thomas, and Kaplan, Robert. *Relevance Lost: The Rise and Fall of Management Accounting*. Boston: Harvard Business School Press, 1987.

Kell, Walter G. "The Commission's Long Run Goals." *The Accounting Review* (April 1958): 198-205.

Kennelly, John W., and Smith, John H. "More on Research and Teaching." *The Journal of Accountancy* (July 1969): 86-87.

Kerr, Donna H. *Barriers to Integrity: Modern Modes of Knowledge Utilization*. Boulder, Colorado: Westview Press, 1984.

Kerrigan, Harry. "Some Current Problems in the Teaching of Accounting." *The Accounting Review* (January 1952): 79-88.

Kester, Roy B. "Education for Professional Accountancy." *The Accounting Review* (June 1936): 99-108.

Knepper, Edwin G. *History of Business Education in United States*. Bowling Green, Ohio: Printed by Edwards Brothers, Inc., 1941.

Knight, Robert G. "Accounting Education--From the Point of View of the Business Employer." *The Accounting Review* (July 1953): 343-349.

Langenderfer, Harold Q. "Foreword." In *Accounting Education: Problems and Prospects*, pp. ix-x. Edited by James Don Edwards. American Accounting Association, 1974.

_____. "Accounting Education's History--A 100-Year Search for Identity." *The Journal of Accountancy* (May 1987): 302-331.

Langenderfer, Harold Q., and Weinwurm, Ernest H. "Bringing Accounting Curricula Up-To-Date." *The Accounting Review* (July 1956): 423-430.

Lanham, James S. "Problems of Professional Education in Accounting." *The Journal of Accountancy* (March 1960): 71-75.

Larson, Kermit D. "Schools of Accountancy: What Should Be Their Objectives?" In *Proceedings of the First National Conference on Professionalization of the Accounting Curriculum*, pp. 21-34. Edited by Joseph A. Silvoso and Raymond C. Dockweiler. Columbia, Missouri: University of Missouri, 1977.

Larson, Rholan E. "For the Members, By the Members." *The Journal of Accountancy* (October 1987): 116-122.

Leland, Thomas W. "Educational Prerequisites for the Certificate." *The Accounting Review* (April 1945): 191-194.

_____, ed. "Student's Department." *The Journal of Accountancy* (May 1947): 440.

Lentilhon, Robert W., and Krzystofik, Anthony T. "Education, Preparation and Examination of the CPA." *The Journal of Accountancy* (June 1984): 129-134.

Littleton, A.C. "The Professional College." *The Accounting Review* (June 1936): 109-116.

_____. "Accounting Rediscovered." *The Accounting Review* (April 1958): 246-253.

Lockley, Lawrence C. "Some Comments Regarding University Education." *The Journal of Accountancy* (May 1969): 94-97.

Lockwood, Jeremiah. "Early University Education in Accountancy." *The Accounting Review* (June 1938): 131-144.

McCrea, Roswell C., and Kester, Roy B. "A School of Professional Accountancy." *The Journal of Accountancy* (February 1936): 106-117.

McGrath, Earl J. "Education, Profession and Public Affairs." *The Journal of Accountancy* (April 1958): 44-49.

_____. *Liberal Education in the Professions*. Teachers College, Columbia University, 1959.

MacNeill, James H. "A Readback on 'Horizons for a Profession.'" *The Journal of Accountancy* (April 1970): 66-69.

Madden, Donald L., and Phillips, Lawrence C. "An Evaluation of the Common Body of Knowledge Study and its Probable Impact Upon the Accounting Profession." *The Journal of Accountancy* (February 1968): 86-89.

Mautz, Robert K. "The Fifth Year--But Later." *The Journal of Accountancy* (February 1964): 88-92.

_____. "Challenges to the Accounting Profession." *The Accounting Review* (April 1965): 299-311.

_____. "The Practitioner and the Professor." *The Journal of Accountancy* (October 1965): 64-66.

_____. "Where Do We Go From Here?" *The Accounting Review* (April 1974): 353-360.

_____. "The Over-Intellectualization of Accounting Education." In *Accounting Education: Problems and Prospects*, pp. 30-37. Edited by James Don Edwards. American Accounting Association, 1974.

May, Gordon S., and May, Claire B. "Communication Instruction: What Is Being Done to Develop the Communication Skills of Accounting Students?" *Journal of Accounting Education* (Fall 1989): 233-244.

Mayhew, Lewis B., and Ford, Patrick J. *Reform in Graduate and Professional Education.* San Francisco: Jossey-Bass Publishers, 1974.

Meonske, Norman R., and Madison, Roland L. "Questioning the 150 Hours," *New Accountant* (September 1991): 40-43, 60.

Middle Atlantic Association of Colleges of Business Administration. "Statement of Policy Relative to a Fifth Year in the Accounting Curriculum." *The Accounting Review* (October 1961): 635-637.

Miller, Herbert E. "Accreditation: Two Views; Where Such Education Standard Setting Is Headed." *The Journal of Accountancy* (March 1978): 56-61.

Miller, Hermann C. "Interim Report of the Standards Rating Committee." *The Accounting Review* (January 1951): 19-21.

Miller, Jay W. *A Critical Analysis of the Organization, Administration and Function of the Private Business Schools of the United States.* Cincinnati: South-Western Publishing Co., 1939.

Mills, Robert H. "Views on Education and Experience Requirements." *The Journal of Accountancy* (October 1985): 106-114.

Montgomery, Robert H. "An Accountancy Laboratory." *The Journal of Accountancy* (June 1914): 405-411.

Moonitz, Maurice. "The Beamer Committee Report--A Golden Opportunity for Accounting Education." *The Journal of Accountancy* (August 1973): 64-71.

Moriarty, Shane. "Perspectives on Educating Future Accounting Practitioners." In *Future of Accounting Education*, pp. 7-14. Edited by Teddy L. Coe and Barbara D. Merino. Denton, Texas: North Texas State University, 1987.

Mueller, Gerhard G., ed. *A New Introduction to Accounting: A Report of the Study Group Sponsored by the Price Waterhouse Foundation, July 1971.*

Mueller, Gerhard G., and Simmons, John K. "Change in Accounting Education." *Issues in Accounting Education* (Fall 1989): 247-251.

Nelson, A. Tom. "A New Direction in Accounting Education--The AICPA Steps Out." *Issues In Accounting Education* (Spring 1989): 211-217.

Nelson, Edward G. "Science and Accounting." *The Accounting Review* (October 1949): 354-359.

Newcomer, Hale L. "The CPA Examination." *The Accounting Review* (April 1949): 128-135.

Noble, Paul L. "A Quantitative Evaluation of Accounting Curricula." *The Accounting Review* (April 1950): 163-169.

Nye, Paul E. "Training For an Accounting Career: A Public Accountant's View." *The Accounting Review* (April 1958): 187-192.

Paton, William A. "Some Reflections on Education and Professoring." *The Accounting Review* (January 1967): 7-23.

_____. "Accounting's Educational Eclipse." *The Journal of Accountancy* (December 1971): 35-37.

Pearson, David B. "Will Accreditation Improve the Quality of Education?" *The Journal of Accountancy* (April 1979): 53-58.

Pedelahore, J. Earl. "The Case For the Dissent." *The Journal of Accountancy* (December 1956): 38-41.

Perry, Donald P. "Training for the Profession." *The Journal of Accountancy* (November 1955): 66-71.

Pierson, Frank C., and Others. *The Education of American Businessmen: A Study of University-College Programs in Business Administration*. New York: McGraw-Hill, 1959.

Planning Committee of the AICPA. "Education of Certified Public Accountants." *The Journal of Accountancy* (April 1968): 48-52.

Poe, C. Douglas, and Viator, Ralph E. "AACSB Accounting Accreditation and Administrators' Attitudes Toward Criteria for the Evaluation of Faculty." *Issues in Accounting Education* (Spring 1990): 59-77.

Porter, W. Thomas, Jr. *Higher Education and the Accounting Profession: A Summary Report on the Haskins & Sells 75th Anniversary Symposiums*, a pamphlet, 1971.

Previts, Gary John, and Merino, Barbara Dubis. *A History of Accounting in America*. New York: John Wiley & Sons, 1979.

Previts, Gary John, and Robinson, Thomas R. "In Search of an Identity. " *Accounting Education News* (January 1991): 2-3.

Pye, Malcolm L. "The Undergraduate Accounting Curriculum." *The Accounting Review* (April 1955): 284-289.

Rayburn, Frank R., and Bonfield, E.H. "Schools of Accountancy: Attitudes and Attitude Structure." *The Accounting Review* (July 1978): 752-765.

Rebele, James E. "An Examination of Accounting Students' Perceptions of the Importance of Communication Skills in Public Accounting." *Issues in Accounting Education* (1985): 41-50.

Reeve, James M. "The Five-Year Accounting Program as a Quality Signal." *The Accounting Review* (July 1983): 639-646.

Reininga, Warren. "An Approach to Elementary Accounting." *The Accounting Review* (January 1965): 211-214.

Revzan, David A. "What is a Balanced Curriculum in Accounting?" *The Accounting Review* (October 1949): 409-413.

Roy, Robert H., and MacNeill, James H. "Study of the Common Body of Knowledge for CPAs: A Report of Plans and Progress." *The Journal of Accountancy* (December 1963): 55-58.

_____. *Horizons for a Profession: The Common Body of Knowledge for Certified Public Accountants*. New York: American Institute of Certified Public Accountants, 1967.

Schiff, Michael. "The Business School Establishment Versus the Accounting Profession." *The Journal of Accountancy* (April 1980): 84-89.

Schmidt, Leo A. "Employers' Conference Evaluates Accounting Curriculums, Recruitment, Placement." *The Journal of Accountancy* (October 1948): 292-296.

Schmidt, Richard J. "Accounting Curriculum Responses to the 150-Hour Requirement." *Journal of Accounting Education* (Spring 1993): 15-41.

Schultz, Joseph J. Jr.; Meade, Janet A.; and Khurana, Inder. "The Changing Roles of Teaching, Research, and Service in the Promotion and Tenure Decisions for Accounting Faculty." *Issues in Accounting Education* (Spring 1989): 109-119.

Scovill, H.T. "Education for Public Accounting on the Collegiate Level." *The Accounting Review* (July 1946): 261-267.

Shaulis, L.L. "Instruction in Accounting for Liberal Education." *The Accounting Review* (September 1930): 222-225.

Shenkir, William G. "Comments on the AAA Committee Report." In *Future of Accounting Education*, pp. 74-78. Edited by Teddy L. Coe and Barbara D. Merino. Denton, Texas: North Texas State University, 1987.

_____, ed. *The Future of Accounting Education: A Summary Report on the Seminars Sponsored by the American Accounting Association and the American Institute of Certified Public Accountants*. New York: American Institute of Certified Public Accountants, 1974.

Shute, George E. *Accounting Students and Abstract Reasoning: An Exploratory Study*. Sarasota, Florida: American Accounting Association, 1979.

Sloan, Donald R. "The Education of the Professional Accountant." *The Journal of Accountancy* (March 1983): 56-60.

Smith, C. Aubrey. "Education for the Professional Accountant." *The Accounting Review* (January 1945): 17-23.

_____. "University Offers Degree of Master in Professional Accounting (MPA)." *The Journal of Accountancy* (February 1949): 140-141.

_____. "The Next Step--A Professional School of Accounting." *The Accounting Review* (October 1956): 565 572.

_____. "An Experiment with a Five-year Professional Accounting Program." *The Journal of Accountancy* (May 1961): 86-87.

Smyth, J.E. "A Case for National Income Accounting in the Accounting Curriculum." *The Accounting Review* (July 1959): 376-380.

Soder, Roger. "Studying the Education of Educators: What We Can Learn from Other Professions." Phi Delta Kappan (December 1988): 299-305.

Sondereggen, Emory O. "Qualifications for Accounting Students to Meet the Needs of Business Firms." *The Accounting Review* (January 1959): 112-123.

Special Committee on Standards of Professional Conduct for Certified Public Accountants. *Restructuring Professional Standards to Achieve Professional Excellence In a Changing Environment.* New York: American Institute of Certified Public Accountants, 1986.

Spiceland, J. David; Brenner, Vincent C.; and Hartman, Bart P. "Standards for Programs and Schools of Professional Accounting: Accounting Group Perceptions." *The Accounting Review* (January 1980): 134-143.

Sterling, Robert R. "Accounting Research, Education and Practice." *The Journal of Accountancy* (September 1973): 44-52.

Stewart, A. Frank. "Accounting Education--From the Viewpoint of a Member of a State Board of Accountancy." *The Accounting Review* (July 1953): 350-355.

Strait, A. Marvin, and Bull, Ivan. "Do Academic Traditions Undermine Teaching?" *The Journal of Accountancy* (September 1992): 69-73.

Summerhill, G. Winston. "Administrative Accounting in the Accounting Curriculum." *The Accounting Review* (January 1953): 64-78.

Summers, Edward L. "Accounting Education's New Horizons." *The Journal of Accountancy* (September 1974): 56-63.

_____. "The Professional School in Accounting Education." In *Accounting Education: Problems and Prospects*, pp. 79-93. Edited by James Don Edwards. American Accounting Association, 1974.

Tannery, Fladger F. "The Requirements and Opportunities in Industry for Students of Accounting." *The Accounting Review* (October 1948): 377-384.

Task Force on the Report of the Committee on Education and Experience Requirements for CPAs. "Education Requirements for Entry into the Accounting Profession: A Statement of AICPA Policies." *The Journal of Accountancy* (March 1979): 121-128.

The American Accounting Association Committee on the Future Structure, Content, and Scope of Accounting Education. "Future Accounting Education: Preparing for the Expanding Profession." *Issues in Accounting Education* (Spring 1986): 168-195.

Trump, Guy. "Attributes of a New (Public) Accountant." In *Accounting Education: Problems and Prospects*, pp. 60-63. Edited by James Don Edwards. American Accounting Association, 1974.

_____. "Comments by..." In *Schools of Accountancy: A Look at the Issues*, p. 37. Edited by Allen H. Bizzell and Kermit D. Larson. New York: American Institute of Certified Public Accountants, 1975.

Tyack, David B., ed. *Turning Points in American Educational History*. Waltham, Mass.: Blaisdell Publishing Company, 1967.

Vance, Lawrence L. "Education for Public Accounting: With Special Reference to the Report of the Commission on Standards of Education and Experience for Certified Public Accountants." *The Accounting Review* (October 1956): 573-580.

Vatter, William J. "Education For Accountancy." *The Journal of Accountancy* (January 1964): 88-91.

Veysey, Lawrence R. *The Emergence of the American University*. Chicago: University of Chicago Press, 1965).

Walsh, Lawrence M. "Accounting Education in Review." *The Accounting Review* (April 1960): 183-189.

Walton, Seymour. "Practical Application of Theoretical Knowledge." *The Journal of Accountancy* (October 1917): 276-282.

Watts, Ross L., and Zimmerman, Jerold L. "Toward a Positive Theory of the Determination of Accounting Standards." *The Accounting Review* (January 1978): 112-134.

_____. "The Demand for and Supply of Accounting Theories: The Market for Excuses." *The Accounting Review* (April 1979): 273-305.

Webster, Norman E. "Higher Education for Public Accountants." *The Accounting Review* (June 1938): 117-124.

_____. "College Education as a Requirement for Certified Public Accountants--The New York Experience." *The Accounting Review* (October 1946): 445-450.

Weckstein, Donald T. "Discussion of 'What We Can Learn from Other Countries and Other Professions.'" In *Accounting Education: New Horizons for the Profession*, pp. 55-63. Edited by Donald H. Skadden. Reston, Virginia: The Council of Arthur Young Professors, 1977.

Welsch, Glenn A. "Is Accountancy an Academic Discipline?" *The Journal of Accountancy* (May 1966): 81-83.

Werntz, William W. "Accounting Education and the Ford and Carnegie Reports." *The Accounting Review* (April 1961): 186-190.

Whitehead, Alfred North. *The Aims of Education*. New York: New American Library of World Literature, Inc., 1947.

Williams, Doyle Z. "Reactions to 'Horizons for a Profession.'" *The Journal of Accountancy* (June 1969): 81-84.

_____. *Accounting Education: A Statistical Survey, 1972-73*. New York: American Institute of Certified Public Accountants, 1974.

_____. "Schools of Accounting: Anatomy of a Movement." *Issues in Accounting Education* (1984): 13-32.

_____. "Reforming Accounting Education." *The Journal of Accountancy* (August 1993): 76-82.

Winter, Sidney G. "What is Proper Training for Accountants?" *The Accounting Review* (June 1941): 183-188.

Wyatt, Arthur R. "Professional Education in Accounting." *The Accounting Review* (April 1959): 200-206.

Zeff, Stephen A. "Does Accounting Belong in the University Curriculum?" *Issues in Accounting Education* (Spring 1989): 203-210.

Zlatkovich, Charles T. "Training For an Accounting Career: An Educator's View." *The Accounting Review* (April 1958): 193-197.

Index